Native American Folklore

Native American Folklore in Nineteenth-Century Periodicals

William M. Clements

Swallow Press/Ohio University Press
Athens, Ohio   Chicago   London

Library of Congress Cataloging-in-Publication Data

Native American folklore in nineteenth-century periodicals.

  Includes bibliographies.
   1. Indians of North America—Folklore.   2. Folklore—North America.
I. Clements, William M., 1945–
  E98.F6N38   1986   398.2′08997   86-5409
  ISBN 0-8040-0872-8

For Francie

Contents

* * * * *

Acknowledgments

* * * * *

The preparation of this anthology has resulted in a number of debts. I encountered and copied most of the anthologized essays while working in several libraries around the country: West Virginia University Library; Texas Tech University Library; Perry-Castaneda Library, The University of Texas at Austin; and Doheny Library, University of Southern California. Julia Johnson of the Documents Department at Doheny Library and Margarett Daniels of the Interlibrary Loan Department of the Dean B. Ellis Library, Arkansas State University have been particularly helpful in locating necessary material for me. Although I have not always followed their advice, Dell Hymes, W. K. McNeil, and Rosemary Zumwalt suggested essays for inclusion as well as bibliographic references. Frances M. Malpezzi has been involved at every stage of this project, from conceptualization to proofreading. I appreciate the assistance of these individuals and institutions.

Introduction

*   *   *   *   *

In an essay prepared some thirty years ago, A. Irving Hallowell enumerated some aspects of Euro-American culture that have evinced the effects of contact with Native Americans: "our speech, our economic life, our clothing, our sports and recreations, certain indigenous religious cults, many of our curative practices, folk and concert music, the novel, poetry, drama, even some of our basic psychological attitudes, and one of the social sciences, anthropology."[1] As far as the last item in Hallowell's list is concerned, the relationship between American Indian cultures and social anthropology—as well as its related field of study, folklore—has indeed been close. One can claim that, with very few exceptions, every American anthropologist until well into the twentieth century had a primary interest in studying the indigenous inhabitants of the New World. Anthropology as a scholarly pursuit in America was essentially the study of humanity as represented by the American Indians. Not until the 1920s did American anthropologists in large numbers join their British and continental counterparts in seeking out exotic peoples in remote parts of the world for study. For unlike anthropologists in Europe, Americans lived in relative proximity to groups who could be characterized as "primitive" or "savage," in the anthropological jargon of the not-so-distant past.[2]

Yet interest in American Indian cultures existed long before anthropology achieved status as a true scholarly discipline. The study of those cultures began with Friar Ramon Pane, who accompanied Columbus on his second voyage in 1493,[3] and continued through the sixteenth, seventeenth, and eighteenth centuries in descriptive and polemical works most often written by missionaries, explorers, and casual travelers.[4] But not until the nineteenth century did an anthropologically oriented approach to Native American studies begin to establish itself, perhaps in response to Thomas Jefferson's argument in *Notes on the State of Virginia* that the aboriginal American was a problem for study by natural history, a science, instead of by social philosophy.[5] Early in the century, the anthropological approach was just emerging, and most students of Native American cultures pursued their anthropological interests while directing their primary energies elsewhere. For example, Christian missionaries such as John Heckewelder and David Zeisberger, government officials such as Lewis Cass, and explorers such as Meriwether Lewis and William Clark contributed substantially to the growing knowledge about American Indians while engaged by other responsibilities.

Perhaps the first professional student of American Indian cultures—that is, the first to study those cultures primarily for their own sake and on a relatively full-time basis—was Henry Rowe Schoolcraft, whose publications appeared during the thirty-year period from the 1820s to the 1850s.[6] While most of Schoolcraft's contemporaries were amateurs, working at Native American studies during time off from medical, legal, or other professional careers, their efforts and his created a climate of interest and a body of knowledge that afforded a conducive setting for the establishment of the Bureau of Ethnology at the Smithsonian Institution under John Wesley Powell in

1879. ("American" was added to the official title in the mid-1890s.) For the rest of the century, the Bureau served as a professional center for American anthropological research, though private scholars and researchers affiliated with universities such as Harvard or with other museums were also active.[7]

Even before the nineteenth-century development of an anthropologically oriented Native American studies, researchers had paid some attention to oral literature as exemplified by the stories, songs, orations, chants, and prayers of various tribal groups. While generally unappreciative of the artistry evident in this literature, students of American Indian cultures recognized the Natives' oral art as usable data for the questions which they were asking about the cultures. As Clark Wissler has pointed out, early research on Native Americans operated on two levels: "(1) for practical purposes in trade, government, colonization, education and missionary work; (2) for the sake of pure scence [sic]."[8] One aspect of practical knowledge to which data from oral literature could contribute was linguistic in nature. Initially, the European colonists who settled in the New World faced the necessity of communicating with the peoples who were already resident there. For economic and military reasons and, in many cases, in order to facilitate their perceived mission of spreading Christianity wherever they might go, New Englanders such as John Eliot and Roger Williams compiled grammars and vocabularies of Native languages.[9] One source of language which these early linguists exploited was oral literature.[10] An oration, for instance, afforded an excellent opportunity for the researcher to encounter a wide variety of language forms in a fairly circumscribed context. Similarly, the text of an oral narrative presented a range of language usages that might be difficult to elicit through casual discourse. By the end of the eighteenth century, interest in Native American languages had transcended purely practical ends and become a scholarly avocation. Efforts toward classifying languages into family groups marked a shift in language interest toward Wissler's "pure science."

Another use to which early researchers put Native American oral literature involved the reconstruction of tribal histories and, in fact, speculations about the ultimate origins of the Indian peoples. The presence of these peoples, already established in the New World, posed some difficult intellectual problems. Their existence had to be reconciled with the Old Testament version of history, for the question of Native American origins could potentially challenge the scriptural account of human creation and migration. Quite early in European contact with Native Americans, concerned historians and philosophers posited that the Indians were survivors of the ten tribes of Israel who had inexplicably disappeared from the Old Testament chronicles soon after the Hebrews had reached the Promised Land.[11] This view was doubly useful in that it not only explained the origin of the American Indians but also neatly solved a mystery in the biblical record. Oral literature became a significant exhibit in the attempt to accumulate proof for the hypothesis of the Indians' Hebrew ancestry, for writers such as James Adair cited parallels between Native American and Hebrew oral narratives as well as between other cultural features of the two groups.[12] Well into the nineteenth century, the issue of Native American origins continued to generate controversy, and while the Hebrew theory eventually yielded to the idea of an Asiatic source for the New World Natives, other points of origin—usually in some culture of European antiquity—were advanced.[13]

A less speculative set of historical problems regarding American Indians focused on the histories of individual tribal groups. Quite early in the development of Native American studies, researchers realized that tribal histories were preserved, not in conventional historical documents, but in orally transmitted accounts. The first extensive attempt to reconstruct tribal history through oral literature was probably that of John Heckewelder, a Moravian missionary who prepared his *Account of the History, Manners, and Customs of the Indian Nations, Who Once Inhabited Pennsylvania and Neighbouring States* from orally transmitted material. Heckewelder's work received an unfavorable reception because of its reliance on the oral literature of supposed savages; in fact, the American Philosophical Society delayed the work's publication until 1819, nine years after it had been written. But Heckewelder was far from alone in

placing some reliance on oral records for historical information.[14] Influential students of Native American studies followed
his example, and by the mid-1800s several historical works using oral sources, at least partially, had appeared.[15]

The acceptance of oral literature as an historical resource
grew in parallel with a theory of the development of culture that
came to dominate Native American studies during the final
third of the nineteenth century. Although theories about cultural evolution were proposed by several philosophers during the
1700s, the appearance of Charles Darwin's *Origin of the Species*
in 1849 spawned an increase of interest in the application of
evolutionist thought to anthropological data. Theorizers such as
Lewis Henry Morgan in the United States and Edward Burnett
Tylor in Britain posited unilinear scenarios for the evolutionary
development of human cultures that became widely accepted.[16]
Morgan, for instance, suggested that societies everywhere
passed through the same three stages of evolutionary development: savagery, barbarism, and civilization. A survey of the
world's cultures in 1877, when the first edition of Morgan's *Ancient Society* appeared, would reveal peoples at each evolutionary stage. The aboriginal Americans clearly represented the
savage stage, and even the ancient civilizations in Central and
South America had not advanced beyond barbarism, according
to Morgan's scheme. Morgan became particularly influential in
Native American studies when his ideas were championed by
John Wesley Powell. Virtually every researcher in Powell's Bureau of American Ethnology—as well as many other students of
American Indian cultures—was more or less committed to evolutionary theory. The evolutionists used the oral literature
which they encountered while doing field research to bolster
their ideas, for the myths and songs of the Indians revealed,
they thought, a stage of mental culture demonstrably antece-
dent to the beliefs and behavioral patterns of civilized man. For
the evolutionists, the oral literature of Native Americans proffered an excellent source of data about the mentality of
savages.

Out of the theoretical background of cultural evolutionism,
the study of folklore began to emerge, first as a field of concen-

tration within anthropology and then as an increasingly independent discipline. The term "folk-lore" had been introduced in 1846 by the British antiquarian William J. Thoms as a good Saxon compound to replace the latinate "popular antiquities" then in use.[17] By 1871, when Tylor's *Primitive Culture*, the British landmark in cultural evolutionism, appeared, the term "folklore" was ensconced in the evolutionists' lexicon. For most, it referred to aspects of a civilized culture which had survived from the savage stage out of which that civilization had evolved. The evolutionists believed that just as an adult might retain isolated remnants of childhood in his character, so a civilized culture possessed folklore. Since Native Americans were regarded as savages, they were thought to have no folklore. Savagery pervaded their existence; it was not something that persisted in vestigial survivals of the primitive past.[18] However, evolutionary folklorists were quite interested in the cultures of the Indians because the mythology and rituals of the savages of America provided a context by which to interpret the folklore of civilized Europe. The folktales and superstitions which continued to circulate in Victorian England, for example, represented all that remained of the mythology and rituals of the long-deceased savages of Britain, whose counterparts were still living in the New World.

When the Bureau of Ethnology was established in 1879, the study of Native American oral literature had become a matter of course. Evolutionary anthropologists mined texts of songs, myths, and orations for insights into the purportedly childlike mentalities of the savages they were investigating. Folklorists examined the same material to facilitate their understanding of savage survivals in civilized cultures. Both groups, for the most part, viewed Native American oral literature as a repository of data, not as cultural material worthy of attention for its own sake. But their interests in oral literature among the Indians— as well as the work of researchers studying similar phenomena from other parts of the world—began to generate some questions about the literature itself. Two issues raised by nineteenth-century students of oral literature continue to vex scholars: the issue of multiple occurrence and the issue of irrational fantasy.[19]

For even the most casual student of oral literature, one of its most intriguing features is probably the fact that the same or quite similar stories and songs occur in several different cultures. Students of Native American cultures in the nineteenth century delighted in pointing out the affinities between Siouan or Algonquin myths and those of various Old World cultures.[20] Researchers elsewhere found striking similarities between the oral literary traditions of various cultures. Some investigators attempted to explain these similarities in terms of monogenesis and diffusion. The idea that Hebrew culture had spread to the New World with the ten lost tribes of Israel illustrates this concept. Most monogeneticists based their arguments on fairly unscientific grounds. They perceived correspondences between two bodies of oral literature and assumed that the material had spread, often in a vaguely superorganic fashion, from the culture they viewed as superior to its inferior. Thus, American Indians were frequently regarded as being on the receiving end of cultural diffusion from European cultures of antiquity or from explorers and colonists in post-contact times. But scientific rigor did ultimately become a part of diffusionist principles. Regarding Native American cultures, anthropologist Franz Boas argued for diffusionism as the reason for the occurrence of the same oral literature among various tribes. He believed that when a number of narrative elements combined to form similar stories in several different societies, the combinations had originated at one place and spread from storyteller to storyteller in discernible routes of diffusion. In his first major essay on oral literature, Boas provided some careful guidelines for the study of the diffusion of oral literature among Native American cultures.[21] Meanwhile, scholars in Scandinavia were working out a historic-geographic method of diffusionist study, which imposed a precise methodology upon the investigation of the multiple occurrence of oral literature.[22]

There were others, however, cultural evolutionists, who rejected monogenesis and diffusion as a fit explanation for cross-cultural recurrence of the same or similar stories and songs. Instead, they advocated polygenesis. They believed that if cultures passed through the same stages as they evolved toward civilization, universal cultural traits would exist among all groups at each particular stage. Therefore, a myth found among a Native American group such as the Navajo as well as in a Polynesian culture would be a product of the savagery in which both groups of people were living. The advocates of polygenesis supported the notion of the psychic unity of mankind. Everywhere and at all times, they claimed, humanity experienced the same stimuli, to which they responded in the same fashion as they progressed toward civilization.[23]

The other major issue which students of Native American oral literature began to confront was the irrational fantasy that imbued many stories and songs. Researchers wondered why the American Indians employed so much of the implausible in their literary productions. For cultural evolutionists, the explanation lay firmly in the nature of Native American cultures. For if the savages of America were in their cultural childhood—in fact, not even really having begun to mature toward civilization —naturally their literary productions would be childish, filled with the fantastic and the crude. Childish savages produced childish oral literature, which mirrored their primitive intellectual state.[24] Although this cultural evolutionist view predominated in the late nineteenth century, occasionally other explanations for the irrational fantasy of Native American oral literature would be voiced. For example, Daniel G. Brinton followed the lead of an English philologist and mythographer, Max Müller, and suggested that Indian myths were allegories of natural phenomena. Beneath the fantasy lay symbolic descriptions of the conflict of sunshine with darkness.[25]

As anthropologists and folklorists began to address these two questions about Native American oral literature, some of them realized that the mythology of the Indians and the folklore extant in civilized cultures behaved, in fact, in similar ways. More and more often researchers were expanding the term "folklore" to encompass some aspects of Native American cultures, especially oral literature. And when William Wells Newell in a policy statement as first editor of the *Journal of American Folklore* outlined the periodical's scope, he firmly included "Lore of the Indian Tribes of North America (myths, tales, etc.)."[26] He went so far as to state that Native American folklore "will be generally regarded as the most promising and important part of the work to be accomplished."[27] The idea that American Indians had no folklore was a product of cultural evolutionism, and when that idea lost its grip on anthropological theorizing, the term "folklore" came to apply to Native American oral literature as well as to the stories and songs which circulated orally in civilized cultures. Today many anthropologists and folklorists use the term to refer even to esoteric songs and chants of Indian groups, which may seem more "elite" than "folk," and to Native American oratory, which appears to lack the traditional currency that many insist on as being essential to folklore.

In choosing twenty-one essays to represent pioneering work in the study of Native American folklore, I have regarded folklore in the sense which William R. Bascom employed in an essay in which he elucidated the place of folklore within the discipline of anthropology: "myths, legends, tales, proverbs, riddles, the texts of ballads and other songs, and other forms of lesser importance"[28]—that is, oral literature. Although too narrow when applied to most cultures, Bascom's anthropological delimitation of folklore to include only oral literature provides a handy operational definition when one is working with nonliterate cultures such as those of Native Americans. However, I have expanded the view expressed by Bascom somewhat to include the contexts of oral literary performance. This expansion, which is in keeping with trends in behavioral folkloristics in the 1970s and 1980s,[29] allows essays which treat musical settings for oral literature or which emphasize features of performance other than text alone to be included in the anthology. Working with a view of folklore as "oral literature and its contexts," I have reached back into the periodical literature of the 1800s to locate essays in Native American studies which treat matters that, within my usage of the concept, relate to American Indian folklore.

There are three major reasons for using only periodical essays, instead of excerpts from books and monographs. First, several reprint houses have made available new or facsimile editions of the most important book-length treatments of Native American topics from the nineteenth century. These works are much more accessible to interested students than are periodical pieces, many of which appeared in publications not readily available in even some academic libraries and which often have no adequate indexes to facilitate location of relevant materials. As far as I know, none of the essays included in this anthology has been reprinted in the twentieth century. Second, I have focused on essays because they represent complete statements, while an excerpt from a longer work, to be understood thoroughly, may depend upon the context from which it has been wrenched. Finally, the exclusive use of periodicals positions this anthology in parallel with Bruce Jackson's similar treatment of black American folklore in nineteenth-century periodicals.[30]

Magazines in the 1800s were full of articles about American Indians. The aboriginal inhabitants of the American wilderness were of pressing interest to many Euro-American readers, and writers who had studied Indian cultures first-hand or in the library found a receptive market for their work. Consequently, I have exercised considerable selectivity in choosing essays for inclusion in this anthology. A primary principle has been to choose only essays which make some theoretical point, instead of pieces which merely present texts of stories or songs, often retold in highly embellished language. But I have attempted to be as representative as possible. I have included essays on most of the Native American folklore genres studied in the nineteenth century: oratory, mythology, legend, anecdote, and song and poetry. Furthermore, I have chosen essays representative of most of the theories and issues which interested nineteenth-century students of Native American cultures: origins, diffusion, cultural evolution, irrational fantasy, and translation and presentation. Also, I have used pieces by most of the major figures in Native American studies in the 1800s.

In reproducing the texts of the essays, I have followed the orthography and punctuation of the originals. The only exceptions to this practice involve silent correction of typographical lapses. However, I have made some major changes in the style of documentation of sources used by the essayists. Every reference which an author has made to a book or an article has been converted into the documentation format prescribed by modern usage. This has often meant correction of titles, addition of publication information, and removal of parenthetical documentation from the texts into notes. Moreover, I have added some notes of my own. When a note appeared in the original—albeit in a format different from that used here—I have so indicated. All other notes are mine.

Notes

1. A. Irving Hallowell, "The Backwash of the Frontier: The Impact of the Indian on American Culture," in *The Frontier in Perspective*, ed. Walker D. Wyman and Clifton B. Kroeber (Madison: University of Wisconsin Press, 1957), p. 231. An abbreviated version of this essay appeared as "The Impact of the American Indian on American Culture," *American Anthropologist*, 59 (1957), 201-217.

2. The history of anthropolgy in the New World is a rapidly growing field of study. A good place to start is A. Irving Hallowell, "The Beginnings of Anthropology in America," in *Selected Papers from the American Anthropologist*, ed. Frederica de Laguna (Evanston: Row, Peterson, 1960), pp. 1-90. For a listing of sources, see Robert V. Kemper and John F. S. Phinney, *The History of Anthropology. A Research Bibliography* (New York: Garland, 1977). A *History of Anthropology Newsletter* also appears periodically under the editorship of George W. Stocking, Jr.

3. Edward Gaylord Bourne, "Columbus, Ramon Pane and the Beginnings of American Anthropology," *Proceedings of the American Antiquarian Society*, n. s. 17 (1906), 310-348. This essay has been excerpted in Regna Darnell, ed., *Readings in the History of Anthropology* (New York: Harper and Row, 1974), pp. 18-20.

4. An overview of the interest in American Indians during the 1600s and 1700s appears in Roy Harvey Pearce, *The Savages of America. A Study of the Indian and the Idea of Civilization*, revised edition (Baltimore: Johns Hopkins Press, 1965), pp. 3-49. This work has been reissued in paperback as *Savagism and Civilization. A Study of the Indian and the American Mind*.

5. Joan Mark presents the case for Jefferson's influence on the development of American anthropology in *Four Anthropologists. An American*

Science in Its Early Years (New York: Science History Publications 1980), pp. 5-6. See also Hallowell, "Beginnings of Anthropology . . . ," pp. 15-18.

6. Schoolcraft's claim to primacy is suggested by his being denominated the "father of American ethnology and folklore" in the introduction to Mentor L. Williams, ed., *Schoolcraft's Indian Legends* (East Lansing: Michigan State University Press, 1956), p. xviii.

7. Though far from complete, a beginning effort at a history of the BAE is Neil M. Judd, *The Bureau of American Ethnology. A Partial History* (Norman: University of Oklahoma Press, 1967). In "The American Indian and the American Philosophical Society," *Proceedings of the American Philosophical Society*, 86, no. 1 (September 1942), 189-204, Clark Wissler emphasizes the role of the American Philosophical Society in the development of Native American studies, but points out that the BAE was "the world's greatest team of full-time gatherers of field data in all divisions of anthropology" (p. 199). In *Four Anthropologists*, Joan Mark establishes the prominence of scholars associated with Harvard University as well as with the BAE in the growth of American anthropology.

8. Wissler, p. 190.

9. For example, Roger Williams provides some descriptions of oral literary performances in Chapter 3, "Of *Discourse* and *Newes*," in *A Key into the Language of America. . .* , ed. J. Hammond Trumbull, in *The Complete Writings of Roger Williams* (New York: Russell and Russell, 1963), I, 82-88. Perry Miller praises Williams' early linguistic treatise as "the nearest approach to an objective, anthropological study that anyone was to achieve in America for a century or more." See *Roger Williams. His Contribution to the American Tradition* (1953; rpt. New York: Atheneum, 1966), p. 53.

10. The use of oral literature as a source of knowledge about language continues to be a feature of linguistic research. For example, see the many oral literary texts presented in articles in the *International Journal of American Linguistics*. Using oral literature as a data source was part of the methodology of the linguistic anthropology of Franz Boas.

11. To assign primacy for this idea may be well nigh impossible. In *The Legend of Noah. Renaissance Rationalism in Art, Science, and Letters* (Urbana: University of Illinois Press, 1963), Don Cameron Allen reports that the idea can be found in Gregorio Garcia's *Origen de los Indios de el nuevo mundo*, published in 1607 (pp. 121-122), but in *The Writer and the Shaman. A Morphology of the American Indian*, trans. Raymond Rosenthal (New York: Harcourt Brace Jovanovich, 1973), Elèmire Zolla explicitly assigns the first occurrence of the idea to Lumnius's *De Extremo Dei Judicio et Indorum Vocatione*, which appeared in 1569 (p. 16).

12. James Adair, *The History of the American Indians* . . . (London: E. and C. Dilly, 1775). See also "Traditions of Descent," the essay by William W. Warren included in this volume.

13. For instance, see the following essays in this anthology: "Mythology of the Dakotas" by Stephen Return Riggs, "The Edda Among the Algonquin Indi-

ans" by Charles Godfrey Leland, and "The Borrowed Myths of America" by Stephen D. Peet.

14. A brief, but handy survey of the historical use of oral literature by students of American Indian cultures is W. K. McNeil, "History in American Folklore: An Historical Perspective," *Western Folklore,* 41 (1982), 30-35.

15. The debate over the historicity of Native American oral literature continued to flourish well into the twentieth century. Proponents included John R. Swanton and Roland B. Dixon in "Primitive American History," *American Anthropologist,* 16 (1914), 376-412. Opponents included Robert Lowie in "Oral Tradition and History," *Journal of American Folklore,* 30 (1917), 161-167. Perhaps the most vehement twentieth-century defender of the historical value of oral tradition in general has been folklorist Richard M. Dorson. His arguments have been reiterated in a number of essays, some of the most important appearing in *American Folklore and the Historian* (Chicago: University of Chicago Press, 1971) and *Folklore and Fakelore. Essays Toward a Discipline of Folk Studies* (Cambridge: Harvard University Press, 1976).

16. The influence of evolutionism on the development of anthropological theory is treated in Robert Lowie, *The History of Ethnological Theory* (New York: Holt, Rinehart and Winston, 1937), pp. 54-85.

17. Thoms's brief essay, which introduced his coinage, appeared in *The Atheneum* for August 1846. It has been reprinted in Alan Dundes, ed., *The Study of Folklore* (Englewood Cliffs, New Jersey: Prentice-Hall, 1964), pp. 4-6. The most thorough discussion of the developments which ensued from Thoms's neologism is Richard M. Dorson, *The British Folklorists. A History* (Chicago: University of Chicago Press, 1968). For the contemporary development of folklore studies in the United States, see W. K. McNeil, "A History of American Folklore Scholarship Before 1908," Ph.D. Thesis (Indiana University, 1980).

18. For a discussion of the problems in using "folklore" to refer to the literature of Native American cultures in the 1800s, see two essays by Alan Dundes: "The American Concept of Folklore," *Journal of the Folklore Institute,* 3 (1966), 228-229; and "North American Indian Folklore Studies," *Journal de la Societe des Americanistes,* 56 (1967), 55-57.

19. The issues are identified in Dundes, *The Study of Folklore,* p. 54.

20. Again, see the essays by Riggs, Leland, Peet, and Warren included in this anthology.

21. Franz Boas, "Dissemination of Tales Among the Natives of North America," *Journal of American Folklore,* 4 (1891), 13-20; reprinted in *Race, Language, and Culture* (New York: Macmillan, 1940).

22. The most fully developed statement of the historic-geographic method worked out in Scandinavia is Kaarle Krohn, *Die folkloristische Arbeitsmethode,* translated by Roger L. Welsch as *Folklore Methodology* (Austin: University of Texas Press, 1971). During the twentieth century, the most ardent student of Native America materials using the historic-geographic method has been Stith Thompson. See his *The Folktale* (New York: Dryden Press, 1946)

and especially his model study of a single narrative, "The Star Husband Tale," *Studia Septentrionalia*, 4 (1953), 93-163. The latter has been reprinted in Dundes, *The Study of Folklore*, pp. 414-474.

23. Works by proponents of cultural evolutionism as the theory applied to oral literature are legion. For a clearly worded statement, see "The Method of Folklore," the introductory essay in Andrew Lang, *Custom and Myth* (London: Longmans, Green, 1884), pp. 10-28. For an American perspective, see John Wesley Powell, "The Lessons of Folklore," *American Anthropologist*, 2 (1900), 1-36. See also the following essays in this anthology: Frank Hamilton Cushing, "The Zuñi Social, Mythic, and Religious Systems"; Washington Matthews, "Some Deities and Demons of the Navajos"; and Charles A. Eastman, "The Sioux Mythology."

24. Of course, the cultural evolutionists had no monopoly on considering the Native Americans as children. In *History of the Present State of Virginia* (1705), for example, Robert Beverly writes of the Indians: "happy, I think, in their simple State of Nature, and in their enjoyment of Plenty, without the Curse of Labour." He laments their exposure to Euro-Americans, "by whose means they seem to have lost their Felicity, as well as their Innocence" (quoted in Pearce, p. 43).

25. See Daniel G. Brinton, "The Myths of Manibozho and Ioskeha," reprinted in this anthology.

26. [William Wells Newell], "On the Field and Work of a Journal of American Folk-Lore," *Journal of American Folklore*, 1 (1883), 3. Elsewhere Newell was not as comfortable in writing of Indian *folklore* instead of *mythology*, a distinction he treated in "Folk-Lore and Mythology," *Journal of American Folklore*, 1 (1888), 163. But his initial editorial statement provided a precedent for Americanists who did want to think of Indian *folklore*. See also Michael J. Bell, "William Wells Newell and the Foundation of American Folklore Scholarship," *Journal of the Folklore Institute*, 10 (1973), 7-21; and Susan Adair Dwyer-Schick, "The American Folklore Society and Folklore Research in America," Ph.D. Thesis (University of Pennsylvania, 1979).

27. Newell, "On the Field and Work. . . ," p. 5.

28. William R. Bascom, "Folklore and Anthropology," *Journal of American Folklore*, 66 (1953), 285; reprinted in Dundes, *The Study of Folklore*, pp. 25-33.

29. For example, see Dan Ben-Amos, "Toward a Definition of Folklore in Context," *Journal of American Folklore*, 84 (1971), 3-15; reprinted in Americo Paredes and Richard Bauman, eds., *Toward New Perspectives in Folklore* (Austin: University of Texas Press, 1972), pp. 3-15.

30. Bruce Jackson, *The Negro and His Folklore in Nineteenth-Century Periodicals* (Austin: University of Texas Press, 1967). My anthology should also be viewed within the context of several collections of anthropological essays and excerpts from the period: Margaret Mead and Ruth L. Bunzel, eds., *The Golden Age of Anthropology* (New York: George Braziller, 1960) and Roger C. Owen, James J. F. Deetz, and Anthony D. Fisher, eds., *The North American Indians. A Source Book* (New York: Macmillan, 1967), for example.

Indian Eloquence

* * * * *

Perhaps no genre of oral literature was as apt as oratory to capture the fancies of romantic sympathizers with Native Americans, while at the same time perpetuating their perceived role as obstacle to progress. On one hand, the speeches delivered by Native American leaders confirmed the image of the Noble Savage whose eloquence, though limited by the supposed poverty of his language, reflected a natural gift for concise, yet colorful expression. Unlike myths and legends, with their embarrassing superstitions, or songs, which were largely incomprehensible to European ears, oratory was something that a non-Indian could appreciate and which revealed the best of Native virtues: directness, courage, and spiritual grandeur, to name only a few that observers in the nineteenth century were likely to notice. But at the same time, the oratorical skills of Native American leaders were often employed to encourage resistance to Euro-American progress. Thus, orations served as evidence of

SOURCE: *The Knickerbocker*, 7 (April 1836), 385-390.

1

the real threat that the Indians incorrigibly posed. Their myths and songs might be deemed child-like, but their speeches revealed men set to thwart Euro-American designs as far as possible.

The unknown author of "Indian Eloquence" reflects some prevailing attitudes of his time, especially his assumption that Native American cultures were inevitably on the wane. Though he laments that circumstance only with reservation, he does argue that Native Americans have represented a significant era in human cultural history and that memory of them must be preserved. One value of oratory is that, if recorded, it can assist in that preservation. For oratory mirrors those cultural values that created the Native Americans' distinctive historical role. Moreover, our author speaks of the Indian as "the only true child of nature," whose sparse vocabulary necessitates the development of a rich system of metaphor. Such ideas about the natural poetic tendency of savage speech can be traced at least as far back as the eighteenth-century Italian philosopher Giambattista Vico and comprised a romantic article of faith in the early nineteenth century. Yet the rhetorical analysis which accompanies the text excerpts in this essay reveals an author who is willing to go beyond effusion over Native American oratorical skills to a careful examination of what those skills might be.

Many accounts of American Indian life written during the first half of the nineteenth century included data on oratory, either texts of speeches (often the same ones over and over again) or descriptions of contexts where speeches were made and of their style of delivery. Among some of the more important works on Native American oratory from the 1800s were Samuel G. Drake, Indian Biography, Containing the Lives of More Than Two Hundred Indian Chiefs: Also Such Others of That Race as Have Rendered Their Names Conspicuous in the History of North America from Its First Being Known to Europeans to the Present Period. Giving at Large Their Most Celebrated Speeches, Memorable Sayings, Numerous Anecdotes; and a History of Their Wars. Much of Which Is Taken from Manuscripts Never Before Published (Boston: Josiah Drake, 1832); and William Tracy, "Indian Eloquence," Appleton's Journal, 6 (11 November 1871), 543–545.

Although interest in the subject had somewhat abated by the end of the century, several studies and collections of texts worthy of note have been published in the twentieth century: Virginia Irving Armstrong, ed., I Have Spoken. American History Through the Voices of the Indians

(Chicago: Swallow Press, 1971); Donald Bahr, Pima and Papago Ritual Oratory. A Study of Three Texts *(San Francisco: Indian Historian Press, 1975); Marius Barbeau, "Indian Eloquence,"* Queen's Quarterly, *39 (1932), 451–464; Louis Thomas Jones,* Aboriginal American Oratory. The Tradition of Eloquence Among the Indians of the United States *(Los Angeles: Southwest Museum, 1965); Marjorie N. Murphy, "Silence, the Word, and Indian Rhetoric,"* College Composition and Communication, *21 (1970), 356–363; Jarold Ramsey, ed.,* Coyote was Going There. Indian Literature of the Oregon Country *(Seattle: University of Washington Press, 1977); Edna C. Sorber, "The Noble Eloquent Savage,"* Ethnohistory, *19 (1972), 227–236; and W. C. Vanderwerth,* Indian Oratory. Famous Speeches by Noted Indian Chiefs *(Norman: University of Oklahoma Press, 1971). The last item contains texts of two of the most famous speeches made by Native Americans during the nineteenth century (but after this essay was published in 1836): the response of the Duwamish leader Seattle to the formal organization of Washington Territory by the United States in 1853; the speech which Joseph, Nez Perce leader, delivered in 1879 to an assembly of federal officials when he visited the national capital to plead for his tribe's welfare. A rhetorical analysis of a Native American oration, emphasizing the role of parallel structures, appears in Dell Hymes, "Breakthrough into Performance Revisited," in* "In Vain I Tried to Tell You." Essays in Native American Ethnopoetics *(Philadelphia: University of Pennsylvania Press, 1981), pp. 201–208.*

*   *   *   *   *

A few suns more, and the Indian will live only in history. A few centuries, and that history will be colored with the mellow, romantic light in which Time robes the past, and contrasted with the then present wealth and splendor of America, may seem so improbable, as to elicit from the historian a philosophic doubt of its authenticity. The period may even arrive, when the same uncertainty which hangs over the heroic days of every people may attend its records, and the stirring deeds of the battle-field and council-fire may be regarded as attactive fictions, or at the best as beautiful exaggerations.

This is but in the nature of things. Actions always lose their reality and distinctness in the perspective of ages; time is their charnel-house. And no memorials are so likely to be lost or forgotten, as those of a conquered nation. Of the Angles and Saxons little more than a name has survived, and the Indian may meet no better fate. Even though our own history is so enveloped in theirs, it is somewhat to be feared that, from neglect, the valuable cover will be suffered to decay, and care be bestowed only on the more precious contents. 'Be it so,' exclaim some; 'what pleasure or profit is to be derived from the remembrance? Let the wild legend be forgotten. They are but exhibitions of savage life teeming with disgusting excess, and brutal passion. They portray man in no interesting light, for with every redeeming trait, there rises up some revolting characteristic in horrid contrast. Was he grateful? so was his revenge bloody and eternal. Was he brave?—So was he treacherous. Was he generous?—so was he crafty and cruel.'

But a more philosophic mind would say, 'No! he presents a part of the panorama of humanity, and his extermination is an embodiment of a great principle—the same retreat of the children of the wilderness before the wave of civilization; hence arises a deep interest in his fortune, which should induce us to preserve, carefully and faithfully, the most trifling record of his greatness or his degradation.' At a time when barbarous nations elsewhere had lost their primitive purity, we find him the only true child of nature—the best specimen of man in his native simplicity. We should remember him as a 'study of human nature'—as an instance of a strange mixture of good and evil passions. We perceive in him fine emotions of feeling and delicacy, and unrestrained, systematic cruelty, grandeur of spirit and hypocritical cunning, genuine courage and fiendish treachery. He was like some beautiful spar, part of which is regular, clear, and sparkling, while a portion, impregnated with clay, is dark and forbidding.

But above all, as being an engrossing subject to an American, as coming to us the only relic of the literature of the aborigines, and the most perfect emblem of their character, their glory and their intellect, we should dearly cherish the remains of their

4

oratory. In these we see developed the motives which animated their actions, and the light and shadows of their very soul. The iron encasement of apparent apathy in which the savage had fortified himself, impenetrable at ordinary moments, is laid aside in the council-room. The genius of eloquence bursts the swathing bands of custom, and the Indian stands forth accessible, natural, and legible. We commune with him, listen to his complaints, understand, appreciate, and even feel his injuries.

As Indian eloquence is a key to the character, so is it a noble monument of their literature. Oratory seldom finds a more auspicious field. A wild people, and region of thought, forbade feebleness; uncultivated, but intelligent and sensitive, a purity of idea, chastely combined with energy of expression, ready fluency, and imagery now exquisitely delicate, now soaring to the sublime, all united to rival the efforts of any ancient or modern orator.[1]

What can be imagined more impressive, than a warrior rising in the councilroom to address those who bore the same scarred marks of their title to fame and to chieftainship? The dignified stature—the easy repose of limbs—the graceful gesture, the dark speaking eye, excite equal admiration and expectation. We would anticipate eloquence from an Indian. He has animating remembrances—a poverty of language, which exacts rich and apposite metaphorical allusions, even for ordinary conversation—a mind which like his body has never been trammelled and mechanised by the formalities of society, and passions which, from the very outward restraint imposed upon them, burn more fiercely within. There is a mine of truth in the reply of Red Jacket, when called a warrior: 'A *warrior!*' said he; 'I am an *orator*—I was *born* an orator.'[2]

There are not many speeches remaining on record, but even in this small number there is such a rich yet varied vein of all the characteristics of true eloquence, that we even rise from their perusal with regret that so few have been preserved. No where can be found a poetic thought clothed in more captivating simplicity of expression, than in the answer of Tecumseh to Governor Harrison, in the conference at Vincennes.[3] It contains a high moral rebuke, and a sarcasm heightened in effect by an evident consciousness of loftiness above the reach of insult. At the close of his address, he found that no chair had been placed for him, a neglect which Governor Harrison ordered to be remedied as soon as discovered. Suspecting, perhaps, that it was more an affront than a mistake, with an air of dignity elevated almost to haughtiness, he declined the seat proffered, with the words, 'Your father requests you to take a chair,' and answered, as he calmly disposed himself on the ground: 'My father? The sun is my father, and the earth is my mother. *I will repose upon her bosom.*'

As they excelled in the beautiful, so also they possessed a nice sense of the ridiculous. There is a clever strain of irony, united with the sharpest taunt, in the speech of Garangula to De la Barre, the Governor of Canada, when that crafty Frenchman met with his tribe in council, for the purpose of obtaining peace, and reparation for past injuries.[4] The European, a faithful believer in the maxim that '*En guerre ou la peau du lion ne peut suffire il y faut coudre un lopin de celle du regnard,*' attempted to overawe the savage by threats, which he well knew he had no power to execute. Garangula, who also was well aware of his weakness, replied, 'Yonondio, you must have believed when you left Quebec, that the sun had burnt up all the forests which render our country inaccessible to the French, or that the lakes had so overflowed their banks, that they had surrounded our castles, and that it was impossible for us to get out of them. Yes, surely you must have dreamed so, and the *curiosity* of seeing so great a wonder has brought you so far. Hear, Yonondio: our *women* had taken their clubs, our *children* and *old* men had carried their bows and arrows into the heart of your camp, if our *warriors* had not disarmed them, and kept them back when your messenger came to our castle.' We cannot give a better idea of the effect of their harrangues upon their own people, and at the same time a finer instance of their gratefulness when skilfully touched, than in the address to the Wallah-Wallahs by their young chief, the Morning Star.[5] In consequence of the death of several of their tribe, killed in one of their predatory excursions against the whites, they had collected in a large body for the purpose of assailing them. The stern, uncompromising hostility with which they were animated, may be imagined from the words they chaunted on approaching to the attack: 'Rest, brothers, rest! You will be avenged. The tears of your widows will cease to flow, when they behold the blood of your murderers, and on seeing their scalps, your young children shall sing and leap with joy. Rest, brothers, in peace! Rest, we shall have blood!' The last strains of the death-song had died away. The gleaming eye, burning with the desire of revenge—the countenance, fierce even through an Indian's cloak—the levelled gun, and poised arrow, forbade promise of peace, and their superior force as little hope of successful resistance. At this moment of awful excitement, a mounted troop burst in between them, and its leader addressed his kindred: 'Friends and relations! Three snows have only passed over our heads, since we were a poor, miserable people. Our enemies were numerous and powerful; we were few and weak. Our hearts were as the hearts of little children. We could not fight like warriors, and were driven like deer about the plains. When the thunders rolled, and the rains poured, we had no place save the rocks, whereon we could lay our heads. Is such the case now? No! We have regained possession of the land of our fathers, in which they and their fathers' fathers lie buried; *our hearts are great within us, and we are now a nation.* Who has produced this change? The white man! And are we to treat him with ingratitude? No! *The warrior of the strong arm and the great heart will never rob a friend.'* The result was wonderful. There was a complete revulsion of feeling. The angry waves were quieted, and the savage, forgetting his enmity smoked the calumet with those whom the eloquence of the Morning Star alone had saved from his scalping knife.

Fearlessness and success in battle were the highest titles to honor, and an accusation of cowardice was a deadly insult. A reproach of this kind to a celebrated chief received a chivalric reply. Kognethagecton, or as he was more generally called, White-Eyes, at the time his nation was solicited to join in the war against the Americans, in our struggle for liberty, exerted his influence against hostile measures. His answer to the Senecas, who were in the British interest, and who, irritated by his obstinate adherence to peace, attempted to humble him, by reference to an old story of the Delawares being a conquered people, is a manly and dignified assertion of independence.[6] It reminds one of the noble motto of the Frenchman: '*Je n'éstime un autre plus grand que moi lors que j'ai mon épée.*' 'I know well,' said he, 'that you consider us a conquered nation—as women—as your inferiors. You have, say you, shortened our legs, and put petticoats on us. You say you have given us a hoe and a corn-pounder, and told us to plant and pound for *you—you men— you warriors*. But look at me—am I not full grown? And have I not a warrior's dress? Ay! *I am a man*—and these are the arms of a man—and all that country is mine!' What a dauntless vindication of manhood, and what a nice perception of Indian character, is this appeal to their love of courage, and their admiration for a fine form, vigorous limbs, complete arms, and a proud demeanor! How effective and emphatic the conclusion, 'all that country is mine!' exclaimed in a tone of mingled defiance and pride, and accompanied with a wave of the hand over the rich country bordering on the Alleghany!

This bold speech quelled for a time all opposition, but the desire to engage against the Americans, increased by the false reports of some wandering tories, finally became so vehement, that, as a last resort, he proposed to the tribe to wait ten days before commencing hostilities. Even this was about to be denied him, and the term traitor beginning to be whispered around, when he rose in council, and began an animated expostulation against their conduct. He depictured its inevitable consequences—the sure advance of the white man, and the ruin of his nation; and then, in a generous manner, disclaimed any interest or feelings separate from those of his friends; and added: 'But if you *will* go out in this war, you shall not go without *me*. I have taken peace measures, it is true, with the view of saving my tribe from destruction. But if you think me in the wrong—*if you give more credit to runaway vagabonds than to your own friends— to a man—to a warrior—to a Delaware*—if you insist upon fighting the Americans—go! And I will go with you. *And I will not go like the bear-hunters, who sets his dogs upon the animal, to be beaten about with his paws, while he keeps himself at a safe distance.* No! I will lead you on. I will place myself in the front. I will fall with the first of you. *You* can do as you choose. But as for *me*, I will not survive my nation. I will not live to bewail the miserable destruction of a brave people, who deserved, as you do, a better fate!'

The allusion to their greater confidence in foreigners than in their own kindred, is a fine specimen of censure, wonderfully strengthened by a beautiful climacteric arrangement. Commencing with a friend—and who so grateful as an Indian?—it passes to a man—and who so vain of his birth-right as an Indian?—then to a warrior; and who more glorious to the savage than the man of battles?—and lastly to a Delaware—a word which rings through the hearts of his hearers, starts into life a host of proud associations, and while it deepens their contempt for the stranger and his falsehoods, imparts a grandeur to the orator, in whom the friend, the man, the warrior, the Delaware are personified.

The spirit of the conclusion added to its force. It was the outbursting of that firm determination never to forsake their customs and laws—that brotherhood of feeling which have ever inspired the action of the aborigines—a spirit which time has strengthened, insult hardened to obstinacy, and oppression rendered almost hereditary. It bespeaks a bold soul, resolved to die with the loss of its country's liberties.

We pass by the effect of this speech, by merely stating that it was successful, to notice a letter much of the same character as the close of the last, sent to General Clinch, by the chief who is now setting our troops at defiance in Florida.[7] 'You have arms,' says he, 'and so have we; you have powder and lead, and so have we; you have men, and so have we; your men will fight, and so will ours, *till the last drop of the Seminole's blood has moistened the dust of his hunting ground.*' This needs no comment. Intrepidity is its character.

View these evidences of attachment to the customs of their fathers, and of heroic resolution to leave their bones in the forests where they were born, and which were their inheritance, and then revert to their unavailing, hopeless resistance against the march of civilization; and though we know it is the rightful, natural course of things, yet it is a hard heart which does not feel for their fate. Turn to Red Jacket's graphic description of the fraud which has purloined their territory, and shame mingles somewhat with our pity.[8] 'Brothers, at the treaties held for the purchase of our lands, the white men, with *sweet voices* and *smiling faces*, told us they *loved* us, and that they would not cheat us, but that the king's children on the other side of the lake would cheat us. When we go on the other side of the lake, the king's children tell us your people will cheat us. These things puzzle our heads, and we believe that the Indians must take care of themselves, and not trust either in your people or in the king's children. Brothers, *our seats were once large, and yours very small. You have now become a great people, and we have scarcely a place left to spread our blankets.*' True, and soon their graves will be all they shall retain of their once ample hunting-grounds. Their strength is wasted, their countless warriors dead, their forests laid low, and their burial-places upturned by the plough-share. There was a time when the war-cry of a Powhattan, a Delaware, or an Abenaquis, struck terror to the heart of a pale-face: but now the Seminole is singing his last battle-song.

Some of the speeches of *Skenandoah*, a celebrated Oneida chief, contain the truest touches of natural eloquence.[9] He lived to a great age; and in his last oration in council, he opened with the following sublime and beautiful sentence: 'Brothers—*I am an aged hemlock. The winds of an hundred winters have whistled through my branches, and I am dead at the top.*' Every reader, who has seen a tall hemlock, with a dry and leafless top surmounting its dark green foliage, will feel the force of the simile. 'I am dead at the top.' His memory, and all the vigorous powers of youth, had departed forever.

Not less felicitous was the close of a speech made by *Pushmataha*, a venerable chief of a western tribe at a council held, we believe, in Washington, many years since.[10] In alluding to his extreme age, and to the probability that he might not even survive the journey back to his tribe, he said: 'My children will walk through the forests, and the Great Spirit will whisper in the tree-tops, and the flowers will spring up in the trails—but Pushmataha will hear not—he will see the flowers no more. He will be gone. His people will know that he is dead. The news will come to their ears, *as the sound of the fall of a mighty oak in the stillness of the woods.'*

The most powerful tribes have been destroyed; and as Sadekanatie expressed it,[11] 'Strike at the root, and when the trunk shall be cut down, the branches shall fall of course.' The trunk has fallen, the branches are slowly withering, and shortly the question *'Who is there to mourn for Logan,'*[12] may be made of the whole race, and find not a sympathizing reply.

Their actions *may* outlive, but their oratory we think *must* survive their fate. It contains many attributes of true eloquence. With a language too barren, and minds too free for the rules of rhetoric, they still attained a power of touching the feelings, and a sublimity of style which rival the highest productions of their more cultivated enemies. Expression apt and pointed—language strong and figurative—comparisons rich and bold—descriptions correct and picturesque—and gesture energetic and graceful, were the most striking peculiarities of their oratory. The latter orations, accurate mirrors of their character, their bravery, immoveable stoicism, and native grandeur, heightened as they are in impressiveness by the melancholy accompaniment of approaching extermination, will be as enduring as the swan-like music of Attic and Roman eloquence, which was the funeral song of the liberties of those republics.

Notes

1. An unqualified opinion to this effect has been expressed by JEFFERSON and CLINTON [original note].

2. Red Jacket (c. 1756–1830) was a Seneca leader, who attained considerable fame through his oratorical abilities. He negotiated with several Euro-American leaders, including President Washington. He is the subject of a biography, which also includes texts of some of his orations: William L. Stone, *The Life and Times of Sa-Go-Ye-Wat-Ha (Red Jacket)* (New York: Wiley & Putnam, 1841).

3. Tecumseh (1768–1813), a Shawnee, was a leader of major Native American resistance to Euro-American incursions into the Upper Ohio Valley. The meeting with Harrison occurred in 1810.

4. Garangula (or Grangula) was an Onondaga leader. In 1684 a French Canadian military expedition tried to exact his promise that members of the Iroquois Confederacy would no longer trade with the British. The speech excerpted here is Garangula's reply.

5. I have not been able to identify the Morning Star referred to here. The Walla Walla were a group of Sahaptin-speakers related to the Nez Percé, who were first encountered by Lewis and Clark in 1805.

6. Kognethagecton (Koguethagechton or White Eyes) (c. 1730–1778) was a Delaware leader who opposed his tribe's entering the American War for Independence on the side of the British. His speech was delivered in 1775 in response to Seneca attempts to enlist the Delaware in the British cause. Despite his stance, White Eyes was apparently murdered by American soldiers.

7. Osceola (c. 1804–1838) commanded Native American resistance during the Second Seminole War which began in 1835.

8. The following material actually comes from two of Red Jacket's speeches. The first section (unitalicized) was part of a speech delivered in May 1811 to a representative of a company that wished to buy Seneca lands. The italicized sentences are taken from Red Jacket's response to a missionary who had come to make converts of the Seneca in 1805.

9. Skenandoah (c. 1706–1816) was a noted Oneida chief who died at what was reputed to be over a century in age. He was noted for his conversion to Christianity from a life of dissipation. The ethnologist Lewis Henry Morgan sometimes wrote under the pen name "Skenandoah."

10. Pushmataha (c. 1764–1824) counseled his people to resist Tecumseh's attempts to organize Indian resistance against Euro-American encroachment. The speech excerpted here was probably delivered in the year of his death, when he was in Washington on a mission for his people.

11. Sadekanatie (c. 1640–1701) was an Onondaga chief known as the principal tribal orator.

12. James Logan (c. 1723–1780) led the Mingo, a branch of the Iroquois who had settled outside the group's traditional habitat. In 1774 he presented one of the most memorable addresses in Native American oratorical history. Actually, his comments were read in English translation to an emissary of Lord Dunmore, the governor of Virginia, as a response to the treacherous murder of some of Logan's people by Euro-Americans. Controversy, though, still exists over the authenticity of Logan's speech. For some recent opinions, see James H. O'Donnell III, "Logan's Oration: A Case Study in Ethnographic Authentication," *Quarterly Journal of Speech*, 65 (1979), 150–156; and Ray H. Sandefur, "Logan's Oration—How Authentic?," *Quarterly Journal of Speech*, 46 (1960), 289–296.

Historical and Mythological Traditions of the Algonquins;

with a Translation of the "Walum-Olum," or Bark Record of the Linni-Lenape

by E. G. Squier

* * * * *

As student of American Indian cultures and Central Americana and as an active diplomat, Ephraim George Squier (1821–1888) epitomized the scholar as public person during the middle years of the nineteenth century. He started his career as a journalist, but early in life began to contribute to the study of American Indian cultures. The most important of these early contributions

SOURCE: *American* [Whig] *Review,* 9 (February 1849), 173-193. The essay was reprinted in W. W. Beach, ed., *The Indian Miscellany; Containing Papers on the History, Antiquities, Arts, Languages, Religions, Traditions and Superstitions of the American Aborigines; with Descriptions of Their Domestic Life, Manners, Customs, Traits, Amusements and Exploits; Travels and Adventures in the Indian Country; Incidents of Border Warfare; Missionary Relations; etc.* (Albany: J. Munsell, 1877). "This paper was read before the New York Historical Society, at its regular meeting in June last. It has not been thought necessary to materially alter its original form, although as a general rule, the use of the first person is objectionable" [Squier's note].

were archeological in nature; in 1847 he collaborated with Edwin Hamilton Davis on "Ancient Monuments of the Mississippi Valley," a paper on the remains of the Moundbuilders in Ohio which appeared in the first number of the Smithsonian Contributions to Knowledge. *Squier published a paper on the archeology of his native New York state in the same series in 1851. Meanwhile, in 1849, Squier undertook a diplomatic mission to Central America, where he was instrumental in negotiating a treaty for an interoceanic canal with the government of Nicaragua. During the next decade he spent considerable time in Nicaragua and Honduras, and his familiarity with the region's natural history, the cultures of its peoples, and its archeology made him one of the leading authorities on Central America in the nineteenth century. He published several important books on Central American topics. In the early 1860s Squier became chief editor for the publishing house of Frank Leslie. Until ill health forced his retirement from active life, he combined his editorial work there with further diplomatic duties.*

The Walam Olum, *parts of which are presented and translated in Squier's essay reproduced here, generated some controversy among students of Native American cultures in the 1800s. A poetic chronicle of the Delaware (or Lenni Lenape) which begins with the cosmogonic myth and ends with the arrival of the Europeans in the New World, the* Walam Olum *originally consisted of a bundle of sticks on which were painted pictographs, each representing one of the chronicle's 183 verses. Although the sticks themselves do not survive, a manuscript copy of the pictographs with accompanying text in Delaware was written out in 1833 by Constantine S. Rafinesque, a botanist and natural historian. Rafinesque claimed to have obtained the pictographic material from a "Dr. Ward" in Indiana in 1820. Song texts in Delaware came from two other sources, neither of whom is identified (though Rafinesque cites one John Burns as translator of some of the songs). Rafinesque published his translation of the song texts, but omitted the pictographs and the Delaware originals of the songs in* The American Nations; or, Outlines of Their General History, Ancient and Modern . . . (*Philadelphia: by the Author, 1836). Twelve years later in the essay given here, E. G. Squier retranslated the material and published some of the pictographs and Delaware text. Yet because of Rafinesque's reputation for eccentricity, serious doubts arose about the authenticity of the* Walam Olum. *Fears of a hoax similar to the Ossianic poems of MacPherson surfaced. However, researches of anthropologist Daniel Brinton resulted in his assertion of the material's genuineness. Brinton published all the pictographs, the complete*

14

Delaware text, and a new translation in The Lenâpé and Their Legends: with the Complete Text and Symbols of the Walam Olum, a New Translation, and an Inquiry into Its Authenticity, *volume 5 in his* Library of Aboriginal American Literature *(1885). A new examination of the* Walam Olum, *which agrees with Brinton's verdict of authenticity but does not completely resolve the continuing controversy over its genuineness, includes a facsimile reproduction of Rafinesque's manuscript, now in the University of Pennsylvania Museum, a new translation, and commentaries from the perspectives of ethnology, archeology, linguistics, and history.* Walam Olum or Red Score: The Migration Legend of the Lenni Lenape or Delaware Indians, a New Translation, Interpreted by Linguistic, Historical, Archaeological, Ethnological, and Physical Anthropological Studies *(Indianapolis: Indiana Historical Society, 1954) is the work of a research team involving several relevant disciplines. Quite recently, material from the* Walam Olum *has been adapted for literary use by Daniel Hoffman. His* Brotherly Love *(New York: Random House, 1981) poetically recounts the settling of what is now Pennsylvania by Native Americans and then by Euro-American colonists led by William Penn.*

Squier's essay is primarily designed to present the Walam Olum *in a new, smoother translation, but he does make several theoretical points in his commentary. He is principally concerned with the historical value of the Native American document. In trusting it, he anticipates the stance of twentieth-century ethnohistorians. He also evinces a good deal of regard for Delaware culture. For instance, he suggests that the Delaware had a knowledge of a "high god," a concept which cultural evolutionists in the late 1800s would deny to groups at the savage or primitive stage of cultural development. Perhaps the most important point about the* Walam Olum *for the student of oral literature is also developed briefly by Squier. The role of the pictographs in oral performance of the songs was probably mnemonic, he suggests. The graphics served to remind singers of what came next in what they were singing. Frances Densmore has reported similar mnemonic drawings among the Ojibwa in* Chippewa Music, Bureau of American Ethnology Bulletin No. 45 *(1910); J. Dyneley Prince found mnemonic devices used by the Passamaquoddy, as reported in "The Passamaquoddy Wampum Records,"* Publications of the American Philosophical Society, 36 *(1897), 479–495; Frank Russell found the utilization of sticks as memory cues among the Pima, a phenomenon which he described in "Pima Annals,"*

15

American Anthropologist, *5 (1903), 76–80; and Jack A. Frisch has recently commented on mnemonic devices among the Iroquois in "Folklore, History, and the Iroquois Condolence Cane," in* Trends and New Vistas in Native American Folklore, *ed. Stephen Mannenbach, Folklore Forum Bibliographic and Special Series No. 15 (1976), pp. 19–25. Some parallels may be drawn between the* Walam Olum *and the winter counts kept by some Plains Indian groups. For an example of a winter count, see Martha Warren Beckwith, "Mythology of the Oglala Dakota,"* Journal of American Folklore, *43 (1930), 338–342.*

* * * * *

The discovery of America, in the fifteenth century, constitutes a grand era in the history of the world. From it we may date the rise of that mental energy and physical enterprise, which has since worked so wonderful changes in the condition of the human race. It gave a new and powerful impulse to the nations of Europe, then slowly rousing from the lethargy of centuries. Love of adventure, hope, ambition, avarice,—the most powerful incentives to human action,—directed the attention of all men to America. Thither flocked the boldest and most adventurous spirits of Europe; and half a century of startling events sufficed to lift the veil of night from a vast continent, unsurpassed in the extent and variety of its productions, abounding in treasures, and teeming with a strange people, divided into numberless families, exhibiting many common points of resemblance, yet differing widely in their condition, manners, customs, and civil and social organizations.

Along the shores of the frozen seas of the North, clothed with the furs of the sea-monsters whose flesh had supplied them with food, burrowing in icy caverns during the long polar nights, were found the dwarfed and squalid Esquimaux. In lower latitudes, skirting the bays and inlets of the Atlantic, pushing their canoes along the shores of the great lakes, or chasing the buffalo on the vast meadows of the West, broken up into numerous families, subdivided into tribes, warring constantly, and ever struggling for ascendency over each other, were the active and fearless Hunters, falling chiefly within the modern extended denominations of the Algonquin and Iroquois families. Still lower down, in the mild and fertile regions bordering the Gulf of Mexico, more fixed in their habits, half hunters, half agriculturists, with a systematized religion, and a more consolidated civil organization, and constituting the connecting link between the gorgeous semi-civilization of Mexico and the nomadic state of the Northern families, were the Floridian tribes, in many respects one of the most interesting groups of the continent. Beneath the tropics, around the bases of the volcanic ranges of Mexico, and occupying her high and salubrious plains, Cortez found the Aztecs and their dependencies,—nations rivalling in their barbarous magnificence the splendors of the oriental world,—far advanced in the arts, living in cities, constructing vast works of public utility, and sustaining an imposing, though bloody religious system. Passing the nations of Central America, whose architectural monuments challenge comparison with the proudest of the old world, and attest the advanced condition and great power of their builders,—Pizarro found beneath the equator a vast people, living under a well-organized and consolidated government, attached to a primitive Sabianism, fixed in their habits and customs, and happy in their position and circumstances. Still beyond these to the southward, were the invincible Aurucanians, together with numerous other nations, with distinctive features, filling still lower places in the scale of advancement, and finally subsiding into the squalid counterparts of the Esquimaux in Patagonia.

These numerous nations, exhibiting contrasts so striking, and institutions so novel and interesting, it might be supposed, would have at once attracted the attention of the learned of that day, and insured at their hands a full and authentic account of their government, religion, traditions, customs and modes of life. The men, however, who subverted the empires of Montezuma and the Incas, were bold adventurers, impelled for the most part by an absorbing avarice, and unfitted by habit, as incapable from education and circumstances, of transmitting to us correct or satisfactory information respecting the nations with which they were acquainted. The ecclesiastics who followed in their train, from whom more might have been expected, actuated by a fierce bigotry, and eager only to elevate the symbol of their intolerance over the emblems of a rival priesthood, misrepresented the religious conceptions of the Indians, and exaggerated the bloody observances of the aboriginal ritual, as an apology, if not a justification, for their own barbarism and cruelty. They threw down the high altars of Aztec superstition, and consecrated to their own mummeries the solar symbols of the Peruvian temples. They burned the pictured historical and mythological records of the ancient empire in the public square of Mexico; defaced the sculptures on her monuments, and crushed in pieces the statues of her gods. Yet the next day, with an easy transition, they proclaimed the great impersonation of the female, or productive principle of Nature, who in the Mexican, as in every other system of mythology, was the consort of the Sun, to be no other than the Eve of the Mosaic record, or the Mother of Christ; they even tracked the vagrant St. Thomas in the person of the benign Quetzalcoatl, the Mexican counterpart of the Hindoo Buddha and the Egytian Osiris!

All these circumstances have contributed to throw doubt and uncertainty over the Spanish accounts of the aboriginal nations. Nor were the circumstances, attending European adventure and settlements in other parts of the continent, much more favorable to the preservation of impartial and reliable records. The Puritan of the North and the gold-hunter of Virginia and Carolina, looked with little interest and less complacency upon the "wilde salvages" with which they were surrounded, and of whom Cotton Mather wrote, that "Although we know not *when* nor *how* they first became inhabitants of this mighty continent, yet we may guess the devil decoyed these miserable salvages hither, in hopes that the gospel of the Lord Jesus Christ would never come to destroy his absolute empire over them."[1]

The Jesuits and other enthusiasts, the propagandists of the Catholic faith among the Northern tribes, were more observant and correct, but their accounts are very meagre in matters of the most consequence, in researches concerning the history and religion of the aborigines. All treated the religious conceptions and practices and transmitted traditions of the Indians with little regard. Indeed it has been only during the last century, since European communication with the primitive nations of Southern Asia, and a more intimate acquaintance with Oriental literature, have given a new direction to researches into this history of mind and man, that the true value of the religious notions and the recorded or transmitted traditions of various nations, in determining their origins and connections, and illustrating their remote history, has been ascertained. And even now there are few who have a just estimation of their importance in these respects. It may however be claimed, in the language of an erudite American, that "of all researches which most effectually aid us to discover the origin of a nation or people, whose history is either unknown, or deeply involved in the obscurity of ancient times, none are perhaps attended with such important results, as the analysis of their theological dogmas, and their religious practices. To such matters mankind adheres with the greatest tenacity, and though both modified and corrupted in the revolutions of ages, they still preserve features of their original construction when language, arts, sciences and political establishments no longer retain distinct lineaments of their ancient constitutions."[2]

The traveller Clarke, maintaining the same position, observes, "that by a proper attention to the vestiges of ancient superstition, we are sometimes enabled to refer a whole people to their original ancestors, with as much if not more certainty, than by observations made upon their languages, because the superstition is engrafted upon the stock, but the language is liable to change."[3] However important is the study of military, civil and political history, the science is incomplete without mythological history, and he is little imbued with the spirit of philosophy, who can perceive in the fables of antiquity nothing but the extravagance of a fervid imagination.[4] It is under this view, in the absence of such information derivable from early writers, as may form the basis of our inquiries into the history of the American race, its origin, and the rank which it is entitled to hold in the scale of human development, that the religious conceptions and observances, and authentic traditions of the aboriginal nations, become invested with new interest and importance. And although the opportunities for collecting them, at this day, are limited, and much care and discrimination is requisite to separate that which is original from what is derivative, still they perhaps afford the safest and surest means of arriving at the results desired. Not that I would be understood as undervaluing physical or philological researches, in their bearings upon these questions; for if the human mind can ever flatter itself with having discovered the truth, it is when many facts, and these facts of different kinds, unite in producing the same result.

Impressed with these views, I have, in pursuing investigations in another but cognate department of research, taken considerable pains to collect from all available sources, such information as seemed authentic, relating not only to the religious ceremonies and conceptions, but also to the mythological and historical traditions of the aborigines of all parts of the continent. An analysis and comparison of these have led to some most extraordinary results, which it would be impossible, in the narrow scope of this paper, to indicate with necessary fullness. It may be said generally, that they exhibit not only a wonderful uniformity and concurrence in their elements and more important particulars, but also an absolute identity, in many essential respects, with those which existed among the primitive nations of the old world, far back in the monumental and traditional periods.

Among the various original manuscripts which, in the course of these investigations, fell into my possession, I received through the hands of the executors of the lamented NICOLLET, a series by the late Prof. C. S. RAFINESQUE,—well known as a man of science and of an inquiring mind, but whose energies were not sufficiently concentrated to leave a decided impression in any department of research. A man of unparalleled industry, an earnest and indefatigable collector of facts, he was deficient in that scope of mind joined to severe critical powers, indispensable to correct generalization. While, therefore, it is usually safe to reject his conclusions, we may receive his facts, making proper allowances for the haste with which they were got together.

Among these MSS. (*"rudis indigestaque moles,"*) was one entitled the *"Walum Olum,"* (literally, *"painted sticks,"*)—or painted and engraved traditions of the Linni-Lenape,—comprising five divisions, the first two embodying the traditions referring to the Creation and a general flood, and the rest comprising a record of various migrations, with a list of ninety-seven chiefs, in the order of their succession, coming down to the period of the discovery. This MS. also embraces one hundred and eighty-four compound mnemonic symbols, each accompanied by a sentence or verse in the original language, of which a literal translation is given in English. The only explanation which we have concerning it, is contained in a foot note, in the hand of Rafinesque, in which he states that the MS. and wooden originals were obtained in Indiana in 1822, and that they were for a long time inexplicable, "until with a deep study of the Delaware, and the aid of Zeisberger's[6] manuscript Dictionary, in the library of the Philosophical Society, a translation was effected." This translation, it may here be remarked, so far as I have been able to test it, is a faithful one, and there is slight doubt that the original is what it professes to be, a genuine Indian record. The evidence that it is so, is however rather internal and collateral than direct.[7] The traditions which it embodies coincide, in most important respects, with those which are known to have existed, and which still exist, in forms more or less modified, among the various Algonquin tribes, and the mode in which they are recorded is precisely that which was adopted by the Indians of this stock, in recording events, communicating intelligence, etc., and which has not inaptly been denominated *picture-writing.*

The scope of this system of picture-writing, and the extent to which it was applied, have not been generally understood nor fully recognized. Without, however, going into an analysis of the system, its principles and elements,—an inquiry of much interest,—it may be claimed, upon an array of evidence which will admit of no dispute, that under it the Indians were not only able to communicate events and transmit intelligence, but also to record chants and songs, often containing abstract ideas,—allusions to the origin of things, the power of nature, and to the elements of their religion. "The Indians," says Heckewelder, "have no alphabet, nor any mode of representing words to the eye, yet they have certain hieroglyphics, by which they describe facts in so plain a manner, that those who are conversant with their marks, can understand them with the greatest ease,—as easily, indeed, as they can understand a piece of writing."[8] This writer also asserts that the simple principles of the system are so well recognized, and of so general application, that the members of different tribes could interpret with the greatest facility the drawings of other and remote tribes. Loskiel has recorded his testimony to the same effect. He says: "The Delawares use hieroglyphics on wood, trees and stones, to give caution, for communication, to commemorate events and preserve records. Every Indian understands their meaning, etc."[9] Mr. Schoolcraft also observes of the Ojibwas, that "every path has its blazed and figurated tree, conveying intelligence to all that pass, for all can understand these signs, which," he adds, "are taught to the young as carefully as our alphabet."[10] Testimony might be accumulated upon this point, to an indefinite extent, were it necessary to our present purpose.

Most of the signs used in this system are representations of things: some however were derivative, others symbolical, and still others entirely arbitrary. They however were not capable of doing more than to suggest classes of ideas, which would not be expressed in precisely the same words by different individuals. They were taught in connection with certain forms of expression, by which means they are made essentially *mnemonic*—a simple or compound sign, thus serving to recall to mind an entire sentence or a series of them. A single figure, with its adjuncts, would stand for the verse of a song, or for a circumstance which it would require several sentences to explain.

Thus the famous *Metai song* of the Chippeways, presented by Mr. Catlin,[11] although embracing but about thirty signs, occupied, in the slow, monotonous chant of the Indians, with their numerous repetitions, nearly an hour in its delivery. James observes, respecting the recorded Indian songs,—"They are usually carved on a flat piece of wood, and the figures suggest to the minds of those who have learned the songs, the ideas and the order of their succession. The words are not variable, but must be taught; otherwise, though from an inspection of the figure the idea might be comprehended, no one would know what to sing."[12] Most of the Indian lore being in the hands of the priests or medicine-men, the teaching of these songs was almost entirely monopolized by them. They taught them only to such as had distinguished themselves in war and the chase, and then only upon the payment of large prices. Tanner states that he was occupied more than a year in learning the great song for "medicine hunting," and then obtained his knowledge only at the expense of many beaver skins.[13] After the introduction of Christianity, among some of the Western tribes, prayers were inscribed on pieces of wood, in mnemonic symbols, in the making and teaching of which to their followers, some of the Christian chiefs obtained a profitable monopoly.

Admitting then, as we must do upon this evidence, that the Algonquins had the means of imperfectly recording their traditions, songs, etc., we can readily understand how these might be taught by father to son, and perpetuated in great purity through a succession of priests,—the sages of the aboriginal races. The fact that they were recorded, even in the rude way here indicated, would give them a degree of fixedness, and entitle them to a consideration which they would not possess if handed down in a simple oral form.[14]

The MS. under consideration seems to be a series of Indian traditional songs, in the original mnemonic signs, with the words attached to them, written out from the recitations of the Indians, by some person conversant with the Indian tongue, precisely as we find some of the songs recorded by James in his Appendix to Tanner's Narrative.[15] As already observed, it has strong internal evidence of being what it purports to be,— evidence sufficiently strong, in my estimation, to settle its authenticity. I may however add, that, with a view of leaving no means unemployed to ascertain its true value, I submitted it, without explanation, to an educated Indian chief, (Kah-ge-ga-gah-bowh,) George Copway,[16] who unhesitatingly pronounced it authentic, in respect not only to the original signs and accompanying explanations in the Delaware dialect, but also in the general ideas and conceptions which it embodies. He also bore testimony to the fidelity of the translation.

In submitting, therefore, the following paraphrase of these singular records, I feel I am not obtruding the coinage of a curious idler, nor an apocryphal record, but presenting matter deserving of attention, and of important bearing upon many interesting questions connected with the history of our aboriginal nations.

It will be readily understood that I have, in numerous instances, been compelled to adopt forms of expression, not common to the Indian languages; so far as practicable, however, the words have been literally rendered, and the Indian form of expression preserved; and I feel some confidence in saying that no violence has been done to the original in the paraphrase.

For the sake of convenience, I have divided the MS. into two parts; the first embracing the traditions referring to the Creation, etc., and the second those which may be regarded as historical. It will be observed that there are various interruptions or pauses in the narrative, which indicate the individual traditions.

In illustration of the manner in which the MS. is written, the first two songs or chants are presented as they appear in the original. We have first, the original sign; second, the suggested verse or sentence in the Delaware dialect; and third, a literal translation of the same in English.

SONG I.—THE CREATION

1. Sayewitalli   wemiguma   wokgetaki.[17]
   At first there all sea-water above land.

2. Hackung-kwelik   owanaku   wakyutali
   Above much water   foggy (was) and (or also) there

   Kitanitowit-essop.[18]
   Creator he was.

3.[19] Sayewis[20]   hallemiwis[21]   nolemiwi
First-being,   Eternal-being,   invisible

Kitanitowit-essop.
Creator he was.

4. Sohalawak   kwelik   hakik
He causes them   much water   much land

owak   awasagamak.
much air (or clouds)   much heaven.

5. Sohalawak   gishuk   nipanum   alankwak.
He causes them   the Sun   the moon   the stars.

6. Wemi-sohalawak   yulik yuch-aan.
All he causes   these well to move.

7. Wich-owagan   kshakan   moshakwat
With action (or rapidly)   it blows (wind)   it clears up

kwelik   kshipelep.
great waters   it ran off.

8. Opeleken   mani-menak   delsin-epit.
It looks bright   made islands   is there at.

9. Lappinup   Kitanitowit   manito   manitoak.
Again when   Creator   he made   spirits or makers.

10. Owiniwak   Angelatawiwak   chichankwak   wemiwak.
First beings also   and Angels   Souls also   and all.

11. Wtenk-manito   'jinwis[22]   lennowak   mukom.
After he made   beings   men and   grandfather.

12. Milap   netami-gaho   owini-gaho.
He gave them   the first mother   first-being's mother.

13. Namesik-milap   tulpewik   awesik   cholensak.
     Fishes he gave him   turtles   beasts   birds.

14. Makimani-shak   sohalawak   makowini   n'akowak
     Bad Spirit but   he causes them   bad beings   black snakes

     amangamek.
     monsters (or large reptiles).

15. Sohalawak   uchewak   sohalawak   pungusak.
     He causes them   flies   he causes them   gnats.

16. Nitisak   wemi-owini   w'delsinewuap.
     Friends   all beings   were then.

17. Kiwis,   wunand   wishi-manitoak   essopak.
     Thou being   good God   good spirits   were there.

18. Nijini   netami   lennowak   nigoha   netami
     The beings   the first   men   mothers   first

     okwewi   nantinewak.
     wives   little spirits (fairies).

19. Gattamin   netami   mitzi   nijini
     Fat fruits   the first   food   the beings

     nantiné.
     little spirits.

20. Wemi   wingi-namenep   wemi-ksin   elandamep
     All   willingly pleased   all easy   thinking

     wullatemanuwi.
     happy.

21. Shukand   eli-kimi   mekenikink   wakon
     But then   while secretly   on earth   snake-god[23]

     powako   init'ako.
     priest-snake   worship snake.

22. Mattalugas   pallalugas   maktatin   owagan
    Wickedness   crime   unhappiness   actions

    payat-chikutali.
    coming there then.

23. Waktapan-payat   wihillan   mboagan.
    Bad weather coming   distempers   death.

24. Wonwemi wiwunch-kamik   atak-kitahikan   netami-epit.
    This all very long aforetime   beyond great waters   first land at.

PARAPHRASE OF THE ABOVE SONG.

1. At the first there were great waters above all the land,
2. And above the waters were thick clouds, and there was God the Creator:
3. The first being, eternal, omnipotent, invisible, was God the Creator.
4. He created vast waters, great lands, and much air and heaven;
5. He created the sun, the moon and the stars;
6. He caused them all to move well.

7. By his power he made the winds to blow, purifying, and the deep waters to run off:
8. All was made bright and the islands were brought into being.

9. Then again God the Creator made the great Spirits,
10. He made also the first beings, angels and souls:
11. Then made he a man being, the father of men;
12. He gave him the first mother, the mother of the early born,
13. Fishes gave he him, turtles, beasts and birds.
14. But the Evil Spirit created evil beings, snakes and monsters:
15. He created vermin and annoying insects.
16. Then were all beings friends:
17. There being a good God, all spirits were good—
18. The beings, the first men, mothers, wives, little spirits also.
19. Fat fruits were the food of the beings and the little spirits:
20. All were then happy, easy in mind and pleased.

21. But then came secretly on earth the snake (evil) God, the snake-priest and snake worship:
22. Came wickedness, came unhappiness,
23. Came then bad weather, disease and death.

24. This was all very long ago, at our early home.

The grand idea of a Supreme Unity, a Great, Good, Infinite and Eternal Creator, so clearly indicated in the foregoing song, may be regarded by many as the offspring of European intercourse, or as a comparatively late engraftment upon Algonquin tradition. Without denying that the teachings of the early missionaries had the effect of enlarging this conception, and of giving it a more definite form, it may at the same time be unhesitatingly claimed that the idea was an original one with the Indian mind. The testimony of the earliest travellers and of the earliest missionaries themselves, furnishes us abundant evidence of the fact. "Nothing," says Charlevoix, "is more certain than that the Indians of this continent have an idea of a Supreme Being, the First Spirit, the Creator and Governor of the World."[24] And Loskiel, not less explicit in his testimony, observes, "The prevailing opinion of all these nations is, that there is one God, a great and good Spirit, who created the heavens and the earth; who is Almighty; who causes the fruits to grow, grants sunshine and rain, and provides his children with food."[25] Says Schoolcraft, "They believe in the existence of a Supreme Being, who created material matter, the earth and heavens, men and animals, and filled space with subordinate spirits, having something of his own nature, to whom he gave part of his power."[26] From this great and good being, it was believed, no evil could come; he was invested with the attribute of universal beneficence, and was symbolized by the sun. He was usually denominated *Kitchi-Manitou* or *Gitchy-Monedo*, literally, Great, Good Spirit. Various other names were employed to designate him under his various aspects, as *Wāskeánd*, Maker; *Wāosemigōyan*, Universal Father.

Subordinate to this Supreme, Good Being, was an Evil Spirit, *Mitchi-Manitou*, or *Mudje-Monedo*, (Great Bad Spirit), who, according to Mr. Schoolcraft, was a subsequent creation, and not co-existent with the *Kitchi-Manitou*. This seems implied in the song, where he is first spoken of after the creation of men and beings. Great power was ascribed to him, and he was regarded as the cause and originator of all the evils which befall mankind. Accordingly his favor was desired, and his anger sought to be averted by sacrifices and offerings. The power of the Mitchi-Manitou was not, however, supposed to extend to the future life.[27] He is represented in the text as the creator of flies and gnats, and other annoying insects, an article of belief not exclusively Indian. While the symbol of the Good Spirit was *the Sun*, that of the chief of the Evil Spirits was *the Serpent*, under which form he appears in the Chippeway tradition of his contest with the demi-god Manabozho.

The idea of a destruction of the world by water seems to have been general amongst the Algonquin nations. The traditionary details vary in almost every instance where they have been recorded, but the traditionary event stands out prominently. The catastrophe is in all cases ascribed to the Evil Spirit; who, as already observed, was symbolized as a great Serpent. He is generally placed in antagonism to Manabozho, a powerful demigod or intermediate spirit, whose nature and character have already been indicated.[28] These two mythological characters have frequent conflicts, and the flood is usually ascribed to the final contest between them. In these cases the destruction of the world is but an incident. As recorded in the "*Walum-Olum*," it originates in a general conflict between the Good Spirits, "the beings," and the Evil Spirit, *Maskinako*. The variation is, however, unimportant, for in this as in all the other versions of the tradition, Manabozho appears in the character of Preserver. The concurrence in the essential parts of the several traditions, is worthy of remark.

SONG II.—THE DELUGE.

1. Wulamo   maskan-ako-anup   lennowak   makowini
   Long ago   powerful snake when   men also   bad beings

   essopak.
   had become.

2. Maskanako   shingalusit   nijini-essopak
   Strong snake   enemy   beings had become

   shawalendamep   ekin-shingalan.
   became troubled   together hating.

29

3. Nishawi   palliton,   nishawi   machiton,   nishawi
   Both   fighting,   both   spoiling,   both

   matta   lungundowin.
   not   peaceful (or keeping peace.)

4. Mattapewi   wiki   nihanlowit   mekwazuan.
   Less men   with   dead keeper   fighting.

5. Maskanako   gichi   penauwelendamep   lennowak
   Strong snake   great   resolved   men

   owini   palliton.
   beings   to destroy (fight).

6. N'akowa   petonep,   amangam   petonep
   Black snake   he brought,   monster   he brought

   akopehella   petonep.
   rushing snake water   he brought.

7. Pehella-pehella,   pohoka-pohoka,   eshohok-eshohok,
   Much water rushing,   much go to hills,   much penetrating,

   palliton-palliton.
   much destroying.

8. Tulapit   menapit
   At Tula (or turtle land)   at that island

   Nanaboush, maska-boush,   owinimokom
   Nanabush (strong)   of beings the grandfather

   linowimokom.
   of men the grandfather.

9. Gishikin-pommixin   tulagishatten-lohxin.
   Being born creeping   at Tula he is ready to move and dwell.

10. Owini   linowi   wemoltin   pehella   gahani
    Beings   men   all go forth   flood   water

    pommixin   nahiwi   tatalli
    creeping (floating?)   above water   which way (where)

    tulapin.
    turtle-back.

11. Amangamek makdopamek alendguwek
Monsters of the sea they were many some of them

metzipannek.
they did eat.

 12. Manito-dasin mokol-wichemass palpal
Spirit daughters boat helped come, come

payat payat wemichemap.
coming coming all helped.

 13. Nanaboush, Nanaboush, wemimokom
Nanabush, Nanabush, of all the grandfather,

winimokom linnimokom
of beings the grandfather, of men the grandfather,

tulamokom.
of turtles the grandfather.

 14. Linapima tulapima tulapewi tapitawi.
Man then turtle then turtle they altogether.

 15. Wishanem tulpewi pataman tulpewi
Frightened (startled?) turtle he praying turtle he

paniton wuliton.
let it be to make well.

16. Kshipehelen penkwihilen kwamipokho
Water running off it is drying plain and mountain

sitwalikho maskan wagan palliwi.
path of cave powerful or dire action elsewhere.

PARAPHRASE.

1. Long ago came the powerful Serpent, (*Maskanako*,) when men had become evil.
2. The strong serpent was the foe of the beings, and they became embroiled, hating each other.
3. Then they fought and despoiled each other, and were not peaceful.
4. And the small men (*Mattapewi*) fought with the keeper of the dead (*Nihanlowit*).
5. Then the Strong Serpent resolved all men and beings to destroy immediately.
6. The Black Serpent, monster, brought the snake-water rushing.
7. The wide waters rushing, wide to the hills, everywhere spreading, everywhere destroying.

8. At the island of the turtle (*Tula*) was Manabozho, of men and beings the grandfather—
9. Being born creeping, at turtle land he is ready to move and dwell.
10. Men and beings all go forth on the flood of waters, moving afloat, every way seeking the back of the turtle (*Tulapin*).
11. The monsters of the sea were many, and destroyed some of them.
12. Then the daughter of a spirit helped them in the boat, and all joined, saying, Come help!
13. Manabozho, of all beings, of men and turtles, the grandfather!
14. All together, on the turtle then, the men then, were all together.
15. Much frightened, Manabozho prayed to the turtle that he would make all well again.
16. Then the waters ran off, it was dry on mountain and plain, and the great evil went elsewhere by the path of the cave.

The allusion to the turtle, in the tradition, is not fully understood. The turtle was connected, in various ways, with the mythological notions of the upper Algonquins. According to Charlevoix and Hennepin, the Chippeways had a tradition that the mother of the human race, having been ejected from heaven, was received upon the back of a tortoise, around which matter gradually accumulated, forming the earth.[29] The Great Turtle, according to Henry, was a chief Spirit of the Chippeways, the "Spirit that never lied," and was often consulted in reference to various undertakings. An account of one of these ceremonies is given by this author.[30] The island of *Michilimakanak* (literally, Great Turtle) was sacred to this Spirit, for the reason, probably, that a large hill near its centre was supposed to bear some resemblance, in form, to a turtle.[31] The Turtle tribe of the Lenape, says Heckewelder, claim a superiority and ascendency, because of their relationship to the "Great Turtle," the Atlas of their mythology, who bears this great island (the earth) on his back.[32]

With these few illustrative observations, which might be greatly extended, I pass to the second or historical portion of the traditional record, with the simple remark that the details of the migrations here recounted, particularly so far as they relate to the passage of the Mississippi and the subsequent contest with the Tallegwi or Allegwi, and the final expulsion of the latter, coincide, generally, with those given by various authors, and known to have existed among the Delawares.

The traditions, in their order, relate first to a migration from the north to the south, attended by a contest with a people denominated Snakes or Evil, who are driven to the eastward. One of the migrating families, the *Lowaniwi*, literally Northlings, afterwards separate and go to the snow land, whence they subsequently go to the east, towards the island of the retreating Snakes. They cross deep waters, and arrive at *Shinaki*, the Land of Firs. Here the *Wunkenapi*, or Westerners, hesitate, preferring to return.

A hiatus follows, and the tradition resumes, the tribes still remaining at *Shinaki* or the Fir land.

They search for the great and fine island, the land of the Snakes, where they finally arrive, and expel the Snakes. They then multiply and spread towards the south, to the *Akolaki* or beautiful land, which is also called shore-land, and big-fir land. Here they tarried long, and for the first time cultivated corn and built towns. In consequence of a great drought, they leave for the *Shillilakiny* or Buffalo land. Here, in consequence of disaffection with their chief, they divide and separate, one party, the *Wetamowi*, or the Wise, tarrying, the others going off. The *Wetamowi* build a town on the *Wisawana* or Yellow River, (probably the Missouri,) and for a long time are peaceful and happy. War finally breaks out, and a succession of warlike chiefs follow, under whom conquests are made, north, east, south and west. In the end *Opekasit* (literally East-looking) is chief, who, tired with so much warfare, leads his followers towards the sunrising. They arrive at the *Messussipu*, or Great River, (the Mississippi,) where, being weary, they stop, and their first chief is *Yagawanend*, or the Hut-maker, under whose chieftaincy it is discovered that a strange people, the *Tallegwi*, possess the rich east land. Some of the *Wetamowi* are slain by the *Tallegwi*, and then the cry of *palliton! palliton!!* war! war!! is raised, and they go over and attack the *Tallegwi*. The contest is continued during the lives of several chiefs, but finally terminates in the *Tallegwi* being driven southwards. The conquerors then occupy the country on the Ohio below the great lakes,—the *Shawanipekis*. To the north are their friends, the *Talamatun*, literally *not-of-themselves*, translated Hurons. The Hurons, however, are not always friends, and they have occasional contests with them.

Another hiatus follows, and then the record resumes by saying that they were strong and peaceful at the land of the Tallegwi. They built towns and planted corn. A long succession of chiefs followed, when war again broke out, and finally a portion under *Linkewinnek*, or the Sharp-looking, went eastward beyond the *Talegachukung* or Alleghany Mountains. Here they spread widely, warring against the *Mengwi* or Spring-people, the *Pungelika*, Lynx or Eries, and the *Mohegans* or Wolves. The various tribes into which they became divided, the chiefs of each in their order, with the territories which they occupied, are then named,—bringing the record down until the arrival of the Europeans. This latter portion we are able to verify in great part from authentic history.

SONG III.—MIGRATIONS.

1. After the flood the true men (*Lennapewi*) were with the turtle, in the cave house, the dwelling of Talli.
2. It was then cold, it froze and stormed, and
3. From the Northern plain, they went to possess milder lands, abounding in game.
4. That they might be strong and rich, the new comers divided the land between the hunters and tillers, (*Wikhichik, Elowichik.*)
5. The hunters were the strongest, the best, the greatest.
6. They spread north, east, south and west;
7. In the white or snow country, (*Lumowaki*,) the north country, the turtle land and the hunting country, were the turtle men or *Linapiwi*.
8. The snake (evil) people being afraid in their cabins, the snake priest (*Nakopowa*) said to them, let us go away.
9. Then they went to the East, the snake land sorrowfully leaving.
10. Thus escaped the snake people, by the trembling and burned land to their strong island, (*Akomenaki.*)
11. Free from opposers, and without trouble, the Northlings (*Lowaniwi*) all went forth separating in the land of snow, (*Winiaken,*)
12. By the waters of the open sea, the sea of fish, tarried the fathers of the eagle (tribe?) and the white wolf.

13. Our fathers were rich; constantly sailing in their boats, they discovered to the eastward the Snake Island.
14. Then said the Head-beaver (*Wihlamok*) and the Great-bird, let us go to the snake land.
15. All responded, let us go and annihilate the snakes.
16. All agreed, the Northerlings, the Easterlings, to pass the frozen waters.
17. Wonderful! They all went over the waters of the hard, stony sea, to the open snake waters.
18. In vast numbers, in a single night, they went to the eastern or snake island; all of them marching by night in the darkness.
19. The Northerlings, the Easterlings, the Southerlings, (*Shawanapi*,) the Beaver-men, (*Tamakwapis*,) the Wolf-men, the Hunters or best men, the priests, (*Powatapi*,) the *Wiliwapi*, with their wives and daughters, and their dogs.
20. They all arrived at the land of Firs, (*Shinaking*,) where they tarried; but the Western men (*Wunkenapi*) hesitating, desired to return to the old Turtle land, (*Tulpaking*.)

It may be suggested that the account of the second migration, across frozen waters, is so much in accordance with the popular prejudice, as to the mode in which the progenitors of the American race arrived in America, that it throws suspicion upon the entire record. It is not impossible, indeed, that the original tradition may have been slightly modified here, by the dissemination of European notions among the Indians. McKenzie, however, observes of the traditions of the northern Chippeways:—"The Indians say that they originally came from another country, inhabited by a wicked people, and had traversed a great lake, which was shallow, narrow and full of islands, where they suffered great hardships and much misery, it being always winter, with ice and deep snows. * * * They describe the deluge when the waters spread over the whole earth, except the highest mountain, on the top of which they were preserved."[33]

The preceding songs have something of a metrical character, and there is in some of the verses an arrangement of homophones which has a very pleasing effect. For instance, the last verse of the above song is as follows:

Wemipayat guneunga shinaking
Wunkenapi chanelendam payaking
Allowelendam kowiyey-tulpaking.

How far this system was carried it is difficult to say, but it is not unlikely that most of the transmitted songs or chants had something of this form.

The next song resumes, after the lapse of an indefinite period, as follows:—

SONG IV.—THE CHRONICLE.

1. Long ago our fathers were at *Shinaki* or Firland.
2. The White Eagle (*Wapalanewa*) was the path-leader of all to this place.
3. They searched the great and fine land, the island of the Snakes.
4. The hardy and the friendly spirits met in council.
5. And all said to *Kalawil* (Beautiful-head) be thou chief (*Sakima*) here.
6. Being chief he commanded they should go against the Snakes.
7. But the Snakes were weak and hid themselves at the Bear hills.
8. After Kalawil, *Wapagokhas* (White-owl) was Sakima at Firland.
9. After him *Jantowit* (Maker) was chief.
10. And after him *Chilili* (Snow-bird) was Sakima. The South, he said
11. To our fathers, they were able, spreading, to possess.
12. To the South went *Chilili*; to the East went *Tamakwi*, (the Beaver.)
13. The Southland (*Shawanaki*) was beautiful, shore-land, abounding in tall firs.
14. The Eastland (*Wapanaki*) abounded in fish; it was the lake and buffalo land.
15. After Chilili, *Agamek* (Great Warrior) was chief.
16. Then our fathers warred against the robbers, snakes, bad men, and stony men, *Chikonapi, Akhonapi, Makatapi, Assinapi* (Assiniboins?)
17. After Agamek came ten chiefs, and then were many wars, south, east and west.
18. After them was *Langundowi* (the Peaceful) Sakima, at the *Aholaking*, (Beautiful land.)
19. Following him *Tasukamend*, (Never-bad,) who was a good or just man.
20. The chief after him was *Pemaholend*, (Ever-beloved,) who did good.
21. Then *Matemik* (Town-builder) and *Pilwihalen*.

22. And after these, in succession, *Gunokeni*, who was father long, and *Mangipitak*, (Big-teeth.)
23. Then followed *Olumapi*, (Bundler-of-sticks,) who taught them pictures, (records.)
24. Came then *Takwachi*, (Who-shivers-with-cold,) who went southward to the corn land, (*Minihaking.*)
25. Next was *Huminiend*, (Corn-eater,) who caused corn to be planted.
26. Then *Alko-ohit*, (the Preserver,) who was useful.
27. Then *Shiwapi*, (Salt-man,) and afterwards *Penkwonowi*, (the Thirsty,) when
28. There was no rain, and no corn, and he went to the East, far from the great river or shore.
29. Passing over a hollow mountain (*Oligonunk*) they at last found at *Shililaking*, the plains of the buffalo-land.
30. After *Penkwonowi*, came *Mekwochella*, (the Weary,) and *Chingalsawi*, (the Stiff.)
31. After him *Kwitikwund*, (the Reprover,) who was disliked and not willingly endured.
32. Being angry, some went to the eastward, and some went secretly afar off.
33. The wise tarried, and made *Makaholend* (the Beloved) chief.
34. By the *Wisawana* (Yellow river) they built towns, and raised corn on the great meadows.
35. All being friends, *Tamenend* (the Amiable, literally *beaver-like*) became the first chief.
36. The best of all, then or since, was *Tamenend*, and all men were his friends.
37. After him was the good chief, *Maskansisil*, (Strong-buffalo,) and
38. *Machigokhos*, (Big-owl,) and *Wapikicholen*, (White-crane.)
39. And then *Wingenund*, (the Mindful or Wary,) who made feasts.
40. After him came *Lapawin*, (the White,) and *Wallama*, (the Painted,) and
41. *Waptiwapit*, (White-bird,) when there was war again, north and south.
42. Then was *Tamaskan*, (Strong-wolf,) chief, who was wise in council and
43. Who made war on all, and killed *Maskensini*, (Great-stone.)
44. *Messissuwi* (the Whole) was next chief, and made war on the Snakes, (*Akowini.*)
45. *Chitanwulit* (Strong-and-good) followed, and made war on the northern enemies, (*Lowanuski.*)
46. *Alkouwi* (the Lean) was next chief, and made war on the father-snakes, (*Towakon.*)

47. *Opekasit* (East-looking) being next chief, was sad because of so much warfare,
48. Said, let us go to the sun-rising, (*Wapagishek;*) and many went east together.
49. The great river (*Messussipu*) divided the land, and being tired, they tarried there.
50. *Yagawanend* (Hut-maker) was next *Sakima*, and then the Tallegwi were found possessing the east.
51. Followed *Chitanitis*, (Strong-friend,) who longed for the rich east-land.
52. Some went to the east, but the *Tallegwi* killed a portion.
53. Then all of one mind exclaimed, war, war!
54. The *Talamatan* (Not-of-themselves,) and the *Nitilowan*, all go united (to the war.)
55. *Kinnehepend* (Sharp-looking) was their leader, and they went over the river.
56. And they took all that was there, and despoiled and slew the *Tallegwi.*
57. *Pimokhasuwi* (Stirring-about) was next chief, and then the *Tallegwi* were much too strong.
58. *Tenchekensit* (Open-path) followed, and many towns were given up to him.
59. *Paganchihilla* was chief, and the *Tallegwi* all went southward.
60. *Hattanwulatou* (the Possessor) was *Sakima*, and all the people were pleased.
61. South of the lakes they settled their council-fire, and north of the lakes were their friends the *Talamatan*, (Hurons?)
62. They were not always friends, but conspired when *Gunitakan* was chief.
63. Next was *Linniwalamen*, who made war on the *Talamatan*.
64. *Shakagapewi* followed, and then the *Talamatan* trembled.

SONG V.—THE CHRONICLE CONTINUED.

1. All were peaceful, long ago, at the land of the *Tallegwi.*
2. Then was *Tamaganend* (Beaver-leader) chief at the White river, (*Wapalaneng*, Wabash.)
3. *Wapushuwi* (White-lynx) followed, and much corn was planted.
4. After came *Walichinik*, and the people became very numerous.
5. Next was *Lekhihitin*, and made many records, (*Walum-Olumin*, or painted-sticks.)

6. Followed *Kolachuisen,* (Blue-bird,) at the place of much fruit or food, (*Make-liming.*)
7. *Pematalli* was chief over many towns.
8. And *Pepomahemen,* (Paddler,) at many waters, (or the great waters.)
9. And *Tankawon* (Little-cloud) was chief, and many went away.
10. The *Nentegos* and the *Shawanis* went to the south lands.
11. *Kichitamak* (Big-beaver) was chief at the White lick, (*Wapahoning.*)
12. The good prophet (*Onowatok*) went to the west.
13. He visited those who were abandoned there and at the south-west.
14. *Pawanami* (Water-turtle) was chief at the *Talegahonah* (Ohio) river.
15. *Lakwelend* (Walker) was next chief, and there was much warfare.
16. Against the *Towako,* (father Snakes,) against the *Sinako,* (stone or mountain Snakes,) and against the *Lowako,* (north Snakes.)
17. Then was *Mokolmokoni* (grandfather of boats) chief, and he warred against the Snakes in boats.
18. *Winelowich* (Snow-hunter) was chief at the north-land, (*Lowashkin.*)
19. And *Linkwekinuk* (Sharp-seer) was chief at the Alleghany Mountains, (*Talegachukang.*)
20. And *Wapalawikwan* (East-settler) was chief east of the *Tallegwi* land.
21. Large and long was the east land;
22. It had no enemies, (snakes,) and was a rich and good land.
23. And *Gikenopalat* (Great-warrior) was chief towards the north;
24. And *Hanaholend* (Stream-lover) at the branching stream, (*Saskwihanang* or Susquehanna.)
25. And *Gattawisi* (the Fat) was Sakima at the Sassafras-land, (*Winaki.*)
26. All were hunters from the big Salt Water (*Gishikshapipek,* Chesapeak, or literally Salt Sea of the Sun,) to the again (or other) sea.
27. *Makliuawip* (Red-arrow) was chief at tide water, (*Lapihaneng.*)
28. And *Wolomenap* was chief at the Strong Falls, (*Maskekitong,* Trenton?)
29. And the *Wapenend* and the *Tumewand* were to the north.
30. *Walitpallat* (Good-fighter) was chief and set out against the north—
31. Then trembled the *Mahongwi,* (the Iroquois?) and the *Pungelika,* (lynx-like, or Eries.)
32. Then the second *Tamenend* (Beaver) was chief, and he made peace with all.

33. And all were friends, all united under this great chief.
34. After him was *Kichitamak* (Great-good-beaver) chief in the Sassafras-land.
35. *Wapahakey* (White-body) was chief at the Sea-shore, (*Sheyabi*.)
36. *Elangonel* (the Friendly) was chief, and much good was done.
37. And *Pitemunen* was chief, and people came from somewhere.
38. At this time from the east sea came that which was white, (vessels?)
39. *Makelomush* was chief and made all happy.
40. *Wulakeningus* was next chief, and was a warrior at the south.
41. He made war on the *Otaliwako*, (Cherokee snakes or enemies,) and upon the *Akowetako*, (Coweta? snakes.)
42. *Wapagamoski* (White-otter) was next chief, and made the *Talamatans* (Hurons) friends.
43. *Wapashum* followed, and visited the land of Tallegwi at the west.[34]
44. There were the *Hiliniki*, (Illinois,) the *Shawanis*, (Shawanoes,) and the *Kenowiki*, (Kenhawas?)
45. *Nitispayat* was also chief, and went to the great lakes.
46. And he visited the *Wemiamik*, (Beaver-children, or Miamis,) and made them friends.
47. Then came *Packimitzin*, (Cranberry-eater), who made the *Tawa* (Ottawas) friends.
48. *Lowaponskan* was chief, and visited the noisy-place, (*Ganshowenik*.)
49. And *Tashawinso* was chief at the Sea-shore, (*Shayabing*.)
50. Then the children divided into three parts, the *Unamini*, (Turtle tribe,) the *Minsimini*, (Wolf tribe,) the *Chikimini*, (Turkey tribe.)
51. *Epallahchund* was chief, and fought the *Mahongwi*, but failed.
52. *Laugomuwi* was chief, and the *Mohongwi* trembled.
53. *Wangomend* was chief, yonder between. (?)
54. The *Otaliwi* and *Wasiotowi* were his enemies.
55. *Wapachikis* (White crab) was chief and a friend of the shore people.
56. *Nenachipat* was chief towards the sea.
57. Now from north and south came the *Wapagachik*, (white-comers,)
58. Professing to be friends, in big-birds, (ships.) Who are they?

Here stop the pictured records. There is, however, a fragment in the original MSS., which may be taken as a continuation, and concerning which Rafinesque says nothing more than that it "was translated from the Lenape by John Burns." The references, so far as I am able to verify them, are historically correct. It is here given in its original form, with no attempt at paraphrase. It resumes with an answer to the question which concludes the last song, "who are these *Wapsinis?*"

SONG VI.—THE MODERN CHRONICLE.

1. Alas, alas! we now know who they are, these *Wapsinis*, (East-people), who came out of the sea to rob us of our lands. Starving wretches! they came with smiles, but soon became snakes, (or enemies.)
2. The *Walumolum* was made by *Lekhibit*, (the writer,) to record our glory. Shall I write another to record our fall? No! Our foes have taken care to do that; but I speak what they know not or conceal.
3. We have had many other chiefs since that unhappy time. There were three before the friendly *Mikwon* (*Miquon* or Penn) came. *Mattanikum*[35] (not strong) was chief when the *Winakoli* (Swedes) came to *Winaki: Nahumen* (Raccoon) when the *Sinalwi* (Dutch) came, and *Ikwahon* (Fond-of-women) when the *Yankwis* (English) came. *Miquon* (Penn) and his friends came soon after.
4. They were all received and fed with corn; but no land was ever sold to them: we never sold any land. They were allowed to dwell with us, to build houses and plant corn, as friends and allies. Because they were hungry and we thought them children of *Gishaki*, (or sun-land,) and not serpents and children of serpents.
5. And they were traders, bringing fine new tools, and weapons, and cloth, and beads, for which we gave them skins and shells and corn. And we liked them and the things they brought, for we thought them good and made by the children of *Gishaki*.
6. But they brought also fire-guns, and fire-waters, which burned and killed; also baubles and trinkets of no use, for we had better ones before.
7. After Mikwon, came the sons of *Dolojo-Sakima*, (King George,) who said, more land, more land we must have, and no limit could be put to their steps.
8. But in the North were the children of *Lowi-Sakima*, (King Louis,) who were our good friends, friends of our friends, foes of our foes; yet with *Dolojo* wished always to war.
9. We had three chiefs after Mikwon came,—*Skalichi*, who was another *Tamenend*, and *Sasunam-Wikwikhon*, (Our-uncle-

the-builder,) and *Tutami*, (Beaver-taker,) who was killed by a *Yankwako*, (English snake,) and then we vowed revenge.

10. *Netatawis* (First-new-being) became chief of all the nations in the west. Again at *Talligewink* (Ohio, or place of Tallegwi) on the river Cuyahoga, near our old friends the *Talamatans*. And he called on all them of the east (to go to war).

11. But *Tadeskung* was chief in the east at *Mahoning*, and was bribed by *Yankwis*; then he was burnt in his cabin, and many of our people were killed at *Hickory* (Lancaster) by the land-robber *Yankwis*.

12. Then we joined *Lowi* in war against the *Yankwis*; but they were strong, and they took *Lowanaki* (North-land, Canada) from *Lowi*, and came to us in *Talegawink*, when peace was made, and we called them *Kichikani*, (Big-knives).

13. Then *Alimi* (White-eyes) and *Gelelenund* (Buck-killer) were chiefs, and all the nations near us were friends, and our grandchildren again.

14. When the Eastern-fires began to resist *Dolojo*, they said we shoud be another fire with them. But they killed our chief *Unamiwi* (the Turtle) and our brothers on the Muskingum. Then *Hopokan* (Strong-pipe) of the Wolf tribe was made chief, and he made war on the *Kichikani-Yankwis*, and became the friend of *Dolojo*, who was then very strong.

15. But the Eastern-fires were stronger; they did not take *Lowinaki*, but became free from *Dolojo*. We went to *Wapahani* (White river) to be further from them; but they followed us everywhere, and we made war on them, till they sent *Makhiakho*, (Black-snake, General Wayne,) who made strong war.

16. We next made peace and settled limits, and our chief was *Hacking-pouskan*, (Hard-walker,) who was good and peaceful. He would not join our brothers, the *Shawanis* and *Ottawas*, nor *Dolojo* in the next war.

17. Yet after the last peace, the *Kichikani-Yankwis* came in swarms all around us, and they desired also our lands of *Wapahani*. It was useless to resist, because they were getting stronger and stronger by joining fires.

18. *Kithtilkand* and *Lapanibit* were the chiefs of our two tribes when we resolved to exchange our lands, and return at last beyond the *Masispek*, near to our old country.

19. We shall be near our foes the *Wakon*, (Osages,) but they are not worse than the *Yankwisakon* (English-snakes) who want to possess the whole Big-island.

20. Shall we be free and happy, then, at the new *Wapahani*? We want rest, and peace, and wisdom.

So terminate these singular records. It is unfortunate that they lack that kind of authentication, which depends upon a full and explicit account of the circumstances under which they were found, transcribed and translated. Rafinesque was not particular in these matters, and his carelessness and often extravagant assumptions, have rendered his name of little weight in matters of research. Still, upon neither of these grounds may we reject these records. As already observed, they have the internal evidence of genuineness, and are well supported by collateral circumstances. Some of these circumstances were presented at the outset, and need not be recapitulated. Rafinesque himself has anticipated, and thus disposes of one objection, not among the least formidable: "That so many generations and names can be remembered, may appear doubtful to some; but when symbolical signs and paintings are accompanied with songs, and carefully taught from generation to generation, their retention and perpetuation is not so remarkable." To this may with propriety be added the subjoined observations of Loskiel: "The Delawares delight in describing their genealogies, and are so well versed in them, that they mark every branch of the family with the greatest precision. They also add the character of their forefathers: such an one was a wise and intelligent counsellor; a renowned warrior, or rich man, etc. But though they are indifferent about the history of former times, and ignorant of the art of reading and writing, yet their ancestors were well aware that they stood in need of something to enable them to convey their ideas to a distant nation, or preserve the memory of remarkable events. To this end they invented something like hieroglyphics, and also strings and belts of wampum, etc."[36]

I have alluded to the general identity of the mythological traditions here recorded, with those which are known to have been, and which are still current among the nations of the Algonquin stock. The same may be observed of the traditions which are of a historical character, and particularly that which relates to the contest with the people denominated the *Tallegwi*. The name of this people is still perpetuated in the word *Alleghany*, the original significance of which is more apparent, when it is written in an unabbreviated form, *Tallegwi-henna,* or *Tallegwi-hanna,* literally "River of the Tallegwi." It was applied to the Ohio, (the present name is Iroquois, and literally rendered by the French *La Belle Rivière,*) and is still retained as the designation of its northern or principal tributary. The traditionary contest between the Lenape and the Tallegwi is given by Heckewelder, and is adduced in further illustration of the general concurrence above mentioned. The details vary in some points, but I am inclined to give the first position to the tradition as presented in the *Walum-olum;* it being altogether the most simple and consistent. It must be observed, that Mr. Heckewelder's diffuse account is much condensed in the following quotations, and that part which refers to the wars with the Cherokees, etc., is entirely omitted:—

"The Lenni-Lenape (according to the traditions handed down to them from their ancestors) resided many hundred years ago, in a very distant country, in the western part of the American continent. For some reason which I do not find accounted for, they determined on migrating to the eastward, and accordingly set out together in a body. After a very long journey, and many nights' encampment, ('nights' encampment' is a halt of a year in a place) they at length arrived on the *Namaesi-Sipu,*[37] where they fell in with the Mengwi, (Iroquois,) who had likewise emigrated from a distant country, and had struck upon this river higher up. Their object was the same with that of the Delawares; they were proceeding to the eastward, until they should find a country that pleased them. The spies which the Lenape had sent forward for the purpose of reconnoitering, had long before their arrival discovered that the country east of the Mississippi was inhabited by a very powerful nation, who had many large towns built on the great rivers flowing through the land. These people (as I was told) called themselves *Tallegwi* or *Talligewi.* Col. John Gibson, however, a gentleman who has a thorough knowledge of the Indians, and speaks several of their languages, is often of opinion that they were called *Alligewi.*" * * * * * * * *

"Many wonderful things are told of this famous people. They are said to have been remarkably tall and stout, and there are traditions that there were giants among them. It is related, that they had built to themselves regular fortifications or entrenchments, from whence they would sally out, but were generally repulsed.

* * * When the Lenape arrived on the banks of the Mississippi, they sent a message to the *Alligewi*, to request permission to settle themselves in their neighborhood. This was refused them; but they obtained leave to pass through the country, and seek a settlement further to the eastward. They accordingly commenced passing the Mississippi, when the *Alligewi* discovering their great numbers became alarmed, and made a furious attack upon those who had crossed. Fired at their treachery, the Lenape consulted on what was to be done; whether to retreat, or try their strength against their oppressors. While this was going on the Mengwi, who had contented themselves with looking on from a distance, offered to join the Lenape, upon condition that they should be entitled to a share of the country, in case the combination was successful. Their proposal was accepted, and the confederates were able, after many severe conflicts, to drive the Alligewi down the Mississippi river. The conquerors divided the country between themselves; the Mengwi selecting the lands in the vicinity of the Great Lakes, and on their tributary streams, while the Lenape took possession of the country below them. For a long period of time, some say many hundreds of years, the two nations lived peaceably, and increased their numbers with great rapidity. Ultimately some of the most adventurous among them crossed the mountains towards the rising sun, and falling on streams running to the eastward, followed them to the great Bay River, (Susquehanna,) and thence to the Bay (Chesapeak) itself. As they pursued their travels, partly by land and partly by water, sometimes near and sometimes on the great-salt-water Lake, (as they call the sea,) they discovered the great river which we call the Delaware; and still further to the eastward, the *Sheyicbbi* country, now called New Jersey. Afterwards they reached the stream now called the Hudson. The reports of the adventurers caused large bodies to follow them, who settled upon the four great rivers, the Delaware, Hudson, Susquehanna and Potomac, making the Delaware, which they call '*Lenapewihittuck* (the river of the Lenape)' the centre of their possessions.

"They add that a portion of their people remained beyond the Mississippi, and still another portion tarried between the Mississippi and the Mountains. The largest portion, they supposed, settled on the Atlantic. The latter were divided into three tribes, two of which were distinguished as *Unámis*, or Turtle, and *Wnalachigo*, or Turkey. These chose the lands lying nearest the coast. Their settlements extended from the *Mohicanittuck* (river of the *Mohicans*, or Hudson) to beyond the Potomac. * * * The third great tribe, the *Minsi*, (which we have corrupted into *Monseys*,)

or tribe of the wolf, lived back of the others, forming a kind of bulwark, and watching the nations of the *Mengwi*. They were considered the most active and warlike of all the tribes. They extended their settlements from the *Minisink*, where they had their council-fire, quite to the Hudson on the east, and westward beyond the Susquehanna, and northward to the head waters of that stream and the Delaware. * * * From the above three divisions or tribes, comprising together the body of the people called Delawares, sprung many others, who, having for their own convenience chosen distinct spots to settle in, and increasing in numbers, gave themselves names, or received them from others.
* * * Meanwhile trouble ensued with the *Mengwi*, who occupied the southern shores of the Lakes, and resulted in fierce and sanquinary wars. The reverses of the *Mengwi* induced them to confederate, after which time the contests with the Lenape were carried on with vigor until the arrival of the French in Canada."

It will be seen that there is a difference between the traditions, as given by Heckewelder, and the *Walum-olum*, in respect to the name of the confederates against the Tallegwi. In the latter the allies are called *Talamatan*, literally Not-of-themselves, and which, in one or two cases, is translated Hurons, with what correctness I am not prepared to say.[38] Heckewelder calls them *Mengwi*, Iroquois. This must be a mistake, as the Mengwi are subsequently and very clearly alluded to in the *Walum-olum*, as distinct from the *Talamatan*.

It is remarkable that the traditions of almost all the tribes, on the eastern shore of the continent, refer, with more or less distinctness, to a migration from the westward. "When you ask them," says Lawson, speaking of the Carolina Indians, "whence their fathers came, that first inhabited the country, they will point to the westward and say, 'Where the sun sleeps, our fathers came thence.' "[39] Most of the nations speak of the passage of the Mississippi river. The Natchez, who assimilated more nearly to the central American and Peruvian stocks, (the *Toltecan* family,) informed Du Pratz that they once dwelt at the south-west, "under the sun."[40] The Muscogulges or Creeks, according to Bartram's manuscript,[41] assert that they formerly lived beyond the Mississippi, and that they relinquished that country in obedience to a dream in which they were directed to go to the country where the sun rises. They claim that they crossed the river in their progress eastward, about the period that De Soto visited Florida. The Cherokees (a cognate tribe) have a similar tradition. They assert that "a long time ago all the Indians travelled a great distance and came to a great water. Upon arriving there, and immediately before or immediately after crossing, it is not remembered which, a part went north and another part south. Those who went northwards settled in two towns called *Ka-no-wo-gi* and *Nu-ta-gi*; the others at *Ka-ga-li-u*, or old town, and because they took the lead in the journey were considered the grandfathers of the Indians."[42] Roger Williams informs us that the south-west, or *Sawaniwa*, was constantly referred to by the Indians of New England. "From thence, according to their traditions, they came. There is the court of their great God, *Cawtantowit*; there are all their ancestors' souls; there they also go when they die, and from thence came their corn and beans, out of *Cawtantowit's* field."[43]

It will thus be seen that the general tenor and some of the more important details of the traditions of the Indians of the Algonquin stock, as they have been presented to us by various authorities, are the same with those of the foregoing remarkable records. These records are peculiar, chiefly as giving us a greater number of details than we before possessed. Whatever their historical value, they possess the highest interest, as coming to us through the medium of a rude system of representation, which may be taken as the first advance beyond a simple oral transmission of ideas, and from which we may trace upwards the progress of human invention to its highest and noblest achievement, the present perfected form of written language.

Notes

1. The Puritan divine Cotton Mather (1663–1728) wrote a number of works dealing with life in the New World. I have not located precisely where in his works this quotation may be found.

2. I have not been able to identify the "erudite American" quoted here.

3. Edward Daniel Clarke (1769-1822) was an English mineralogist and traveler. It is unclear from which of his several travel books Squier is quoting here.

4. "The existence of similar religious ideas in remote regions, inhabited by different races, is an interesting subject of study; furnishing as it does, one of the most important links in the great chain of communication which binds together the distant families of nations."—William H. Prescott, *History of the Conquest of Mexico, with a Preliminary View of the Ancient Mexican Civilization and the Life of the Conqueror, Hernando Cortés* (New York: Harper, 1843), 1, 59 [Squier's note].

5. Rafinesque's translation of the *Walam Olum* material appears in *The American Nations; or, Outlines of Their General History, Ancient and Modern* . . . (Philadelphia: by the author, 1836).

6. This is a misprint for David Zeisberger, a missionary who compiled considerable linguistic and ethnographic data on the American Indian groups to whom he spread the gospel. See *Zeisberger's Indian Dictionary. English, German, Iroquois—the Onondaga and Algonquin—the Delaware; Printed from the Original Manuscript in Harvard College Library* (Cambridge, Mass.: J. Wilson, 1887).

7. Since the above was written, a copy of Rafinesque's "American Nations," published in 1836, has fallen under my notice. It is a singular jumble of facts and fancies, and it is perhaps unfortunate for the MS., spoken of in the text, that it falls in such a connection. The only additional information we have respecting it, is that it was "obtained by the late Dr. Ward of Indiana, of the remnant of the Delawares on the White River" [Squier's note].

8. John Heckewelder, "An Account of the History, Manners, and Customs, of the Indian Nations, Who Once Inhabited Pennsylvania and the Neighbouring States," *Transactions of the American Philosophical Society*, 1 (1819), 118 [Squier's note].

9. George Henry Loskiel, *History of the Mission of the United Brethren Among the Indians in North America*, trans. Christian Ignatius LaTrobe (London: Brethren's Society for the Furtherance of the Gospel, 1794), p. 25 [Squier's note].

10. I have been unable to determine from which of Schoolcraft's writings this statement is taken.

11. Presumably the reference is to George Catlin, *The Manners, Customs and Condition of the North American Indians* (London: by the author, 1841).

12. Edwin James edited John Tanner's *A Narrative of the Captivity and Adventures of John Tanner, (U. S. Interpreter at the Saut de Ste. Marie,) During Thirty Years Residence Among the Indians in the Interior of North America* (New York: Carvill, 1830).

13. Tanner; see note 12.

14. "Were it not," says Dr. Barton, in his paper on the 'Origin of the American Nations,' published in the Transactions of the Philosophical Society,—"Were it not for the traditions of many of the American nations, we might for ever

remain in doubt concerning their real origin. These traditions are entitled to much consideration; for, notwithstanding the rude condition of most of the tribes, they are often perpetuated in great purity, as I have discovered by much attention to their history" [Squier's note]. The reference is to Benjamin Smith Barton, *New Views of the Origin of the Tribes and Nations of America* (Philadelphia: John Bioren, 1797).

15. James; see note 12.

16. George Copway (1818–1863), an Ojibwa convert to Christianity, published some sixty books and articles, most of which dealt with the rewards of his religious experiences.

17. The terminal *aki* is a contraction of *hakki*, land, and frequently denotes *place*, simply [Squier's note].

18. Written *Getanitowit* by Heckewelder, p. 422 [Squier's note].

19. Figure 3 is a representation of the sun, which was the Algonquin symbol of the Great Spirit [Squier's note].

20. The termination *wiss* or *iss* makes, according to Mr. Schoolcraft, whatever precedes it personal, (*Algic Researches, Comprising Inquiries Respecting the Mental Characteristics of the North American Indians* [New York: Harper and Brothers, 1839], I, 201). The better translation would therefore be, "The First," "The Eternal," &c [Squier's note].

21. *Allowini*, more, and *wulik*, good, enter into most designations of the Supreme. Heckewelder, p. 422 [Squier's note].

22. In the Chippeway, according to McKenzie and Long, *ninnee* or *inini* means *man*. Mr. Schoolcraft states that *ininee* is the diminutive form of the word, signifying *little-men*, as Puck-wudj-*ininee*, "vanishing little men," the fairy-men of Algonquin story. The cognate term of the text seems to have a slightly different meaning: it is translated *beings*, and is written *nijini* or *'jini*, beings; *owini*, first beings, *mako-wini*, evil beings, etc. In the Delaware dialect *lenno* or *lenna* meant man, and is so tranlated in the text. The true designation of the Delawares was "Linni-Lenape," which is usually understood to mean "Original" or "True men." It is not impossible that it is compounded of "*nijini*," beings, and *lenno*, men; literally, men-beings. This compound may have been suggestive of something superior to men in general or collectively [Squier's note]. The initial reference in the note is to Alexander MacKenzie, *Voyages from Montreal, on the River St. Laurence, Through the Continent of North America, to the Frozen and Pacific Oceans; in the Years 1789 and 1793* (London: Cadell and Davies, 1801). The precise work by Schoolcraft to which Squier refers is unknown.

23. The snake among the Algonquins was symbolical of evil or malignant force [Squier's note].

24. Pierre F. X. de Charlevoix, *Histoire et description generale de la Nouvelle France, avec le Journal historique d'un voyage fait par ordre du roi dans l'Amérique Septentrionnale* (Paris: Chez Pierre-François Giffart, 1744), 2, 141 [Squier's note].

25. Loskiel, p. 34 [Squier's note].

26. Again, the specific Schoolcraft work is unknown.

27. Jonathan Carver, *Travels Through the Interior Parts of North America in the Years, 1766, 1767, and 1768* (London: J. Walter, 1778), p. 381 (Squier's note).

28. *American [Whig] Review*, 2 (1842), 392 [Squier's note].

29. Charlevoix, 2, 143; Louis Hennepin, *Description de la Louisiane, nouvellement decouverte au sud 'oüest de la Nouvelle France, par ordre du roy. Avec la carte du pays: Les moeurs & la manière de vivre des sauvages* (Paris: Chez la veuve Sebastien Huré, 1683), p. 55 [Squier's note].

30. Alexander Henry, *Travels and Adventures in Canada and the Indian Territories Between the Years 1760 and 1776* (New York: I. Riley, 1809), p. 168 [Squier's note].

31. Henry, pp. 37, 110 [Squier's note].

32. Heckewelder, p. 246 [Squier's note].

33. MacKenzie, p. 113 [Squier's note].

34. "At present," says Loskiel (p. 127), "the Delawares call the whole country as far as the entrance of the river Wabash into the Ohio, *Alligewi-nengk*, that is, a land into which they came from distant parts" [Squier's note].

31. *Note by Rafinesque*. "*Mattanikum* was chief in 1645. He is called *Mattahorn* by Holm, who by a blunder, has made his name half Swedish. *Horn* is not Lenapi. Mattawikum means *Not-horned*, without horns, emblem of having little strength" [Squier's note].

36. Loskiel, p. 24 [Squier's note].

37. This differs from the foregoing record, and is undoubtedly incorrect. It is difficult to derive Mississippi from *Namaesi-Sipu*, which is made up of *Namaes*, a fish, and *Sipu*, river. The etymology is clearly *Messu, Messi*, or *Michi*, signifying *great*, or as Mr. Gallatin suggests, the *whole*, and *Sipu*, river" (Squier's note). Albert Gallatin edited "Hale's Indians of North-West America and Vocabularies of North America" for the *Transactions of the American Ethnological Society* in 1848.

38. In Heckewelder we find the Hurons sometimes called *Delamattenos*, which is probably but another mode of writing *Talamatan*. Although speaking a dialect of the Iroquois language, the Hurons seem to have generally maintained friendly relations with the Lenape [Squier's note].

39. John Lawson, *The History of Carolina; Containing the Exact Description and Natural History of That Country: Together with the Present State Thereof. And a Journal of a Thousand Miles, Travel'd thro' Several Nations of Indians. Giving a Particular Account of Their Customs, Manners, &c.* (London: Taylor and Baker, 1714), p. 170 [Squier's note].

40. Le Page du Pratz, *The History of Louisiana, or of the Western Parts of Virginia and Carolina: Containing a Description of the Countries That Lye on Both Sides of the River Mississipi* [sic]: *With an Account of the Settlements, Inhabitants, Soil, Climate, and Products* (London: T. Becket and P. A. De Hondt, 1763), p. 292 [Squier's note].

41. Squier edited William Bartram's "Observations on the Creek and Cherokee Indians," which had apparently been written in 1789. The edited version appeared in the *Transactions of the American Ethnological Society* in 1853.

42. J. H. Payne, MSS. [Squier's note]. John Howard Payne (1791–1852), best known as an actor and dramatist, became interested in the Cherokee removal from the Carolinas and in their leader John Ross. His history of the Cherokee is still in manuscript.

43. Roger Williams, *A Key into the Language of America* . . . (London: G. Dexter, 1643) [Squier's note].

Mental Character
of the Aborigines

by Henry Rowe Schoolcraft

* * * * *

Although most students of American letters remember the ethnological work of Henry Rowe Schoolcraft (1793–1864) as the source of Hiawatha, Longfellow's attempt at an American Indian epic, this geologist-turned-ethnologist must be ranked as the most important figure in Native American studies during the first two-thirds of the nineteenth century. Schoolcraft's early interest lay in the natural sciences, especially geology and mineralogy, and his early

SOURCE: This material appeared in two parts. The first part, to the beginning of the corn origin myth, appeared in the *Southern Literary Messenger*, 28 (June 1859), 466-467. The rest of the material, under the title "Mental Traits of the Aborigines," appeared in the *Southern Literary Messenger*, 29 (July 1859), 12-13. Both parts are signed "H. R. S." I have confirmed in David K. Jackson, *The Contributors and Contributions to the Southern Literary Messenger (1834–1864)* (Charlottesville, Virginia: Historical, 1936), p. 143, that this does indeed refer to Henry Rowe Schoolcraft. At the end of the second part of the reprinted material is the dateline, *"Washington*, May 24th, 1859." Schoolcraft published over and over again the Native American oral narra-

explorations along the Mississippi Valley frontier focused on the region's mineral resources. As a geologist, he toured Missouri and Arkansas in 1817–1818 and then joined Lewis Cass's expedition to the Lake Superior region in 1820. But even this early in his career, Schoolcraft was evincing interest in American Indians, for in 1822 he received an appointment as Indian agent for the tribes in the upper Midwest.

Like most of his contemporaries, Schoolcraft made language the foundation for his investigations of Native American cultures. Yet he soon broadened his interests to encompass the full scope of those cultures, including oral literature. His special concern was the Algonquin-speaking groups such as the Ojibwa, and his ingress into their culture was ensured by his marriage to an Ojibwa in 1823. Through his wife's family, especially her mother, Schoolcraft began to gather a vast body of ethnographic data. Much of this material was published in a periodical edited by Schoolcraft, The Muzziniegan or Literary Voyager *(1826–1829), perhaps the first ethnological magazine in the United States. Articles by Schoolcraft and by members of his wife's family were included. (*The Muzziniegan or Literary Voyager *was re-edited by Philip P. Mason for publication by Michigan State University Press in 1962.) In 1839, Schoolcraft gathered all of his materials together for publication in the two-volume* Algic Researches, Comprising Inquires Respecting the Mental Characteristics of the North American Indians *(New York: Harper and Brothers, 1839), the first of several books which described aspects of the cultures of Native Americans whose habitat embraced the Atlantic seaboard and extended westward through the Allegheny watershed to the Mississippi River. (Schoolcraft's term "Algic" combines "Allegheny" with "Atlantic.")*

---

tives which he had collected. The corn origin myth reproduced here had appeared in print at least four times prior to its inclusion in "Mental Traits of the Aborigines": in *Algic Researches, Comprising Inquires Respecting the Mental Characteristics of the North American Indians* (New York: Harper and Brothers, 1839), I, 122–128; *Historical and Statistical Information Respecting the History, Conditions and Prospects of the Indian Tribes of the United States* (Philadelphia: Lippincott, Grambo, 1852), II, 230–231; *The Myth of Hiawatha, and Other Oral Legends, Mythologic and Allegoric, of the North American Indians* (Philadelphia: Lippincott, 1856), pp. 99–104; and *The Indian Fairy Book, from the Original Legends* (New York: Mason Brothers, 1856), pp. 330–338. See A. Irving Hallowell, "Concordance of Ojibwa Narratives in the Published Works of Henry R. Schoolcraft," *Journal of American Folklore*, 59 (1946), 144.

Yet Schoolcraft's contribution to nineteenth-century American Indian studies goes beyond his own collecting, editing, and publishing. He also encouraged others to engage in research similar to his and helped to organize the Historical Society of Michigan in 1828, the Algic Society of Detroit in 1832, and the American Ethnological Society in 1842. Moreover, he developed plans for a large-scale, systematic project in collecting Native American traditions, which he submitted to the recently established Smithsonian Institution. Part of his plan included the administration of questionnaires, a collecting technique adopted from Lewis Cass, and he was able to show the efficacy of the sort of project he was proposing in the results of similar work he had already done with the Iroquois and published in Notes on the Iroquois; or Contributions to American History, Antiquities, and General Ethnology *(Albany: Erastus H. Pease, 1847). The primary results of Schoolcraft's proposal to the Smithsonian constitute the data appearing in the six-volume* Information Respecting the History, Condition and Prospects of the Indian Tribes of the United States: Collected and Prepared Under the Direction of the Bureau of Indian Affairs *(Philadelphia: Lippincott, Grambo, 1851–1857). This massive work is mostly a compendium of materials which investigators of various American Indian groups had submitted in response to Schoolcraft's questionnaires. Though uneven in quality, the work paved the way for the organized research on the American Indian which eventuated in the establishment of the Bureau of American Ethnology.*

Schoolcraft's major theoretical contribution to the study of Native American folklore was his insistence that oral literature provided a key to the aboriginal mind. Although the piece included here reflects his specific interest in Algonquin-speakers, he means for his conclusions to have more general applications. While his insights about the "mental traits" of the American Indian seem grossly simplistic today, his use of folklore as a way of discovering how people think and what they think about remains a standard practice in the way anthropologists handle oral literature. The piece suggests that Schoolcraft had planned to publish a series of Native American oral narratives and songs in the Southern Literary Messenger, *but the material here represents everything he published in that periodical.*

For more on Native American myths about the origin of corn, see W. M. Beauchamp, "Indian Corn Stories and Customs," Journal of American Folklore, *11 (1898), 195–202; George F. Will and George E. Hyde,* Corn Among the Indians of the Upper Missouri *(St. Louis: Harvey*

Miner, 1917); and Gudmund Hatt, "The Corn Mother in America and in Indonesia," Anthropos, *46 (1951), 853–914. For further information on Schoolcraft's work, see C. S. Osborn and Stellanova Osborn,* School-craft—Longfellow—Hiawatha *(Lancaster, Pennsylvania: Jacques Cattell, 1942); J. F. Freeman, "Religion and Personality in the Anthropology of Henry Schoolcraft,"* Journal of the History of the Behavioral Sciences, *1, no. 4 (1965), 301–313; and Rosemary Zumwalt, "Henry Rowe Schoolcraft—1783–1864. His Collection and Analysis of the Oral Narratives of American Indians,"* Kroeber Anthropological Society Papers, *53 and 54 (Spring and Fall 1976), 44–57.*

∗ ∗ ∗ ∗ ∗

The Algonquin family of tribes, under their various names and dialects, occupied at the period of discovery the greatest part of the territorial area of the United States, lying between the Atlantic and the Mississippi River, north of a line drawn from Pamlico Sound to the mouth of the Ohio. The exceptions were chiefly the Iroquois tribes of New York and their cognate bands in Canada and Maryland, and in Virginia west of the Powhatans.

Of this wide-spread language, the Powhatans constituted a sub-group, marked by the use of the letter *r*; the Lenopees of Pennsylvania another marked by the interchangeable letter *l*, and the Mohegans of southern New York, and of all New England, in which the *l* is changed to *n*. It is not, however, the object of these remarks, to describe the ethnographical spread of this great stock of language, but to call attention to some mental developments in their character, which have received but little notice.

The two great objects of fame, in all our Indian tribes, are bravery or military renown and eloquence. Forest-life left them but little beside. Achievements in hunting were the every-day events and topics of conversation, and of every-day boasts. But triumphs in war, and oratory were the peculiar praises of their great men—their chief warriors and speakers. It is some amelioration of the severities of forest-life to know that, when the purposes of war and hunting are temporarily done, they assemble around the evening lodge-fire, to listen to imaginative recitals of adventures of heroes, giants and dwarfs, or pure creatures of fancy. It gives them further claims on this score, to ascertain that a particular season was appropriate to the exercise of this story-telling faculty, and that it is the province of certain old or recognized men to tell these legends, and that these persons are also the chroniclers of the respective tribes, and the depositories of traditions. This appropriate season is the winter, when snow covers the ground, and leaves do not conceal approach. No war parties are formed in the winter.

These oral stories are, generally, very extravagant, often of an allegorical character, and sometimes they even aim at instruction. They are the true presentments of the Indian mind, and show more than any other species of inquiry, or research, their opinions and beliefs on life, death and immortality. The legends denote what is so difficult to obtain, their ideas of a deity, and spiritual existence, and they cannot be perused, without letting one see their cosmogony, and so to call it, their theology.

The war songs, and hieratic chants of this people, and of the tribes generally, reveal traits of a fixed line of thought. Both species of songs are, often, highly allegorical, and difficult to be understood by the uninitiated. No rhyme is ever attempted in these compositions, but there is a melodious, or measured flow of thought and a fixed or proscribed chorus. Mr. Adair[1] has heard, in this chorus, as used among the Creeks, what no other person has, the syllables, Je-ho-vah. Repetition and transposition are often observed to monotony.

There is another trait in the Algonquin family, which denotes the possession of intellect. It is that common wish of the human family to preserve and transmit their deeds to posterity. This was done in the days of Ninevah and Babylon, by the invention of the cuneiform character, and in the valley of the Nile by hieroglyphics. By these means sounds were preserved before the invention of letters. The Indian tribe never reached to any degree of precision of this character. But by this system of pictography, which is purely ideographic, they represent events, acts, actors. The number of beings slain, whether men or beasts, is denoted on barks, scarified trees, or painted rocks, and thus is preserved a recognized memoir of battles and hunting scenes. A tabular stick placed at the grave of a warrior denotes, symbolically, his name, or tribe, and the number of scalps he has taken in war. Such memorials satisfy the Indian.

Believing that these traits of the Indian mind and character will be best understood and illustrated by examples, it is proposed to submit some specimens of each, originally derived from actors in the forest.

MONDAMIN; OR, THE ORIGIN OF INDIAN CORN

Onz was the son of a poor Indian hunter, who lived in a beautiful part of the country. The streams ran clear and sparkling from the mountains,—the wild pigeon, the omemee, flitted from tree to tree, and the deer ran through the forest. Notwithstanding this abundance of life and beauty around him, the father often failed to find game sufficient for his wants, but he never failed to be thankful to the Great Spirit for all he got. And his wigwam was known for the cheerful welcome he gave to every visitor. Though poor, in the estimation of his friends, he ever received them with a smile, and he made amends by his kind manners for what he sometimes lacked on his board. And his wife was always known for her cleanly swept fire-place.

Onz was the eldest son, and he had now reached that age, between youth and manhood, when a fast must be kept, to choose a guardian spirit. His parents had brought him up strictly to respect and worship the Great Spirit, and to be thankful for every gift, however small. They had, in this way, prepared his mind for the importance and solemnity of this fast, which is called *Ke-ig-wish-im-o-win.*

When the day arrived, he took his hatchet to build his fasting-lodge in the woods, and a little bark dish to dip drink-water, as this is the only article allowed to be taken during the fast. He walked through the forest a long distance, till he found a retired and beautiful spot on elevated grounds, where, by a few turns, he could command an extensive view of woods and waters. Here he erected his lodge of branches, built a small fire of dry sticks, and spread out his mat of rushes for a couch. Before lying down he walked about among the trees, plants and flowers, and resting himself on a high peak, fixed his gaze intensely on the moving canopy of clouds above, tinged by the rays of the setting sun, which is believed to be type of the Great Spirit, and the beautiful blue firmament around. He then returned to his lodge, and as the shades of evening closed around laid down on his mat, having turned up one end of it in the form of a pillow by putting a few short cedar branches under it. In this way he continued his fast for several days, walking about during the day and reposing at night, till he began to grow weak from exhaustion and want of food. In this state he kept his bed altogether, and while thus reposing passed in review his prior thoughts of the goodness of the Great Spirit in creating and sustaining all things. He thought strongly on the object of his fast, and wished for a dream which might reveal to him the way of accomplishing his desires. He admired the mysterious power of the Great Master of Life in creating all animal and vegetable things; and in seeking a boon from him personally, wished, also, his fellow-foresters might be shewn an easier way of obtaining their food than by the uncertainties of the chase.

On the third day of his fast, while lying thus exhausted in his lodge gazing at the sky, he saw a handsome young man descending from the blest abodes. He was richly dressed in waving garments of light green and yellow, with nodding plumes of the same colors on his head.

"I am sent to you," he said, "by the Great Spirit, to grant your request. He knows your motives in fasting, and sees that your object is to procure a benefit for your people, and not for strength in war, or the prowess of warriors. I am sent to instruct you how you may succeed. Arise, and wrestle with me."

Onz was weak from fasting, but felt his courage rising at these words and determined to try. He immediately arose and began the proposed trial. After a protracted struggle he was nearly exhausted, when the celestial messenger, with a smiling countenance, said, "It is enough for once. I will come again to try you." So saying he ascended to the sky.

Next day the messenger re-appeared at the same hour and renewed the contest. Onz felt that his strength was even less than before, but his mind derived secret support from the presence of the visitor in proportion as his body became weaker, and he felt sustained when he heard his adversary say, "Faint not, but be strong, for this is the only way in which you can succeed." He then retired again to the blue skies.

Two days had now been given to the contest, and every day the young forester had become weaker and weaker. But on the third day the trial was again renewed. The poor youth was very faint, but as soon as he arose he appeared to be strengthened, and he determined in his mind to prevail or perish. For a long time he exerted his utmost strength. At last the celestial stranger released his hold, and the next moment he declared himself conquered. He then entered the lodge and began to deliver his instruction.

"You have won your desires," he said, "you have wrestled manfully. To-morrow will be the seventh day of your fasting. I will come and wrestle with you for the last time. You will prevail over me and throw me down. When you have done so you must strip off my garments, make the earth clean and soft by removing the roots and weeds, and bury me in it. Leave my body in the ground, go away and do not disturb it, but come occasionally to visit the place, to see whether I have come to life, and be careful never to let the grass or weeds grow on my grave. When you see me arise put fresh earth around me once a month. Teach others what I have taught you, and your people will be benefitted."

He then shook him affectionately by the hand and left him; but the next day he punctually returned at the same hour, renewed the struggle, and was thrown down as it had been predicted. Onz pulled off the garments and plumes and carefully buried the body in fresh earth, being satisfied that his friend would again come to life.

Having thus finished his fast, he returned home to his father's lodge, and partook sparingly of a meal which had been prepared for him, and told his father that he had successfully accomplished his fast. But he never for a moment forgot his friend, nor his injunctions, but carefully visited the place of burial from time to time.

Joy was depicted in the face of each member of the family after this happy announcement.

Spring had now passed away and summer was drawing to its

close, when he, one day, invited his father to accompany him through the woods to the retired spot where he had undergone his fast. On reaching this place they saw, where the lodge had stood, a tall and graceful plant. Long, green leaves waved on each side of it, and from its top hung a plume of yellow, silken hair. Golden clusters of grain were revealed on the stalk. The whole waved in the gentle, warm breeze with a indescribable grace.

"It is my friend, come to life again," shouted the lad. "It is Mondamin—it is the Spirit's grain,[2]—the gift of the Great Spirit to mankind."

Notes

1. James Adair, *The History of the American Indians: Particularly Those Nations Adjoining to the Mississippi, East and West Florida, Georgia, South and North Carolina* . . . (London: E. and C. Dilly, 1775), [Schoolcraft's note].

2. Such is the meaning of *Mondámin,* the Algonquin name for Indian corn [Schoolcraft's note].

The Myths of Manibozho and Ioskeha

by Daniel Garrison Brinton

* * * * *

Although many of his ideas about Native Americans and their cultures (an insistence on their European rather than Asiatic derivation and the belief that polygenesis accounted for cultural similarities even among closely related tribal groups, for example) have long been discarded by anthropologists, Daniel Garrison Brinton (1837–1899) remains a major pioneer in American anthropology. Educated as a physician, he practiced medicine in West Chester, Pennsylvania, and later in Philadelphia. But his true interests lay in ethnology and archeology. He began to publish in these fields in 1859 and resumed his studies of Native American cultures after Civil War service. His diverse

SOURCE: *Historical Magazine and Notes and Queries*, n. s. 2 (1867), 3–6. "From a work in preparation on American Mythology" (Brinton's note). This essay was incorporated into *The Myths of the New World. A Treatise on the Symbolism and Mythology of the Red Race of America*, 2nd edition (New York: Henry Holt, 1876), pp. 175–186. Brinton's notes to the piece are taken from the book rather than from its periodical appearance.

concerns included the traditional literatures of the Maya and Nahuatl of Central America, the identity of the Moundbuilders of the midwestern United States, linguistic interrelationships among tribal groups in both North and South America, and the approach to myth interpretation articulated by Oxford don Max Müller. Brinton's major publication in this last area, which is most relevant to the essay reproduced here, was The Myths of the New World. A Treatise on the Symbolism and Mythology of the Red Race of America *(New York: Henry Holt, 1868). He was also responsible for editing a several volume series,* Library of Aboriginal American Literature, *which presented texts, translations, and some analyses of Native American literature from throughout the New World. Moreover, Brinton was instrumental in gaining a foothold for anthropology in American academe and taught the subject at the University of Pennsylvania.*

Max Müller's approach to myth interpretation—presented most thoroughly in Comparative Mythology, *in* Oxford Essays *(London, 1856)—arises from his perception of the close interrelationships between myth and language among the prehistoric Aryans. According to Müller, the Aryan (or Indo-European) language was incapable of abstraction and thus compelled its speakers to deal with all phenomena through concrete circumlocutions. Since the rising and setting of the sun—the interplay of light with darkness—were vital concerns for the Aryans, much of their verbalization dealt with those events. In their non-abstract way, the Aryans might refer to a phenomenon such as sunset using the figurative devices of personification and metaphor: "The sun god goes to bed behind the western mountains." Thus, Müller asserted, each time as Aryan spoke, he generated a myth. As centuries passed and the Aryan language gave way to such descendants as Sanscrit, the original meaning of the primitive concrete phrases were forgotten. By the time the Vedas, the Sanscrit religious books, were compiled, stories had developed to explain the obscure Aryan phrases. So a second layer of myth tried to explicate the first. For instance, the names of the Aryan gods and phrases about them produced mythic narratives which tried to account for these names and phrases. The task of the scholar, as Müller saw it, was to determine the original meanings of gods' and heroes' names. Thus Dyaus, the chief god of the Vedas, was shown to be associated with the Aryan word for "sun, light, warmth," and Dyaus became a metaphor for the sun. Accounts of Dyaus's activities, then, were solar myths which recounted the sun's struggles with the forces of darkness. Müller's method became particularly appealing to western scholars when he demonstrated that the gods of classical Greece were linguistically related to the Vedic gods and consequently had the same associations with Aryan terminology. Zeus, as linguistic equivalent of Dyaus, became a solar symbol.*

In "The Myths of Manibozho and Ioskeha," Daniel G. Brinton uses Müller's method to show how the Algonquin Trickster joins Dyaus and Zeus in the gallery of solar gods and heroes. In suggesting that the Algonquin root wab, *which appears in Trickster's name, has multiple denotations, he invokes Müller's theory of polyonomy, the Aryan characteristic that one word could carry several meanings. Brinton sees a similar situation in Algonquin, a primitive language analogous to Aryan. Since one category of denotations of* wab *deals with "light," Trickster becomes the spirit of light. Although Müller's method, as practiced by Brinton, has long been rejected, its use by the Americanist can remind the modern student of Native American oral literatures of the levels of meaning that may be suggested in the original languages of the oral texts. While Manibozho may not be the sun god posited by Brinton, a full understanding of this figure may require the sort of linguistic analysis undertaken by this American advocate of Müller's comparative mythology.*

For a brief, but thorough, treatment of Müller's ideas, see Richard M. Dorson's frequently reprinted essay, "The Eclipse of Solar Mythology," Journal of American Folklore, *68 (1955), 393–416. Besides Brinton, the leading American exponents of Müller's theory were Horatio Hale and John Fiske; for example, see Horatio Hale, " 'Above' and 'Below': A Mythological Disease of Language,"* Journal of American Folklore, *3 (1890), 177–190, and John Fiske,* Myths and Mythmakers. Old Tales and Superstitions Interpreted by Comparative Mythology *(Boston: J. R. Osgood, 1873). A modern perspective on Brinton's work is available in two articles by Regna Darnell: "An Anthropological Reputation in Historical Retrospect. The Case of Daniel Garrison Brinton,"* Bulletin of the Philadelphia Anthropological Society, *9, no. 2 (1968), 7–13; and "Daniel Brinton and the Professionalization of American Anthropology," in* American Anthropology. The Early Years, *ed. J. V. Murra, Publications of the American Ethnological Society (St. Paul: West, 1976), pp. 69–98. Becky Vorpagel has focused specifically on Brinton's relationship to nineteenth-century folklore studies in "Daniel Brinton's Concept of Folklore,"* New York Folklore, *9, nos. 3 and 4 (Winter 1983), 31–42.*

$*$ $*$ $*$ $*$ $*$

From the remotest wilds of the Northwest to the coast of the Atlantic, from the Southern boundaries of Carolina to the cheerless swamps of Hudson's Bay, the Algonkins were never tired of gathering around the winter fire and repeating the story of Manibozho or Michabo, the Great Hare. With like unanimity their various branches, the Powhattans, of Virginia, the Lenni Lenape, of the Delaware, the warlike hordes of New England, the Ottawas of the far North, and the Western tribes, perhaps without exception, spoke of "this chimerical beast," as one of the old missionaries calls it, as their common ancestor, and the totem or clan that bore his name was looked up to with peculiar respect.

In many of the tales which the whites have preserved of Michabo he seems half a wizard, half a simpleton. He is full of pranks and wiles, but often at a loss for a meal of victuals; ever itching to try his arts magic on great beasts, and often meeting ludicrous failures therein: envious of the powers of others, and constantly striving to outdo them in what they did best; in short, little more than a malicious buffoon, delighting in practical jokes, and abusing his superhuman powers for selfish and ignoble ends. But this is a low, modern, and corrupt version of the character of Michabo, bearing no more resemblance to his real and ancient one than the language and acts of our Saviour and the Apostles in the coarse Mystery Plays of the Middle Ages do to those recorded by the Evangelist.

What he really was we must seek in the accounts of older travelers, in the invocations of the Jossakeeds or Prophets, and in the part assigned to him in the solemn mysteries of religion. In these we find him portrayed as the patron and founder of the Meda worship,[1] the inventor of picture writing, the father and guardian of their nation, the ruler of the winds, even the maker and preserver of the world, and creator of the sun and moon. From a grain of sand brought from the bottom of the primeval ocean he fashioned the habitable land and set it floating on the waters. Under the name Michabo Ovisaketchak, the Great Hare who created the Earth, he was originally the highest divinity recognized by them, "powerful and beneficent beyond all others, maker of the heavens and the world." He was founder of the medicine hunt, in which, after appropriate ceremonies and incantations, the Indian sleeps, and Michabo appears to him in a dream, and tells him where he may readily kill game. He himself was a mighty hunter of old; one of his footsteps measured Eight leagues; the Great Lakes were the beaver dams he built; and when the cataracts impeded his progress he tore them away with his hands. Attentively watching the spider spread its web to trap unwary flies, he devised the art of knitting nets to catch fish, and the signs and charms he tested and handed down to his descendants are of marvelous efficacy in the chase. Sometimes he was said to dwell in the skies with his brother the snow, or like many great spirits to have built his wigwam in the far North on some floe of ice in the Arctic Ocean; while the Chippewas localized his birth-place and former home to the island Michilimakinac, at the outlet of Lake Superior. But in the oldest account of the missionaries he was alleged to reside toward the East, and in the holy formulas of the Meda craft, when the winds are invoked to the Medicine lodge, the East is summoned in his name, the door opens in that direction, and there, at the edge of the earth, where the sun rises, on the shore of the infinite ocean that surrounds the land, he has his house, and sends the luminaries forth on their daily journeys.[2]

It is passing strange that such an insignificant creature as the rabbit should have received this apotheosis. No explanation of it in the least satisfactory has ever been offered. Some have pointed it out as a senseless, meaningless brute worship. It leads to the suspicion that there may lurk here one of those confusions of words which have so often led to confusion of ideas in theology. Manibozho, Nanibojon, Missibizi, Michabo, Messon, all variations of the same name, in different dialects, rendered according to different orthographies, scrutinize them close as we may, they all seem composed, according to well ascertained laws of Algonkin euphony, from the words corresponding to *great* and *hare* or *rabbit*, or the first two perhaps from *spirit* and *hare*, (*michi*, great, *nabos*, hare, *manito nabos*, spirit hare, Chippewa dialect), and so they have been invariably translated even by the Indians themselves. But looking more narrowly at the second member of the word, it is clearly capable of another and very different interpretation—of an interpretation which discloses at once the origin and secret meaning of the whole story of Michabo, in the light of which it appears no longer the incoherent fable of savages, but a true myth, instinct with nature, pregnant with matter no wise inferior to those which fascinate in the chants of the *Rig Veda*, or the weird pages of the *Edda*.

I have elsewhere emphasized with what might have seemed superfluous force, how prominent in primitive Mythology is the East, the source of the morning, the day-spring on high, the cardinal point which determines and controls all others. But I did not lay as much stress on it as others have. "The whole theogony and philosophy of the ancient world," says Max Müller, "centered in the Dawn, the mother of the bright gods, of the sun in his various aspects, of the morn, the day, the spring; herself the brilliant image and visage of immortality."[3] Now it appears on attentively examining the Algonkin root *wab* that it gives rise to words of very diverse meanings; that like many others in all languages, while presenting but one form it represents ideas of wholly unlike origin and application; that in fact there are two distinct roots having ths sound. One is the initial syllable of the word translated *Hare* or *Rabbit*, but the other means *White*, and from it are derived the words for the East, the Dawn, the Light, the Day, and the Morning.[4] Beyond a doubt this is the compound in the names Michabo and Manibozho, which therefore mean the Great Light, the Spirit of Light, of the Dawn, or the East, and, in the literal sense of the word, the Great White One, as indeed he has sometimes been called.

In this sense, all the ancient and authentic Myths concerning him are plain and full of meaning. They divide themselves into two distinct cycles. In the one, Michabo is the Spirit of Light, who dispels the darkness; in the other, as chief of the cardinal points, he is lord of the winds, prince of the powers of the air, whose voice is the thunder, whose weapon the lightning, the supreme figure in the encounter of the air currents, in the un-ending conflict which the Dakotas described as being waged by the waters and the winds.

In the first, he is grandson of the Moon, his father is the West Wind, and his mother, a maiden, dies in giving him birth at the moment of conception. For the Moon is the goddess of Night, the Dawn is her daughter who brings forth the Morning and per-ishes herself in the act, and the West, the Spirit of Darkness as the East is of Light, precedes and as it were begets the latter, as the evening does the morning. Straightway, however, continues the legend, the son sought the unnatural father to revenge the death of his mother, and then commenced a long and desperate struggle. "It began on the mountains. The West was forced to give ground. Manibozho drove him across rivers and over mountains and lakes, until at last he came to the brink of this world. 'Hold,' cried he, 'my son, you know my power and that it is impossible to kill me.' "[5] What is this but the diurnal combat of light and darkness carried on from what time "the jocund morn stands tiptoe on the misty mountain tops," across the wide world to the sunset, the struggle that knows no end, for both the opponents are immortal? In the second, and evidently to the native mind more important cycle of legends, he was repre-sented as one of four brothers, the North, the South, the East, and the West, all born at a birth, whose mother died in ushering them into the world.[6] For hardly has the kindling orient served to fix the cardinal points than it is lost and dies in the advancing day. Yet it is clear that he was something more than a personifi-cation of the East or the East wind, for it is repeatedly said that it was he who assigned their duties to all the winds, to that of the East as well as the others. This is a blending of his two char-acters. Here too his life is a battle. No longer with his father, indeed, but with his brother Chokanipok, the flint stone, whom he broke in pieces and scattered over the land, changing his entrails into fruitful vines. The conflict was long and terrible. The face of nature was desolated as by a tornado, and the gigan-tic boulders and loose rocks found on the prairies [7] are the mis-siles hurled by the mighty combatants.[8] Or else his foe was the glittering Prince of Serpents, whose abode was the lake; or the shining Manito, whose home was guarded by fiery serpents and a deep sea; or the great King of Fishes; all symbols of the atmospheric waters, all figurative descriptions of the wars of the elements. In these affrays the thunder and lightning are at his command, and with them he destroys his enemies. For this reason the Chippewa pictography represents him brandishing a rattlesnake, the symbol of the electric flash,[9] and sometimes called him the Northwest Wind, which in the region they inhabit brings the thunder-storms.

As ruler of the winds he was like Quetzalcoatl, father and protector of all species of birds, their symbols.[10] He was patron of hunters, for their course is guided by the cardinal points. Therefore when the medicine hunt had been successful the prescribed sign of gratitude to him was to scatter a handful of the animal's blood toward each of these.[11] As daylight brings vision, and to see is to know, it was no fable that gave him as the author of their arts, their wisdom, and their institutions.

In effect, his story is a world-wide truth veiled under a thin garb of fancy: it is but a variation of that narrative which every race has to tell out of gratitude to that beneficent Father who everywhere had cared for his children. Michabo, giver of life and light, creator and preserver, is no apotheosis of a prudent chieftain, still less the fabrication of an idle fancy or a designing priestcraft, but in origin, deeds and name, the not unworthy personification of the purest conceptions they possessed concerning the Father of All.

To him at early dawn the Indian stretched forth his hands in prayer, and to the sky or the sun as his homes he first pointed the pipe in his ceremonies, rites often misinterpreted by travelers as indicative of sun worship. As later observers tell us, this day the Algonkin Prophet builds the Medicine lodge to face the sunrise, and in the name of Michabo, who there has his home, summons the Spirits of the four quarters of the world and Gizhigooke, the day maker, to come to his fire and disclose the hidden things of the distant and the future. So the earliest explorers relate that when they asked the native priest who it was they invoked, what demon or familiar, the invariable reply was, "the Kichigouai, the genii of Light, those who make the day."[12]

Our authorities on Iroquois traditions, though numerous enough, are not so satisfactory. The best, perhaps, is Father Brebeuf, a Jesuit missionary who resided among the Hurons, in 1626. Their culture myth, which he has recorded is strikingly similar to that of the Algonkins. Two brothers appear in it, Ioskeha and Tawiscava, names which find their meaning in the Oneida dialect as the White One and the Dark One.[13] They are twins born of a virgin mother, who died in giving them life. Their grandmother was the Moon, called by the Hurons *Ataeusic*, a word which signifies literally, *she bathes herself*, and which, in the opinion of Father Bruyas, a most competent authority, is derived from the word for water.[14]

The brothers quarreled, and finally came to blows, the former using the horns of a stag, the latter the wild rose. He of the weaker weapon was very naturally discomfited and sorely wounded. Fleeing for life, the blood gushed from him at every step, and as it fell turned into flint stones. The victor returned to his grandmother and established his lodge in the far East, on the borders of the great ocean whence the sun comes. In time he became the father of mankind and special guardian of the Iroquois. The earth was at first arid and sterile, but he destroyed the gigantic frog which had swallowed all the waters, and guided the torrents into smooth streams and lakes.[15] The woods he stocked with game, and having learned from the great tortoise who supports the world how to make fire, taught his children, the Indians, this indispensable art. He it was who watched and watered their crops, and indeed without his aid, says the old missionary, quite out of patience with such puerilities, "they think they could not boil a pot." Sometimes they spoke of him as the sun, but this only figuratively.[16]

From other writers of early date we learn that the essential outlines of this myth were received by the Tuscaroras and the Mohawks, and as the proper names of the two brothers are in the Oneida dialect, we cannot err in considering this the national legend of the Iroquois stock. There is strong likelihood that the Taronhiawagon, *He who comes from the Sky*, of the Onondagas, who was their supreme God, who spoke to them in dreams, and in whose honor the chief festival of their calendar

69

was celebrated about the winter solstice, was in fact Ioskeha under another name.[17] As to the legend of the Good and Bad Minds given by Cusic, the native historian of the Tuscaroras, and the latter and wholly spurious myth of Hiawatha, first made public by Mr. Clark in his *History of Onondaga* (1849),[18] and which, in the graceful poem of Longfellow, is now familiar to the world, they are but pale and incorrect reflections of the early native traditions. So strong is the resemblance Ioskeha bears to Michabo, that what has been said in explanation of the latter will be sufficient for both. Yet I do not imagine that the one was copied or borrowed from the other. We cannot be too cautious in adopting such a conclusion. The two nations were remote in everything but geographical position. I call to mind another similar myth. In it a mother is also said to have brought forth twins or a pair of twins, and to have paid for them with her life. Again the one is described as the bright, the other as the dark twin; again it is said that they struggled one with the other for the mastery. Scholars likewise have interpreted the Mother to mean the Dawn, the twins either Light and Darkness, or the Four Winds. Yet this is not Algonkin theology; nor is it at all related to that of the Iroquois. It is the story of Sarama in the *Rig Veda*, and was written in Sanscrit, under the shadow of the Himalayas, centuries before Homer.

Notes

1. The *meda* worship is the ordinary religious ritual of the Algonkins. It consists chiefly in exhibitions of legerdemain, and in conjuring and exorcising demons. A *jossakeed* is an inspired prophet who derives his power directly from the higher spirits, and not as the *medawin*, by instruction and practice [Brinton's note].

2. For these particulars see F. Le Mercier, *Relation de ce qui s'est passé de plus remarquable aux Missions des Pères de la Compagnie de Jesus, en la Nouvelle France, les années mil six cens soixante six, & mil six cens soixante sept* (Paris: Sebastien Cramoisy, 1668), p. 12; F. Le Mercier, *Relation de ce qui s'est passé de plus remarquable . . . les années 1669. & 1670* (Paris: Sebastien Cramoisy, 1671), p. 93; P. F. X. Charlevoix, *Histoire et description generale de la Nouvelle France, avec le Journal Historique d'un Voyage fait par*

THE MYTHS OF MANIBOZHO AND IOSKEHA

ordre du Roi dans l'Amérique Septentrionnale (Paris: Chez Pierre-François Giffart, 1744), p. 344; Henry Rowe Schoolcraft, *Historical and Statistical Information, Respecting the History, Condition and Prospects of the Indian Tribes of the United States: Collected and Prepared Under the Direction of the Bureau of Indian Affairs per Act of Congress of March 3d, 1847* (Philadelphia: Lippincott, 1851–1857), 5, 420ff.; and Alexander Henry, *Travels and Adventures in Canada and the Indian Territories Between the Years 1760 and 1776* (New York: I. Riley, 1809), pp. 212ff. These are decidedly the best references of the many that could be furnished. Peter Jones, *History of the Ojebway* [sic] *Indians; with Especial Reference to Their Conversion to Christianity. With a Brief Memoir of the Writer; and Introductory Notice by the Rev. G. Osborn* (London: A. W. Bennett, [1861]), p. 35; Nicolas Perrot, *Memoire sur les Moeurs, Coustumes et Relligion des Sauvages de l'Amérique Septentrionale* (Leipzig: Librairie A. Franck, 1864), pp. 12, 19, 339; and Richard Blomes, *The Present State of His Majesties Isles and Territories in America, viz. Jamaica, Barbadoes, S. Christopher, Meris, Antego, S. Vincent, Dominica, New-Jersey, Pensilvania, Monserat, Anguilla, Bermudas, Carolina, Virginia, New-England, Tobago, New-Found-Land, Mary-Land, New-York* . . . (London: Dorman Newman, 1687), p. 193 [Brinton's note].

3. Max Müller, *Lectures on the Science of Language. Second Series* (London: Longman, Green, Longman, Roberts, & Green, 1864), p. 518 [Brinton's note].

4. Dialectic forms in Algonkin for white, are *wabi, wape, wompi, waubish, oppai*; for morning, *wapan, wapaneh, opah*; for east *wapa, waubun, waubamo*; for dawn, *wapa, waubun*; for day *wompan, oppan*; for light, *oppung*; and many others similar. In the Abnaki dialect, *wanbighen*, it is white, is the customary idiom to express the breaking of the day (Eugene Vetromile, *The Abnakis and Their History. Or, Historical Notes on the Aborigines of Acadia* [New York: J. B. Kirker, 1866], p. 27). The loss in composition of the vowel sound represented by the English w, and in the French writers by the figure 8, is supported by frequent analogy [Brinton's note].

5. Henry Rowe Schoolcraft, *Algic Researches, Comprising Inquiries Respecting the Mental Characteristics of the North American Indians* (New York: Harper and Brothers, 1839), 1, 135–142 [Brinton's note].

6. The names of the four brothers, Wabun, Kabun, Kabibonokka, and Shawano, express in Algonkin both the cardinal points and the winds which blow from them. In another version of the legend, first reported by Father de Smet and quoted by Schoolcraft without acknowledgment, they are Nanaboojoo, Chipiapoos, Wabosso, and Chakekenapok. Lederer gives the names in the Oenock dialect in Virginia as Pash, Sepoy, Askarin and Maraskarin (*The Discoveries of John Lederer, in Three Several Marches from Virginia, to the West of Carolina, and Others Parts of the Contenent* . . . [London: Samuel Heyrick, 1672], p. 4). He calls them ignorantly "four women." When Captain Argoll visited the Potomac in 1610 a chief told him: "We have five gods in all; our chief god appears often unto us in the form of a mighty great hare; the other four have no visible shape, but are indeed the four winds which keep the four

corners of the earth." (William Strachey, *The Historie of Travaile into Virginia Britannia; Expressing the Cosmographie and Comodities of the Country. Togither with the Manners and Customes of the People* [London: The Hakluyt Society, 1849], p. 98) [Brinton's note].

7. Schoolcraft, *Algic Researches*, 1, 135-142 (Brinton's note, from the periodical version of the essay).

8. Schoolcraft, *Algic Researches*, 2, 214; *Historical and Statistical Information*, 1, 317 (Brinton's note, from the periodical version of the essay).

9. *A Narrative of the Captivity and Adventures of John Tanner, (U. S. Interpreter at the Saut de Ste. Marie), During Thirty Years Residence Among the Indians in the Interior of North America*, ed. Edwin James (New York: Carvill, 1830), p. 351 [Brinton's note].

10. Schoolcraft, *Algic Researches*, 1, 216 [Brinton's note].

11. *Narrative of John Tanner*, p. 354.

12. Compare P. Le Jeune, *Relation de ce qui s'est passé en la Nouvelle France, en l'année 1634* (Paris: Sebastien Cramoisy, 1635), p. 14, and P. Le Jeune, *Relation de ce qui s'est passé en la Nouvelle France en l'année 1637* (Rouen: Jean le Boullenger, 1638), p. 46, with Schoolcraft, *Historical and Statistical Information*, 5, 419. *Kichigouai* is the same word as *Gizhigooke*, according to a different orthography [Brinton's note].

13. The names I8skehe and Ta8iscara I venture to identify with the Oneida *owisske* or *owiska*, white, and *tetiucalas* (*tyokaras*, *tewhgarlars* Mohawk), dark or darkness. The prefix i to *owisske* is the impersonal third person singular; the suffix *ha* gives a future sense, so that *i-owisske-ha* or *iouskeha* means "it is going to become white." Brebeuf gives a similar example of *gaon*, old; *a-gaon-ha*, *il va devenir vieux* (*Relation de ce qui s'est passé en la Nouvelle France en l'année 1636* [Paris: Sebastien Cramoisy, 1637], p. 99). But "it is going to become white," meant to the Iroquois that the dawn was about to appear, just as *wanbighen*, it is white, did to the Abnakis (see note 5), and as the Eskimos say, *kau ma wok*, it is white, to express that it is daylight (John Richardson's Vocabulary of Labrador Eskimo in *Arctic Searching Expedition: A Journal of a Boat-Voyage Through Rupert's Land and the Arctic Sea, in Search of the Discovery Ships Under Command of Sir John Franklin* [London: Longman, Brown, Green, & Longmans, 1851]). Therefore, that Ioskeha is an impersonation of the light of the dawn admits of no dispute [Brinton's note].

14. The orthography of Brebeuf is *aataentsic*. This may be analyzed as follows: root *aouen*, water; prefix *at*, *il y a quelque chose là dedans; ataouen, se baigner;* from which comes the form *ataouensere*. (See James Bruyas, *Radices Verborum Iroquaeorum* [New York: J. M. Shea, 1863], pp. 30, 31.) Here again the mythological role of the moon as the goddess of water comes distinctly to light [Brinton's note].

15. This offers an instance of the uniformity which prevailed in symbolism in the New World. The Aztecs adored the goddess of water under the figure of a frog carved from a single emerald; or of human form, but holding in her hand

the leaf of a water lily ornamented with frogs. (Charles, l'Abbe Brasseur de Bourbourg, *Histoire de Nations Civilisées du Mexique et de l'Amérique-centrale, durant les siècles antériers à Christophe Colomb; écrite sur des documents originaux et entièrement inédits, prisés aux anciennes archives des indigènes* [Paris: Arthus Bertrand, 1857–1859], 1, 324.) [Brinton's note].

16. P. Le Jeune, *Relation de ce qui s'est passé en la Nouvelle France en l'année 1636* (Paris: Sebastien Cramoisy, 1637), p. 101 [Brinton's note].

17. Claude d'Ablon, *Relation de ce qui s'est passé de plus remarquable aux Missions des Pères de la Compagnie de Jesus en la Nouvelle France, les années 1670 & 1671* (Paris: Sebastien Mabre-Cramoisy, 1672), p. 17. Cusic spells it *Tarenyawagon*, and translates it Holder of the Heavens. But the name is evidently a compound of *garonhia*, sky, softened in the Onondaga dialect to *taronhia* (see Albert Gallatin, ed., "Hale's Indians of North-West America and Vocabularies of North America," *Transactions of the American Ethnological Society*, 2 [1848], 1–130, under the word sky), and *wagin*, I come [Brinton's note].

18. Brinton's references are to Davis Cusick, *Sketches of Ancient History of the Six Nations, Comprising—First—A Tale of the Foundation of the Great Island (Now North America,) the Two Infants Born, and the Creation of the Universe. Second—A Real Account of the Early Settlers of North America, and Their Dissensions. Third—Origin of the Kingdom of the Five Nations, Which Was Called a Long House: The Wars, Fierce Animals, &c.* (Lockport, New York: Turner & McCollum, 1848); and Joshua V. H. Clark, *Onondaga; or Reminiscences of Earlier and Later Times; Being a Series of Historical Sketches Relative to Onondaga; with Notes on the Several Towns in the County, and Oswego* (Syracuse: Stoddard and Babcock, 1849).

The Poetry of Indians

by James S. Brisbin

* * * * *

James S. Brisbin (1837-1892) was a man of many interests and attainments. Educated in the classics, he taught school and achieved notoriety as an abolitionist orator. At the outbreak of the Civil War, he joined a Pennsylvania regiment with the rank of private. He served with distinction in several of the war's major campaigns and at the close of fighting was Chief of Staff to General Stephen G. Burbridge, who commanded the Districts of Kentucky and Tennessee. After the war Brisbin continued his military career, rising to the rank of colonel and participating in the Little Big Horn campaign of 1876. But military life did not prevent Brisbin from pursuing literary fame. In addition to biographies of Presidents Grant and Garfield, he wrote The Beef Bonanza; or, How to Get Rich on the Plains. Being a Description of Cattle-Growing, Sheep-Farming, Horse-Raising, and Dairying in the West *(Philadelphia: Lippincott, 1881), his most successful book. Brisbin's most important contribution to Native American studies was*

SOURCE: *Harper's New Monthly Magazine*, 57 (1878), 104-108.

editing the memoirs of trader-scout George P. Belden: Belden, The White
Chief: or, Twelve Years Among the Wild Indians of the Plains.
From the Diaries and Manuscripts of George P. Belden *(Cincinnati:
C. F. Vest, 1870. Reissued by Ohio University Press in 1974.)*

*Although Brisbin's contributions to the study of American Indian cultures
were limited, the essay presented here identifies a problem in the field that has
continued to plague its students. The translation of American Indian oral
literature into English has presented significant difficulties. Not only are there
the problems of translating from one language to another that occur whenever
poetry is being dealt with (and commentators on Native American oral literature such as Dennis Tedlock have argued that even Indian myths and folk-
tales must be treated as poetry). One must also decide on a method for convert-
ing oral verbalizations into print. Brisbin's solution to the translator's
problem—the use of standard English poetry to represent American Indian
oral poetry—is faulty on several counts. First, such a solution ignores the*
oral *nature of the material being translated. As Brisbin has noted, gestures
and nonverbal vocalizations—features that cannot be communicated through
conventional English poetics—comprise part of the performance of oral literature. Moreover, English poetry derives from an aesthetic alien to Native
American cultures. The special diction, meter, and rhyme which distinguished nineteenth century poetry in English represented ideas about verbal art
peculiar to English-speaking culture. Native American groups had their own
aesthetics of verbal art, and these aesthetics included features of language not
incorporated into the notions about what constituted poetry in English. Finally, Brisbin generalizes about "Indian" poetry, apparently not realizing
that various tribal groups may have conceived of poetic language in different
ways. Most of his examples are from Algonquin languages; but Brisbin does
not distinguish Algonquin poeticizing from similar verbal artistry among
Siouan-speakers or members of other linguistic groupings.*

*To suggest that Brisbin has not solved the problem of translating Native
American oral literature should not detract from his insightful recognition that
such a problem exists. In fact, many other approaches to the problem have
been almost as unsuccessful. The approach of most anthropologists and linguists, for instance, often robs oral literature of its artistry on even the most basic
verbal level. The convention has been to present Native American texts with
interlinear translations (virtually unreadable) and sometimes with free translations, which serve to make the content of stories and songs accessible, but do
little to represent them as art.*

More recently—within the past two decades—experiments have been aimed at capturing in printed English the full artistry of American Indian oral literature. Poet Jerome Rothenberg has developed the concept of "total translation" as a way of achieving this goal. In two anthologies, Technicians of the Sacred. A Range of Poetries from Africa, America, Asia & Oceania *(Garden City, New York: Doubleday, 1968) and* Shaking the Pumpkin. Traditional Poetry of the Indian North Americas *(Garden City, New York: Doubleday, 1972), he has provided translated texts of Native American oral poetry using concrete poetry and typographic gimmickry to alert the reader that the material is different from conventional English poetry. The result, though, is an experience more visual than oral and is therefore unsuccessful in conveying the real nature of the translated material. Another experimental methodology is that of Dennis Tedlock, who uses typographic signals—spacing, uneven alignment of words, capitalization, and the like—to represent precise features of oral literary performance such as changes in dynamics, tempo, and voice timbre. Tedlock has effectively demonstrated his techniques on Zuni oral narratives in* Finding the Center. Narrative Poetry of the Zuni Indians *(New York: Dial, 1972) and has discussed his theories of translation and presentation in* The Spoken Word and the Work of Interpretation *(Philadelphia: University of Pennsylvania Press, 1983).*

Perhaps the most influential student of Native American poetics and the problems of translating and analyzing Native American poetry has been Dell H. Hymes. In numerous essays—many of them collected in "In Vain I Tried to Tell You." Essays in Native American Ethnopoetics *(Philadelphia: University of Pennsylvania Press, 1981)—he has articulated a perspective that combines linguistic, literary, and ethnographic theory with Native insights and appreciations of the verbal artistry. Hymes's approach to the problems raised by Native American oral poetry is difficult to master, but his influence is apparent in the recent spate of books and essays which confront those problems. Among these publications are Karl Kroeber, ed.,* Traditional Literatures of the American Indian. Texts and Interpretations *(Lincoln: University of Nebraska Press, 1980); Jarold Ramsey,* Reading the Fire. Essays in the Traditional Indian Literatures of the Far West *(Lincoln: University of Nebraska Press, 1983); and Brian Swann, ed.,* Smoothing the Ground. Essays on Native American Oral Literature *(Berkeley: University of California Press, 1983). The periodical* Alcheringa *publishes translations of oral literature (not only from*

Native Americans) by translators using methods similar to those of Rothenberg, Tedlock, and Hymes.

For some critical responses to the efforts of the modern translators, see William Bevis, "American Indian Verse Translations," College English, 35, no. 6 (March 1974), 693–703; H. S. McAllister, " 'The Language of Shamans': Jerome Rothenberg's Contribution to American Indian Literature," Western American Literature, 10, no. 4 (Winter 1976), 293–309; and William M. Clements, "Faking the Pumpkin: On Jerome Rothenberg's Literary Offenses," Western American Literature, 16, no. 3 (November 1981), 193–204. An effort at relating the creative works of contemporary Native American writers to traditional aesthetic concepts is Kenneth Lincoln, Native American Renaissance *(Berkeley: University of California Press, 1983).*

* * * * *

The Indians have no books, and their history is wholly oral. The tales and traditions handed down from father to son are the only connecting link between the present and the past. It is the songs, ceremonies, and poetry of the Indians that form their principal history. The difficulty of rendering these songs will be apparent to every one, when it is remembered that the Indian has no grammar or well-defined sounds in his language. Motion of the hands and gutturals constitute much of his tongue, and these, of course, are not easily defined on paper. There is, however, something to be gleaned in the field of Indian poetry, though the task is so difficult that one may well undertake it with feelings of hesitation, for never was a subject more intricate.

The clouds, the sun, moon, stars, storms, the lightnings, the voice of the thunder—these are the fruitful themes that fill the savage soul with song, and from which he draws symbols in his chants and stories.

War, love, and the chase burst from his lips in weird music, but it is impossible to reduce to metre and connect the flashes of his genius. His monosyllables, his eye, the nod of his head and waving of hands—all these are potential in his song, and mean more than mere words. Viewed in this light, the winds have voices, the leaves of the trees utter a language, and even the earth is animated with a crowd of unseen but beautiful spirits. Hence many of the Indian songs are accompanied with intangible music that can neither be caught nor written.[1] No two languages could be more dissimilar than Indian and English, and it is only the meanest kind of Indian poetry that can be caught and set to words of our tongue.

The Indian girl dancing before her warrior utters not a word, yet she clearly conveys the meaning of her dance.[2] Would she have him go to the chase, she skips like a deer, pointing with outstretched hands to the imagined flying game, and finally, after circling and heading him, launches the fatal spear that is to slay him.[3] Would she have him go to war, with slow and measured step the preparations are made, arrows headed, placed in the quiver, and she briskly marches away.[4] Presently the enemy is seen and the fight begins; then the enemy flies, is overtaken, and, snatching an arrow from her lover's quiver, she fires it through the heart of the imaginary foe, and while he lies bleeding at her feet she imitates the removing of the scalp; and placing it in triumph at her belt, the dance is ended. All this is done without uttering a word, yet every motion of that wild savage fantasia is clearly intelligible, and through it the warrior learns the will of his mistress in language more powerful and exciting than mere words.

So it is of Indian song; the motion forms the poetry, and the words are but the dull filling up of a mystical and beautiful conception. How shall we translate such a language? It is impossible, and we can at best only gather the chaff, leaving the golden grain to be imagined—to be heard like the sighing of winds, the whispering of leaves, but never to be reduced to the dull theory of created matter and material form.

In time of war Indians pay great attention to the flight of birds,[5] and hence frequent allusions are made to them in their battle songs. If the bird is carnivorous, and flies toward the enemy, it indicates that the party will be victorious from which it flies, and that the bird had gone to pick the bones of the foes they are to slay in battle. It is thus the Sioux sing when they see the flight of eagles toward their enemies:

The eagles scream on high,
 They whet their forked beaks:
Raise, raise the battle cry,
 'Tis fame our leader seeks.

Or if it is desired to arouse their young men to deeds of noble daring, they cry:

The birds of the brave take flight round the sky,
 They cross the enemy's line:
Full happy am I that my body shall lie
 Where brave men love to die.[6]

Bah-bam-wa-zehig-equa, the Indian poet, wrote a song on "The Frog in Spring," which, if it could be rendered into good English, would undoubtedly equal some of Tom Hood's or Edgar A. Poe's best productions. In blank verse it runs thus:

See how the white spirit presses us—
Presses us—presses us, heavy and long—
Presses down to the frost-bitten earth.
Alas! you are heavy, ye spirits so white;
Alas! you are cold, you are cold, you are cold.
Ah! cease, shining spirits that fell from the skies—
Ah! cease so to crush us and keep us in dread.
Ah! when will ye vanish, and spring-time return?

This song, by a slight transposition of the original language, may also be rendered into metre, and made to read as follows:

Robed in his mantle of snow from the sky,
 See how the white spirit presses our breath;
Heavily, coldly, the masses they lie;
 Sighing and panting, we struggle for breath.
Spirit! O spirit! who first in the air
 The Great Master Monedo[7] wondrously made,
Cease to be pressing the sons of his care,
 And fly to the blue heights from whence ye have strayed.

Then we shall cheerfully, praisingly sing,
Okógis,[8] Okógis, the heralds of spring,
First to announce to the winter-bound ball
Sunshine and verdure and gladness to all.

The Indians believe that birds are intelligent creatures, and can foretell man's destiny, and they therefore regard their presence as indicative of good or evil, and often undertake to interpret the messages they bring. The Saginaw Indians have a hawk chant, which they sing, and which best illustrates this strange conception of the savage mind:

> The hawks turn their heads nimbly round,
> They turn to look back in their flight;
> The spirits of sun-place have whispered them words,
> They fly with their messages swift;
> They look as they fearfully go,
> They look to the farthermost end of the earth,
> Their eyes glancing bright, and their beaks boding harm.

There is a beautiful bird song, in the same language, written about the falcon—a bird which the Saginaws say lives in the open air with the Great Spirit, and possesses a mysterious knowledge of His will. Here it is:

> Birds! ye wild birds, whom the high gods have made,
>   And gifted with power of wondrous kind,
> Why turn ye so fearfully, shy and dismayed,
>   To gaze on the heavens ye are leaving behind?
>
> Come ye with news of a mystical cast,
>   Speaking of enemies crouched in the wood,
> Who on our people shall burst like a blast,
>   Heralding ruin, destruction, and blood?
>
> Come ye with messages sent from on high,
>   Warning of what the wild heavens shall pour—
> Whirlwinds, tornadoes, or pestilence nigh,
>   Wailing, starvation, or death on our shore?
>
> Come ye with words from the Master of Life,
>   Bringing intelligence good in your track?—
> Ah, then, ye bright birds with messages rife,
>   Why do you turn your heads doubtingly back?

The story of Shingebris has often been published in books, but I do not know that I have ever seen it rendered in verse, and I am sure the poetry gives strongest evidence of the capacity of the Indian mind to form beautiful theories.

Kabibonocca, the God of Winter, froze up all the country, and drove the inhabitants to the South; yet one poor man, Shingebris, in defiance of the icy god, remained by the side of a lake. Kabibonocca, offended at the fellow's perverseness, blew his bitterest blasts, determined if possible to drive him away; but Shingebris, the brave man, declared he would not go, and continued to subsist on fish. "Shall he withstand me?" cried the enraged Ice God; and summoning all his power, he said, "I will go and see this fellow, and freeze him stiff." So he went to the cabin of Shingebris, who, knowing of his coming, had a roaring fire on his hearth, and when Winter knocked at his door, he said, quite blithely, "Come in, Sir." The god entered, and did his best to freeze Shingebris, but he only poked the fire, and never minded him. Finally, Winter, finding unless he made off he should be melted, with tears in his eyes cried out, "Egad, I can not stand this! I am roasting!" and began his retreat, when Shingebris struck up his song of defiance:

> Windy god, I know your plan:
> You are but my fellow-man;
> Blow you may your coldest breeze,
> Shingebris you can not freeze;
> Sweep the strongest breeze you can,
> Shingebris is still your man.
> Heigh for life, and ho for bliss!
> Who so free as Shingebris?

What conception could be more beautiful or more typical of the Indian in his lodge and by the side of his warm fire defying the cold blasts of winter?

Waub Ojeeg, a Chippewa chief, composed the following war-song in commemoration of his expedition against the Sioux, and to encourage his warriors to again go on the war-path:

> On that day when our heroes lay low, lay low—
> On that day when our heroes lay low,
> I fought by their side, and thought ere I died

Just vengeance to take on the foe, the foe—
Just vengeance to take on the foe.

On the day when our chieftains lay dead, lay dead—
On that day when our chieftains lay dead,
I fought hand to hand at the head of my band,
And here on my breast have I bled, have I bled—
And here on my breast have I bled.

Our chiefs shall return no more, no more—
Our chiefs shall return no more,
Nor their bretheren of war, who can show scar for scar,
Like women their fate shall deplore, deplore—
Like women their fate shall deplore.

Five winters in hunting we'll spend, we'll spend—
Five winters in hunting we'll spend;
Then our youth, grown to men, we'll to war lead again,
And our days like our fathers' will end, will end—
And our days like our fathers' will end.

Below I shall give some extracts of Indian songs literally translated:

Indian . . . Ningah peendegay aindahyaig
We he heway.—
English . . . I will walk into some one's dwelling.

Indian . . . Ningah peendegay aindahyaig
We he weway.—
English . . . I will walk into somebody's house.

Indian . . . Nenemoshain aindahyaig
Non dah debik ningah peendigay
We he heway.—
English . . . My sweetheart is in that house;
I will walk in in the night.

Indian . . . Nenemoshain nondah pebon
Ningah peendigay
We he heway.—
English . . . My sweetheart, in the winter
I shall walk into your lodge.

Indian . . . Nondah tibik ningah peendigay
We he heway.—
English . . . This night I will walk into your lodge.

The meaning of this in English is at first somewhat obscure, but in the Indian tongue it is very clear. The lover at first indicates that he is in love with some one, or, as he expresses it, "will walk into somebody's house." Then he delicately states whose house it will be; and in the third verse, as if ashamed, he says he will come in the night. In the fourth verse he becomes more bold, and says he will come in winter, and finally he declares he will come that very night. This is making love with a vengeance, and to a white maiden such a serenade would be very alarming, but to the dusky maid of the forest each note is sweetest music and a welcome sound.

> Wi ha ya dinawido
> Wi ha ya dinawido
>   Ki-awa-we.
>
> Wi ha ya dinawido
> Wi ha ya dinawido
>   Ki-awa-we-yo
>
> Ozam gosha Kiwawa nishkon E-do
> Kikomas ninga nadin
> Kikomas nungo nadin
>   Gosha-we-yo.

This can not be easily rendered into either English poetry or prose, though it is a very amusing song in the Indian tongue. The substance of it is that a lover no longer loved his mistress, because she walked with her toes turned in, or, in other words, was somewhat reel-footed. He positively announces that he is going to hunt up her clothing, and that when he brings it to her she must pack off about her business and not bother him. This may be dull enough in English, but in Indian it is quite as lively as "Shoo, fly, don't bodder me," and indeed sounds very much like it, the words being constantly repeated in the same absurd manner:

> She walks, she walks, she walks,
>   She walks with her toes turned in;
> She walks, she walks, she walks,
>   She walks with her toes turned in, etc.

Repetition is one of the peculiarities of Indian song, and we find a fond girl thus lamenting her lover:

Ya-Nindenendon, Ya-Nindenendon
Ya-Nindenendon, Nitchawiyanin
Naninoushen-win
Jibi, Akking-win, Pinossedoog.

Which may be rendered:

Alas! I think,
Alas! I think,
Alas! I think,
Oh, how I think of him!

Of my dear lover
In the land of dreams.
Does he hunt or roam?
Oh! it sets me thinking
Of my dear lover
In the land of dreams,
Where he is roaming.

Again:

Indenaindum makow weyah
Nindemadum
Pahbojeaun nebemanbekoning
Whabi megissun nenemoshain
Nindenaindum, etc., etc., etc.

Which, rendered into literal English, reads:

Ah me! when I think of him,
    My sweetheart!
As he embarked to return
He put white wampum round my neck,
And said, I'll soon be back again.

Shall I go to you, my sweetheart?
Shall I go to your native land?
Alas! it is far away, sweetheart—
Far away is your native land.

84

When I look back where we parted,
Where he stood looking at me,
On a tree that had fallen by the water,
And my sweetheart gazed at me,

Alas! how I think of him!
Alas! how I fret and pine!
Alas! how I think of him,
The sweetheart that was mine!

Or again:

Nyan nin de naidum
Nyan nin de naidum
Nakow e yaun in siaug e ug
Nakow e yaun in siaug e ug
Nakow e yaun in siaug e ug
Nyan inandah man nin
Nyan inandah man nin.

Makow e yaun in
Kaw e go yaum bum
    Nyan, etc., etc.

Pan oje mid kan we ji win
Nin je in ain dum
Nakow e yaum in
Nyan nin de nain dum
    Makow, etc., etc.

Which, in literal language, we read as follows:

Oh dear, thinks I,
Oh dear, thinks I,
Of him whom I remember,
Of him whom I remember.

Oh dear, when my mind thinks,
Oh dear, when my mind thinks
What was said to me
When I was left behind!

When he came and put his hands around my neck,
I'll go with you, my heart replied,
But my lips were still,
And now I can only think of him.

The following is a Chippewa war-song:

> Oshawamong undausewaug
> Panaissee wug ke bain waiwe dung-ig.
>
> Todatabe penaisse
> Kedow wea weyun.
>
> Newabenan neowan
> Newabenan neowan.

In English:

> From the South they come,
> The birds, the warlike birds, with sounding wings.
>
> I wish I could change myself
> To the body of that swift bird.
>
> I'd throw my body in the strife—
> I'd throw my body in the strife.

The warrior speaks to the bird, and says:

> "Nanakawe penessewain"
> ("From time to time I dwell in a bird").

The bird replies:

> "Kenakoomin nozis"
> ("I answer thee, my son-in-law").

The corn-husking season is one of great hilarity among the semi-civilized Indians, and many young people meet together at social huskings. On such occasions if a young female finds a red ear of corn, it is indicative that she has a brave sweetheart, and she must present it to the warrior she likes best. If, however, the ear is *crooked*, or tapering to a point, the whole circle is set in a roar, and it is considered the image of an old man thief who enters life with hers. "Wa-ge-min! wa-ge-min!" is then shouted by all, and the whole merry troop sets up the corn-song:

Wa-ge-min wa-ge-min
  Paimosaid
Wa-ge-min wa-ge-min
  Paimosaid.

Bakau Kewaizee
  Ka saugizzesse.

Wa-ge-min wa-ge-min
  Kinabowid
Wa-ge-min wa-ge-min
  Ninzah nugamood.

Which, being liberally rendered, would read:

Crooked ear, crooked ear,
  Walker at night;
Stop, little old man,
  And take not to flight.

Crooked ear, crooked ear,
  Stand up strong;
Little old crooked man,
  I'll give you a song.

The Cherokees have a song of friendship, which in their language reads thus:

Kan-al-li eh ne was to
  Yai ne no wai ai e noo ho
Ti mai tan na Klai ne was tu
  Yai ne wai E-noo wai hoo.

You resemble a friend of mine,
  And you look like a friend to me;
I think that we are brothers kind,
  And brothers we will be.

There is a beautiful little song in the Chippewa language which is full of pathos and rhyme, and which the little children sing when at play in the evening. A traveller thus describes it:

"One evening while in the Chippewa village I was attracted by shouts of merriment from childish voices, and I walked out to the green lawn skirting the edge of the river to get a full view of the players and hear their songs. A group of children were at play gambolling and chasing the fire-flies, millions of which little insects filled the air, making the plain to literally sparkle with phosphorescent light." The following are the words which they addressed to the insect:

"Wau wau tay see!
Wau wau tay see!
E-now e shin
Tashe bwan ne baun e wee
Bee eghaun-be eghaun-e wee
Wa wan tay see
Wa wan tay see
Was sa koon ain je gun
Was sa koon ain ja gun."

Literally translated, they would read:

Flitting white fire-fly,
Waving white fire-bug,
Give me light to go to bed,
Give me light to go to sleep.

Or, by a slight transposition of the words in the original language, Mr. Goodrich[9] has made them read, when rendered in free translation:

Fire-fly! fire-fly! bright little thing,
Light me to bed while my song I sing;
Give me your light as you fly o'er my head,
That I may merrily go to my bed;
Give me your light o'er the grass as you creep,
That I may joyfully go to my sleep.

Come, little fire-fly, come, little beast,
Come, and I'll make you to-morrow a feast;
Come, little candle, that flies as I sing,
Bright little fairy bug, night's little king;
Come, and I'll dance as you guide me along;
Come, and I'll pay you, my bug, with a song.

The following is the Twenty-third Psalm, written in both the English and Indian (Algonquin) tongue:

Mar teag nukquenaabikoo
Shepse nanaauk Monedo
Nussepsinwahik ashkoshquat
Nutuk ohtopagod.—

The Lord is my shepherd, and I'll not want;
    He makes me down to lie;
In pastures green He leadeth me,
    The quiet waters by.

Nagun nakketeahog kounoh
Watomohkinuh wonk
Nutuss∞unuk ut sampio waay
Newutch ∞wesnok.—

My soul He doth restore again,
    And me to walk doth make
Within the paths of righteousness,
    E'en for His own name's sake.

Wutonkauhtamut pomushaon
Mupp∞ouk ∞nauhkoe
Woskehettuenk mo nukquel tam∞
Newutch k∞ wetomah.

Kuppogkomunk Kutanwohon
Nish n∞nenehiquog
K∞ noch∞ hkah anquabhetti
Wame nummatwomog.—

Yea, though I walk in death's dark vale,
    Yet will I fear none ill,
For Thou art with me, and Thy rod
    And staff me comfort still.

Kussussqunum nuppuhkuk
Weetepummee nashpea
Wonk woi Monedo n∞ tallamwaitch
Pomponetuphos hau.—

My table Thou hast furnished
    In presence of my foes,

My head Thou dost with oil anoint,
    And my cup overflows.

∞niyeuonk monaneteonk
Nulasukkonkqunash
Tohsohke pomatam wekit Monedo
Michem nuttain pish.—

Goodness and mercy all my life
    Shall surely follow me,
And in God's house for evermore
    My dwelling-place shall be.

It will be observed that in rendering the above example from the sacred writings into Indian the figure 8 is used set horizontally. There is a peculiar sound in the Indian tongue that no letter of the English alphabet will express, and to express this Eliot[10] first used the figure 8, and his example has been ever since followed. All other savage sounds can be expressed by the letters of the alphabet. I shall conclude these examples from Indian poetry by giving a verbatim translation of an Indian hymn that was much in use a few years ago among the Chippewa Indians:

Ever let piety and prayer
Be the rule of our lives,
The Great Spirit alone,
Alone let us love.

All evil living of mankind,
All, all that's bad or weak—
All evil living, as a tainted wind,
All, let us all forsake.

Notes

1. Schoolcraft's *Book of Indians* [Brisbin's note]. Perhaps the reference is to *The American Indians. Their History, Condition and Prospects, from Original Notes and Manuscripts*, new revised edition (Rochester: Wanzer, Foot, 1851).

2. *Belden's Letters* [Brisbin's note]. Perhaps he refers to some of the material used in editing *Belden, The White Chief.*

3. *Catlin among the Savages* [Brisbin's note]. Presumably the reference is to George Catlin, *The Manners, Customs and Condition of the North American Indians* (London: by the author, 1841).

4. Father De Smet on Indian ceremonies [Brisbin's note]. Pierre Jean de Smet (1801-1873), missionary to Native American groups on the northern plains and plateau, wrote a number of letters and sketches which were gathered together several times during the nineteenth century.

5. *Old Indian Traditions,* by Schoolcraft [Brisbin's note]. It is unclear to which of Henry Rowe Schoolcraft's many volumes Brisbin is referring.

6. Belden's *Life with the Sioux Indians* [Brisbin's note]. Presumably the reference is to Belden, *The White Chief: or, Twelve Years Among the Wild Indians of the Plains. From the Diaries and Manuscripts of George P. Belden,* ed. James S. Brisbin (Cincinnati: C. F. Vest, 1870).

7. Indian god [Brisbin's note].

8. Okógis, God of Spring [Brisbin's note].

9. Most likely this is S. G. Goodrich, author of *Celebrated American Indians* (Boston: Taggard and Thompson, 1864).

10. The missionary John Eliot (1604-1690) wrote *The Indian Grammar Begun: or, An Essay to Bring the Indian Language into Rules* (Cambridge, Mass.: Marmaduke Johnson, 1666).

The Morning Star:
An Indian Superstition

by Benjamin Alvord

* * * * *

As a career military officer who graduated from West Point in 1833, Ben-jamin Alvord (1813–1884) saw much action in the wartime and the peace-time army. In addition to the Seminole War of the 1830s, he served in the Mexican War and in the Civil War, when he commanded troops in the Oregon Territory. Though far from the scene of fighting, he helped to keep Oregon loyal to the Union and maintained a degree of harmony between Native Americans and Euro-Americans in the area. From 1872 to 1880, Alvord was Paymaster General of the army. He attained the rank of Brigadier General before his retirement. Despite his busy professional life, Alvord was active in several scholarly fields, primarily botany and mathematics. He also did some work in Native American studies, as the essay included here demon-strates.

Alvord's presentation of Halatoochee's brief account of sympathetic magic among the Florida Indians is noteworthy for several reasons. One of these is

SOURCE: *Harper's New Monthly Magazine*, 66 (March 1883), 606-608.

92

the thorough description of the situation which generated the account. Too many students of traditional belief systems are content to present isolated "superstitions" devoid of any context data, but Alvord clearly relates Halatoochee's belief narrative to pertinent features in its milieu. Also, his attitude toward the account reveals a level of objectivity which is still frequently absent from studies of "exotic" beliefs. Although Alvord's list of parallels for the American Indian belief from other cultural matrices derives principally from the evolutionary theories of John Lubbock and Edward Burnett Tylor, the catalogue of analogous beliefs and practices serves to notify the reader of the fact that Halatoochee's logic may not be as exotic as it appears on first glance. Like most of his contemporaries, Alvord saw similarities where they might not really exist and tended to lump all Native Americans into one entity, but his keen observational skills, as evidenced in this essay, make one wish he had written more about the American Indian cultures which military life had brought him into contact with.

The Second Seminole War (so called to distinguish it from a conflict that occurred in the 1810s), during which Alvord knew Halatoochee, was the most costly in terms of both money and lives of any of the Indian wars in American history. For several years beginning in 1835, the Seminole under the leadership of the famous Osceola successfully resisted government attempts to remove them from their native Florida to Indian Territory in what is now Oklahoma. The government eventually abandoned its attempts and left the Seminole in their homeland. For historical data on this conflict, see A Bibliographical Guide to the History of Indian–White Relations in the United States *(Chicago: University of Chicago Press, 1977), where Francis Paul Prucha lists some sixty-five books and articles about the Second Seminole War.*

* * * * *

A fable led to the discovery of Florida. In 1512 Ponce de Leon sailed from Porto Rico with three ships, fitted out at his own expense, in search of a famous fountain which, according to the story of the aborigines, could restore youth and beauty. He expected to find it among the Bahamas. One of the group, the Bemini, was said to contain the marvellous fountain. Island after island was visited in search of it. And the voyage led him to the peninsula of Florida, which he discovered on Easter-

Sunday, April 8, 1512, giving it its name because of the beauty and magnificence of its flowers and vegetation. If his exploration had led him to that remarkable fountain, the Silver Spring, at the head-waters of the Ocklawaha, he might easily have supposed he had there reached the object of his search.

It is difficult to say, in reflecting upon the persistent search for the fountain of youth, who evinced the firmest faith, the Indians who gave the story to the newcomers, or the Spaniards who received it, and for long years showed the reality of their faith by their brave and persevering efforts to discover it.

As we propose to give an example of the faith of the Indians in the power of conjuration, it is well thus to preface it by showing that the white race of that age, whether in Spain or elsewhere, can not plume itself upon its vast superiority to the red men in this respect. In England during the reign of Henry VIII., in 1542, witchcraft or sorcery was declared "felony without benefit of clergy." During the reign of James I. an act of Parliament assigned the death penalty for "invoking any evil spirit, or for killing or otherwise hurting any person by such infernal arts." In 1698, in Salem, Massachusetts, witches were punished under the above-mentioned law. Not until the reign of George II., in 1728 (a century after the death of Shakspeare), was prosecution for sorcery or enchantment prohibited by law. Forty years after that even Blackstone says: "It seems to be the most eligible way, to conclude with an ingenious writer of our own (Addison in No. 117 of the *Spectator*, published in 1711), "that in general there has been such a thing as witchcraft, though one can not give credit to any particular modern instance of it."[1] This was published by Blackstone in 1769, eighty years after the witches were burned at Salem.

I shall give a narration of a Seminole superstition which I obtained from the lips of an Indian chief in Florida, illustrating their firm faith in the distinct existence of soul and body, and which gives a beautiful and remarkable office to the morning star. First let me give a description of the scene and surroundings of this communication.

In December, 1841, I was on a scout with a large command in the Big Cypress Swamp, bordering on the Everglades of Southern Florida. The guide was Halatoochee, nephew of Micanopy, head chief of the whole Seminole nation. He had emigrated to Arkansas, was anxious to compel all the remaining Indians to go there, and his band had been at war with the hostiles (Mickasukies), whose chief in that region was called "the Prophet." He was a marked character, for to the office of priest and prophet he added that of war chief and commander in the field. Indians are superstitious, and apt to put easy faith in the personal power and prestige of such a chief. And we shall see that such influence extended not only to his own followers, but even to his enemies, and haunted the imagination of our guide.

Our scout was in the Big Cypress, a swamp fifty miles in diameter, through which, guided by Halatoochee, we threaded our labyrinthine course in pursuit of the hostiles under the Prophet. We waded all day in the water, encamping at night on pine islands. The most lovely flora was brought to view, especially the numerous and varied air-plants and orchids, with blossoms of vivid and brilliant colors festooning the cypress-trees, and lilies, callas, and other water–plants of every kind and description.

We finally reached the island called "the Prophet's Town," and as this spot will figure in our story, it is incumbent on me to give a picture of the Prophet's hut and vicinity. Near it we found a ponderous vine of luxuriant growth, the *Ficus indica*, often met with on the island of Cuba. It clasped and entwined in its elephantine folds three large trees—one a live-oak, one a palmetto, and the other a cypress. Fit spot for the incantations of a sorcerer!

Before entering the swamp Halatoochee complained of being sick in our camps at night; and when he said he was made sick by the conjurations of the Prophet (the hostile chief), the officers laughed at him and ridiculed his fears. For there he was, safe in the centre of a command of four hundred men. But one evening a brother officer and myself took him aside with an interpreter, determined to treat him with respect, to draw him out, and ask him to describe how it was that he was made sick by the machinations of the Prophet, who was far distant from us.

Halatoochee, encouraged by our kind and respectful language, said, in effect: "You whites have your faith, your creed, and your philosophy; you must permit us of the red race to have also our peculiar ideas and philosophy." To this we assented, and he went on: "When an Indian sleeps, his body alone sleeps, his spirit is moving around over the face of the earth, but the instant the morning star rises, it returns to its body. If a hostile conjurer or medicine-man wishes to injure him—or make him sick, he makes an image of the victim.[2] On the heart he places a tobacco leaf and a splinter from a tree riven by lightning. In a large kettle of water on the camp fire are placed, from time to time, herbs and malign filters having necromantic power. The image is placed at a distance, and at three separate periods during the night it is advanced nearer and nearer toward the fire, the intervals being occupied by weird dances, drumming, and incantations, sufficient of themselves to 'make the night hideous.' If before the completion of the third stage of the incantation the morning star has not yet risen, the victim may be within the power of the sorcerer. But if the morning star arises, lo! instantly the troubled spirit rushes back to the body, and is saved from the power of the enchanter."

This was the story of Halatoochee. But his morbid fancies did not affect his energy or his fidelity. He guided us in our week's campaign into the centre of the swamp, and into contact with the enemy, with whom we had a fight, and whom we drove from his cherished hiding-places. This alone exhilarated Halatoochee, and a few days after we came out of the swamp we noticed that he was in much improved health and spirits, especially after the arrival of the "Old Doctor," a friend and medicine-man of his own tribe. He said that the "Old Doctor" had gotten up counter-conjurations, talismans, and fascinations to attract his spirit at night to our own camp-fires, and thus keep him from the clutches of the Prophet.

Let us return to the camp fire of the Prophet and his attempted incantation. I have given (so far as the interpreter succeeded in conveying his meaning) the very ideas of Halatoochee; but they instantly suggest the scene of the witches in *Macbeth* and their chorus:

"Double, double toil and trouble;
Fire, burn, and caldron, bubble."

From such evil influences the Indian found relief in the powers and magnetism of the friendly conjurer in his own camp.

In classic mythology, Aurora, the goddess of morn, preceded a train of fairies and malign deities: Nox, the goddess of night, represented as veiled in mourning, crowned with poppies, and carried on a chariot drawn by owls and bats; Erebus, son of Chaos and Darkness; Pluto, god of the inferno; Eris, goddess of discord; Parcae, or Fates; Hecate and Circe, goddesses of magic, and celebrated for their knowledge of poisonous herbs; Ate, the spirit of evil; Somnus, the god of doleful dreams, his home a dark cave where the sun never penetrates. Over all these demons bright Aurora triumphs—the glorious harbinger of day, drawn in a golden chariot, opening the gates of the east, pouring the dew upon the earth, and causing the flowers to spring up over its surface.

An Indian always anticipates harm, and not good. Fear and suspicion put double guard upon his unresting soul. His happiness consists in freedom from harm—is therefore negative rather than positive. He believes in the existence of two ruling principles of evil and of good. The Iroquois called them the evil mind and the good mind. The former is buried in darkness, the latter is absorbed in light. The Aztecs worshipped the sun, the symbol of the beneficent Creator, imparting light and warmth for the benefit of mankind.

Our earliest records of the Natchez tribes describe them as worshippers of the sun. Their mythology gave animation and personality to the stars, and they called the Pleiades "Dancers," and the morning star "Day-Bringer." Star souls and star angels were mixed up with their delusions in astrology. Giving a potent personality to the sun, they called sunrise "The Sun slaying the Darkness"; and the natives of New Zealand said (with more force than elegance) "it was done by the blood-stained jaw-bone of morning."[3]

The Apalaches had cave-temples looking east, and within

stood the priests on festival days at dawn, waiting until the first rays entered to begin the appointed rites of chanting and incense and offering.

Living much in the open air (especially the Florida Indians), the sun, moon, stars, and clouds are minutely observed, and they have (like the shepherds who came near to keep vigil at the birth of our Saviour) every inducement to watch the heavens. Darkness and the black orgies of midnight are the horror of the Indian. The approaching dawn raises his hopes; the cheerful and mellow sunshine, in full-orbed effulgence, is his heaven, his delight. Thus naturally their traditions attribute magic power to the morning star as a triumph over darkness and evil.

Notes

1. William Blackstone, *Commentaries on the Laws of England* . . . (Oxford: Clarendon Press, 1769), IV, 61 [Alvord's note].

2. Sir John Lubbock, in his *Pre-historic Times, as Illustrated by Ancient Remains, and the Manners and Customs of Modern Savages* (New York: D. Appleton, 1872), p. 581, says: "Nor is the belief in sorcery easily shaken off, even by the most civilized nations. James the First [1566-1625] was under the impression that by melting little images of wax 'the persons that they bear the name of may be continually melted or dried away by continual sickness' " [Alvord's note].

3. Edward Burnett Tylor, *Primitive Culture. Researches into the Development of Mythology, Philosophy, Religion, Art, and Custom* (London: J. Murray, 1871), I, 339 [Alvord's note].

The Zuñi Social, Mythic, and Religious Systems

by Frank Hamilton Cushing

* * * * *

Generally regarded as a pioneer in the participant observation method of ethno-graphic fieldwork, Frank Hamilton Cushing (1857–1900) revealed a precocious interest in the scholarly study of American Indians by publishing his first paper on the subject when he was eighteen years old. Four years later, in 1879, he joined an expedition to the American Southwest sponsored by the Smithsonian Institution. Cushing was so attracted to the culture of Zuni Pueblo in New Mexico that he left the expedition soon after it arrived in the area and began living at the Pueblo. For several years he immersed himself in Zuni culture, living with the family of the governor and joining some cultic societies. He became so caught up in Zuni life that he supported his hosts in their feuds with the neighboring Apache and Navajo and used the title "1st War Chief of the Zuñi" in his correspondence.

SOURCE: *The Popular Science Monthly*, 21 (June 1882), 186–192. Lecture be-fore the National Academy of Sciences, delivered in Washington, April 22, 1882 (Cushing's note).

   Nevertheless, despite his involvement with the culture, Cushing main-tained his original goal of ethnographic study. During his lifetime Cushing was perceived as an eccentric genius, an image he encouraged through accounts of his life at Zuni and through his flamboyant style. When he returned east, he often affected Zuni costume and punctuated his talks on American Indian life with war whoops. Yet his work had some substance, and although his out-put of written material was slight, most of it was of high quality. Especially interesting is his description of his field experiences, which was serialized in Century Illustrated Monthly Magazine *in 1882 and 1883. In this nar-rative of his adventures at Zuni Pueblo, Cushing raised a number of questions about the nature of the relationships between a researcher and his subjects which still plague anthropologists and other students of culture. Cushing was also particularly interested in Zuni folklore and published several works on oral narratives from the Pueblo, including "Outlines of Zuni Creation Myths," which appeared in the* Annual Report of the Bureau of American Eth-nology *for 1891–1892, and* Zuñi Folk Tales *(New York: Putnam, 1901). But the fact that Cushing was among the first anthropologists to gather data through an extended stay with his subjects remains his most im-portant contribution to Native American studies.*

   Cushing's ideas about American Indian cultures conformed to the empha-sis on cultural evolution which dominated late nineteenth-century anthropol-ogy. Thus, his friends the Zuni were a "lower people" who still responded to the exigencies of their environment mythologically instead of scientifically as would civilized men and women. But Cushing was drawn to the Zuni in spite of his perception of them as cultural inferiors, and his intimacy with them yielded some theoretical insights. While many other students theorized about American Indian folklore on the basis of what they read in their libraries or uncovered in relatively brief collecting forays, Cushing was living among the Zuni and learning about their lifeways on a day-to-day basis. Such a perspective allowed him to see the integral relationship among various aspects of culture, including oral literature. In the essay reproduced here, his first publication on the Zuni, he characterizes the role which mythology played in their culture, reinforcing and reflecting social structure and religion. Cushing's emphasis on the role of various elements in maintaining the integrity of the culture seems to anticipate the theory of functional relationships in a culture, developed in the twentieth century by Bronislaw Malinowski and A. R. Radcliffe-Brown. This theory suggests that elements in a culture are so closely interrelated that a change in one element will reverberate through the whole culture. For instance, a change in technology may be reflected in developments in religion or the kinship system. Though Cushing does not carry the idea this far, his role as participant observer among the Zuni permitted him to see the vital social role that myth could play.

A generous sampling of Cushing's work has been reprinted in Jesse Green, ed., Zuñi. Selected Writings of Frank Hamilton Cushing *(Lincoln: University of Nebraska Press, 1979). Treatments of Cushing's career include Green's introduction to his anthology; Joan Mark,* Four Anthropologists. An American Science in Its Early Years *(New York: Science History Publications, 1980), pp. 96–130; and John Sherwood, "Life with Cushing: Farewell to Desks," Smithsonian, 10, no. 5 (August 1979), 96–113. For functional theory, see Bronislaw Malinowski,* A Scientific Theory of Culture and Other Essays *(Chapel Hill: University of North Carolina Press, 1944); and A. R. Radcliffe-Brown,* Structure and Function in Primitive Society *(Glencoe, Illinois: Free Press, 1952).*

* * * * *

Gentlemen of the National Academy of Sciences—Ladies and Gentlemen: Let me at once present my Indian friends.* And now let me introduce some remarks on the mythology and religion of the people whom they represent, the Zuñi Indians of Western New Mexico, the largest of the Pueblo nations, the lingering remnants of a vast culture which gave rise to the cliff and *mesa* ruins of the far Southwest, by a few words designed rather to define my own position than to illustrate my subject.

The student of the natural history of mankind finds his most difficult subject in the mythology of the lower peoples. Even our own mythology, including our theisms and superstitions, is hard to understand, yet ours is, thanks to just such bodies as the one which I have the honor to address to-day, the simplest of all mythologies, because its range of superstition is circumscribed by that of definite knowledge, its theism simplified in proportion to the extent of material philosophy.

Perhaps first among the causes of our difficulty is the fact that all mythology deals with those forces and things in nature which are beyond our comprehension; that it ends not here, but attempts to explain the origin of things in themselves incomprehensible. In proportion, then, to the lack of definite knowledge in any people, its mythology becomes more complicated and less readily understood. To the same intellectual germ in humanity which quickens the philosophy of the nineteenth century may we look for the cause of the origin and growth of mythology. And thus it happens that we find the scientist of our own places and times and the Zuñi Indian laboring hand in hand in the same field, both trying to explain the phenomena of nature and their existence, the one by metaphysical, the other by physical research; the one by building up, the other by tearing down, mythology. In order, then, to comprehend the mythology of a people, we must learn their language, acquire their confidence, assimilating ourselves to them by joining in their every-day life, their religious life, even as far as possible in their intellectual life, by remembering with intense earnestness the reasonings of our own childhood, by constantly striking every possible chord of human sympathy in our intercourse with those whose inner life we would study.

I think I have now sufficiently explained why I have entered into relation with the Zuñi Indians, and become a participator in their religious practices and, so far as possible, beliefs, to the extent of acquiring membership in their gentile organization as well as in their priesthood; and my attitude toward the audience before me is that of an imperfect exponent of Zuñi mythology and belief.

Since my return from the Southwest, time has not permitted a sufficient study of those technicalities which have, during the past few years, been introduced into this class of subjects. I shall therefore have to proceed very simply, much as would a Zuñi priest, could he address you, in a discussion of his mythology and religion.

The Zuñi mythology, or theogony, is a reflection of Zuñi sociologic or governmental institutions, with the added feature of an almost univeral spiritualistic philosophy. Hence it follows that a discussion of the one must include at least a brief description of the other. Like all well-known tribes of North American Indians, the Zuñis are divided into *gentes*, there being in their nation fifteen distinct clans or gentes. These again are combined into phratries, not political confederacies as among the Iroquois and Muscogee, but ecclesiastical bands, or, in other words, into secret medicine or sacred orders, of which there are, including the wonderful and supreme organization of the Priesthood of the Bow, thirteen. Based upon this sociologic structure, the government of Zuñi embraces three principles, the ecclesiastic, the martial, and the political, the outgrowths of which, in their order of precedence, are the priesthoods or caciqueships, the war chieftaincies, and the political chieftaincies. Supreme in national as well as in ecclesiastical office is the priest, or cacique of the sun, or *Pekwina*, immediately under whom are four secular as well as ecclesiastical high-priesthoods or caciqueships, the priesthood of the Pueblo, or temple of worship—in Zuñi *kia kwe armosi*—with the auxiliary office *tá shiwan okia*, or "Priestess of Seed." Selected by, yet supreme over the latter four priests in martial and secular matters, are the two high-priests, or caciques of war, who may or may not be at the same time masterpriests—*Pithlan shiwan moson atchi*—of the Order of the Bow. These six priests are designated in Zuñi ecclesiastical language "Priests of the Light or Day"; while resident in those special clans, which by heredity furnish the high-priesthoods (mainly the Clan of the Parrots, itself considered consanguineally descended from the gods), are numerous "Priests of the Night or Darkness," any one of whom may be chosen on the death of a priest of the light by the surviving companions. The two priests of war in turn create both the martial and political head chieftaincies, referring the latter to the four priests of the temple for acceptance or rejection. The martial head chieftaincy, or war chieftaincy, includes the third priesthood of the Order of the Bow, thus combining the ecclesiastical with the martial, and explaining the precedence of the latter over the political office. The third priest of the Order of the Bow, or head war-chief, then names three sub-chiefs, themselves necessarily members of his own order. Likewise the head chief creates his own three subchieftaincies as well as the second political head-chieftaincy or chief, who in turn names his own sub-chiefs. We find, then, that the democracy, or republic, of popular tradition, in its reference to the sedentary Indians of New Mexico and Arizona, is, like most other popular traditions regarding these comparatively unknown peoples, erroneous; that in reality their political fabric is set up and woven by an elaborate priesthood, the only semblance of democracy reposing in the power of the council—itself composed of all adults of good standing in the nation—to reject a political head chief as thus chosen, while the power of choosing a substitute remains still in the hands of the martial priests, and that of confirming him in the hands of the four priests of the temple. The latter are considered the mouth-pieces of the priest of the sun, just as the two priests of war are considered at once the mouth-pieces and, in martial and political affairs, the commanders of the four priests of the temple; and, again, the third priest of war, or head war-chief, and the first political chief, brothers to one another, yet differentiated in their functions, are considered to be the mouth-pieces of the two priests of war, the one in times of national disturbance, the other in times of peace. And yet, again, the sub-chiefs of the war-chief, as well as those of the two political head chiefs, are considered the mouth-pieces of their respective superiors.

Now, the organization of each one of the sacred or medicine orders of Zuñi, less in importance than the order of the priest-hood of the bow, is a miniature representation of the national ecclesiastical and martial organizations—that is, each order has its *pekwina*, or high-priest, its four *kia kwe armosi*, or priests of the temple, its two *pithlan shiwan mosun atchi*, or priests of the bow, and in accordance with its special office its medicine or prayer-priest or master, and its sacred council. Less strictly secret, yet more sacred, and organized upon sim-ilar though more elaborate principles of office, is the church of Zuñi, the order of the sacred dances, or the *ká ká*, which is lodged in six places of worship—the half-underground *estufas* of the north, west, south, and east, the upper and lower regions of the universe. While the *ká ká*, as a whole, has its supreme high-priests, its priests of the temple, its warrior-priests, and its prayer-masters, each one of these six temples of worship has also its like special system of priesthood, with the added offices of song-priests or masters. Both in its organization as a whole and in its lesser organizations, the *ká ká* seems to be a perfect mirror, as it were, of the mythology of the Zuñi nation, just as the mythology is a reflection of the sociologic organization of the same nation. It is, then, to a study of the organization and functions of the *ká ká*, based upon a knowledge of the national sociologic organization, that we are to look for the most complete and clear exemplification of their system of gods, just as we are to look to the traditional rituals, prayers, songs, and sacred epics of this *ká ká* for a comprehensive idea of their mythology. Knowledge gained from both these sources may in turn be vastly added to, strengthened, and corrected by a close study of their most abundant and beautifully imaginative folk-lore.

Supreme over all the gods of Zuñi is *Hano ona wilona*, or holder of the roads of light, corresponding to the earthly *pekwina*, or priest of the sun, and represented by the sun itself. Beneath him is a long line of gods so numerous that I know not half their names, nor have I recorded them, but they are divided into six great classes: the celestial or hero gods (the demongods themselves perhaps the vestiges of a more ancient herogod mythology), the elemental gods, or the gods of the forces of nature, the sacred animal gods, or the *kia pin a hái* and *kia she ma a hái*, the gods of prey, or *wemar a hái*, and the tutelary gods, or divinities of places. While *Hano ona wilona* is supreme over all, he himself, like the earthly sun-priest, is limited by his own high-priests among the gods—the celestial or hero gods, and they, in turn, by the demon-gods, while the two earthly offices of head political and war chiefs are represented, on the one hand, by the *raw* or water-wantings beings, or animal gods; and, on the other, by the *wemár a hái*, or gods of prey, while the priests of the night in the human organization (*tkwi-na-proa-a shi-wa-ni*) seem to be represented by the tutelar gods of the deistic organization. Not less important, then, because they are supposed to act in connection with the latter, are the ancients, or spirits of the ancestors, who form the body-politic of this great system of gods, and are supposed to serve as mediators between the mortals and the gods. In Zuñi belief they have also a definite place of residence assigned to them, notwithstanding which they are supposed to hold constant communion, even to the extent of occasional materialization with those whom they have left behind, to listen attentively to their prayers, and to represent them in some vague way to the higher gods of the Zuñi mythology.

While this great system of gods, like the *ká ká*, is organized, as a whole, not unlike the ecclesiastical and martial systems of the Zuñis, so also has each one of the six systems of gods, like each of the six *estufas* of the Zuñis, its offices of high-priests, priests of the house or temple, warrior-priests, etc. As an example of this special organization, let me speak of the gods of the ocean, who under specific names and attributes are further distinguished as "our beloved *Pe kwi we*, or sun-priest of the ocean; our beloved the *ona ya na k'ia a shi wa ni*, or priests of the temples of the ocean; our beloved mother, the *K'o hak o k'ia*, or the goddess of the white shells; our beloved, the three great warrior-priests of the ocean, *kia chla wa ni*, *ku pish tai a*, and *tsi k'ia hái a*, in whom we do not fail to recognize the two master-priests of the bow, and the third priest of the bow, or head warrior-chief of the martial organization. The lesser personages of Zuñi government are finally represented by the sacred animal gods of the ocean.

Let me give, as illustrations of the deistic conceptions of the Zuñis, without speical reference to their rank in this governmental system of the gods, the names and supposed attributes of a few of the principal gods of Zuñi mythology. *Háno ona wilona*, or the "holder of the roads of our lives," the supreme priest-god of Zuñi mythology, is supposed to hold as in his hands the roads of the lives of his human subjects, is believed to be able (to use the language of a Zuñi) to see (or perceive) not only the visible actions of men, but their thoughts, their prayers, their songs and ceremonials, to will through his lesser deities whether a thing shall be or shall not be in the course of a human life. I once asked a priest in Zuñi, who was about to go forth on a hunt, "Do you think you will lay low a deer this day?" and he said, "*Oothlat háno ona wilona*" (as wills or says the holder of the roads of life). Immediately below *Háno ona wilona* are the gods *Ahai in ta* and *Ma 'tsai le ma*, the two great deities of the priest-hood of the bow, anciently known as *Ua nam atch pi ah ko'a*, the beloved both who fell (for the salvation of mankind). They are supposed to be twin children of the sun, *Háno ona wilona*—mortal, yet divine. They were the guiders of mankind from the four great wombs of earth, the birth-place of the human family, far eastward toward the middle of the world; but, on reaching the eastern portion of Arizona, in the great exodus of the Pueblo races, they are supposed to have been changed by the will of their grandfathers—four great demon-gods—into warriors, and ever since have been the great gods of the order of the priest-hood of the bow, and the rulers of the mountain-passes, and enemies of the world. Just so the young man, in modern Zuñi life, who lives for years in peaceful industrial pursuits, and all at once becomes chosen as a proper person for membership in the Order of the Bow, is induced to take a scalp, and henceforth becomes a ruler of his people and his world, a warrior and a member of that most powerful of priesthoods. These two gods are supposed to have been the immediate ancestors of the two lines of priests who are now their representatives, the high-priests of the Order of the Bow; from them, in one unbroken line, has been breathed the breath of *sa wa nikia*, or the medicine of war, from one to the other of the members of their household, the *a si chlan shi we ni*, or their children, the priests of the bow, just as has been in the belief of the Roman Catholics the un-broken apostolic succession. Through their wills over the *kia sin a hai*, or annual gods, with the consent of *Háno ona wilona*, or the "holder of the roads of life," are the roads of man's life divided, or the light of his life cut off—figurative expressions for death in the highly poetic language of the Zuñis. Prior to their creation war seems to have been a secondary element in the existence of the Pueblo race; such as it previously was, however, it was represented by the great ancient god of war, the hero of hundreds of folk-lore stories, *Atchi a la to sa*, or "he of the knife-feathered wings." He is supposed to carry ever about him his many-colored bow, *a ni 'to lan*, or the goddess of the rainbow, to walk upon his swift arrow, *wi lo lo a 'te*, turquoise-pointed god of lightning, and to be guarded on the right and the left by his warriors, the mountain-lion of the North and the mountain-lion of the West.

Among other beings of ancient Zuñi mythology we have the marvelous example of *Oohe pololon*, or "the god of the north wind," whose breath sends the cold winds from the north re-gion and drives the sands of the southwestern deserts, which have been stirred up by the will of the gods of the mountain. Dark and gloomy, like the clouds of the north-land home, fero-cious with his shining teeth and glaring pendant eyeballs, wild

107

with his iron-gray halo of ever-waving hair and beard, *Oohe po-lolon* is one of the most terrific of Zuñi demon-gods. Then we have the gentle moon, mother of the women of men, through whose will are born the children of women, the representative in this system of deities of the *Shewan okao*, or seed-priestess, younger sister of the priests of the temple; and the sister of the moon, the beautiful goddess of the ocean, through whose ministrations are awakened the loves of the Zuñi youth, and the good fortune of trade is secured.

While those gods in Zuñi mythology remaining unknown to me are legion, yet I might continue for hours to mention gods and their attributes; as for instance, "he who carries the clouds from the ocean of sunrise to the ocean of sunset and scatters them through the heavens between"; *Kwe le le*, or "he who infuses the roots of all trees with the spirit of fire, and swings his torch in mid-air, and it forthwith bursts into flames"; *Te sha mink'ia*, or "he who dwells in the cañons and cliffs of the mountains, ever echoing the cries of his children, men and beasts of mortality."

Interesting among the hero-gods is the great priest of all religious orders save that of the bow, *Poskai ank'ia*. In the days of the new, yet not until after men had begun their journey toward the east, he is supposed to have appeared among the ancestors of the Zuñis, the Taos, the Coconinos, and the Moqui Indians, so poor and ill-clad as to have been ridiculed by mankind. He it was who taught the fathers of the Zuñis their architecture and their arts, their agriculture and their system of worship, by plume and painted stick; but, driven to desperation by the ingratitude of his children, he vanished beneath the world, never to return to the abodes of men—yet he still sits in the city of the sun, ever listening to the prayers of his ungrateful children.

Let me add one more example: that of *Kia nis ti pi*, or "the great water-skate," who with his long legs measured the extent of the earth as with a compass, and between the oceans of sunrise and sunset determined the center of the world as the home of the Zuñis. He is represented by a peculiar figure, and this introduces us to a new department of the subject—the conventional system of pictographs whereby the Zuñi sacred orders illustrate their mythological ideas. It is first to a close study of the mythology and theogony of the Zuñis, and then to that of the conventional forms of art among these and kindred peoples, that we are to look for the key to the mysterious and unnumbered pictographs of the great Southwest.

Interesting for comparison with Eastern mythology is the study of the phallic and the serpent symbolism as they occur in highly developed forms among the Zuñi Indians. Yet, again, interesting because of the light that it throws upon the development of human religions and mythologies is the study of the influence of environment, physical, biologic, and sociologic, as exemplified by the religion and mythology of the Zuñis.

I regret most deeply that in the limited time allowed me today I can not go into a discussion of these various questions, and into a production of the hundreds of facts illustrative of them which I have in my possession; but that I have time only to add that, as further illustrative of the connection between the Zuñi sociologic and the Zuñi mythologic systems is the fact that no general names for chiefs of all the departments—ecclesiastical, martial, and political—are to be found in their language, nor is there a general name for their god-priests, hero, demon, animal, elemental, celestial, or tutelar. Yet the term *awa nu thla* includes the political and martial chiefs in Zuñi government, just as does the name *k'ia pin a há i* include their representatives, the sacred water and prey-gods, of Zuñi mythology.

Notes

*These were five Zuni whom Cushing had brought east with him so that they might take some sacred water from the Atlantic Ocean back to New Mexico. In addition to their appearance in Washington, they accompanied Cushing on a lecture tour that made stops in Boston and at Wellesley College. For an account of this visit, see Sylvester Baxter, "An Aboriginal Pilgrimage," *Century Illustrated Monthly Magazine*, 24 (1882), 526-536.

A Huron Historical Legend

by Horatio Emmons Hale

* * * * *

Horatio Emmons Hale (1817–1896) published his first work on American Indian linguistics in 1834. After graduating from Harvard in 1837, he joined the scientific corps of the Wilkes Exploring Expedition, the first extraterritorial exploring expedition sponsored by the federal government, and got a taste of linguistic fieldwork among Polynesian groups. He was especially interested in the Native Americans who lived in New England, his home region, but a lifetime devoted to legal practice interrupted his ethnological studies. Finally, almost fifty years after his first published work appeared, his local interests bore fruit when he published The Iroquois Book of Rites, *volume 2 in Daniel G. Brinton's Library of Aboriginal American Literature (1883). Like Brinton, Hale was a committed comparative mythologist, espousing the solar theories of Max Müller in much of his work. Hale continued to publish in the fields of linguistics and ethnology almost to the time of*

SOURCE: *Magazine of American History*, 10 (December 1883), 475–483.

his death, and his commitment to the growing field of folklore was evidenced in his service as president of the American Folklore Society in 1893.

The essay reproduced here does not include Hale's solar theorizing but reveals his belief in the historical value of aboriginal traditions, a matter on which he differed from Brinton. For the most part, Hale demonstrates good sense in realizing, as modern ethnohistorians have shown, that the oral traditions of nonliterate cultures can serve as historical records, while remaining cautious enough to withhold total trust in the literal accuracy of everything his Huron informant has told him. He cites motivations such as tribal pride as reasons for certain omissions from the text. If Hale had had the tools of the modern comparative folklorist—especially Stith Thompson's Motif-Index of Folk-Literature, second edition (Bloomington: Indiana University Press, 1955–58)—he probably would not have attempted to explain in historical terms this Huron legend of King Sastaretsi marvelous image. Thompson's work lists several internationally known narrative motifs which are analogous to the behavior of the image in the Huron story. Particularly relevant are D1620ff, Magic automata, and F855.1, Image with pointing finger (which directs someone to a hidden treasure). The image which indicates the way for the Huron migration is probably an accretion onto the strictly historical account from the myths and folktales of the Huron themselves or of some neighboring group.

The question of historicity of folklore—oral narratives in particular—has been one of the major controversies in Native American folklore studies, beginning as early as 1826, when Lewis Cass challenged John Heckewelder's reliance on oral traditions as historical documents. Those who have argued for lore's historical value usually attempt to confirm the accuracy of a myth or legend by drawing upon archeology or Euro-American historical sources. Hale apparently had little doubt regarding the historicity of the Huron legend. In fact, he reverses the procedure of many defenders of folklore's historical significance by using the oral narrative to confirm and explain conventional historical documents.

A few of the major publications which support the historical value of American Indian folklore are George T. Emmons, "Native Account of the Meeting Between La Perouse and the Tlingit," American Anthropologist, 13 (1911), 294–298; John R. Swanton and Roland B. Dixon, "Primitive American History," American Anthropologist, 16 (1914), 376–412; David M. Pendergast and Clement W. Meighan, "Folk Traditions as Historical Fact: A Paiute Example," Journal of American Folklore, 72 (1959), 128–133; and Gordon M. Day, "Oral Tradition as Complement," Ethnohistory, 19 (1972), 99–108. For an important theoretical statement about some general relationships between folklore and history, see Richard M. Dorson, American Folklore and the Historian (Chicago: University of Chicago Press, 1971).

Perhaps the leading opponent of the historical value of Native American folklore during this century has been Robert H. Lowie. For example, see "Oral Tradition and History," Journal of American Folklore, 30 (1917), 161–167. An interesting account of the "mythologizing" of a historical incident recounted in American Indian oral tradition is Jarold Ramsey, "Simon Fraser's Canoe; or, Capsizing into Myth," in Reading the Fire. Essays in the Traditional Indian Literatures of the Far West (Lincoln: University of Nebraska Press, 1983), pp. 121–132. A survey of some of the literature on historical uses of Native American folklore is W. K. McNeil, "History in American Folklore: An Historical Perspective," Western Folklore, 41 (1982), 30–35.

Heckewelder's work which elicited Lewis Cass's early criticisms of folklore's historicity is An Account of the History, Manners, and Customs, of the Indian Nations, who Once Inhabited Pennsylvania and the Neighbouring States, which was published by the American Philosophical Society in 1819. Cass's comments may be found in North American Review, 22 (1826), 53–119; 24 (1828), 357–403. A discussion of Horatio Hale's influence on late nineteenth-century anthropology, especially that of Franz Boas, is Jacob W. Gruber, "Horatio Hale and the Development of American Anthropology," Publications of the American Philosophical Society, 111, no. 1 (February 1967), 5–37.

* * * * *

The wonderful tenacity with which uncivilized tribes frequently retain the memory of ancient events in their history is an interesting fact, which of late years has begun to receive attention from philosophical inquirers. Judge Fornander, of Hawaii, and Sir George Gray, in New Zealand, in their works on the Polynesian race and mythology, have shown how distinctly the people of that race, scattered over the many islands of the Pacific Ocean, have preserved the reminiscences of voyages, settlements, wars, alliances and family successions, during a period of nearly two thousand years.[1] The Lenni Lenape, or Delawares, had a clear tradition of the war which ended in the overthrow of the Alligewi, or Moundbuilders, of Ohio, an event which could not have occurred much less than a thousand years ago.[2] The Iroquois had also a traditional record of the same event, and they had preserved with remarkable minuteness the details of the formation of their confederacy, which preceded by about fifty years the era of Columbus.[3] Their congeners and ancient enemies, the Hurons, were not less careful in retaining and transmitting their oral records. I had the good fortune to obtain from an authentic source one of these traditions, which clears up a doubtful question of some interest relating to the earliest intercourse between the Indians and the European settlers of North America.

When the enterprising French explorer, Jacques Cartier, in 1535, first sailed up the St. Lawrence, he found the sites of what are now the cities of Quebec and Montreal occupied by two Indian settlements, named Standaconé and Hochelaga. They were permanent towns, composed of large houses, fifty yards or more in length, framed of saplings, and cased with bark. Encircling the town was a strong fortification, formed of trunks of trees, set in a triple row, and sustaining galleries furnished with magazines of stones to be hurled against their assailants. This construction of dwellings and defenses, as Mr. Parkman remarks (in his "Pioneers of France in the New World"),[4] was identical with that which was practiced among the tribes of the Huron-Iroquois family, but was not in use among those of Algonkin lineage. This evidence of the stock to which the inhabitants of Hochelaga and Stadaconé belonged was confirmed by two brief vocabularies of their language which Cartier preserved, and which leave no doubt that they were members of the widespread family comprehending the Huron and Iroquois nations, along with the Eries, Andastes, Tuscaroras, and other tribes of the west and south.

Not quite seventy years later, in 1603, when the founder of Canada, the illustrious Champlain, revisited the scenes of Car-

113

tier's discoveries, not a trace of the two populous and well-fortified towns remained. In place of their commodious dwelling and well-cultivated fields he found only some wretched wigwams, in which were huddled a few half starved Indians of the wandering Algonkin race. What had become of their more civilized predecessors? It is remarkable that neither Champlain, nor any of the intelligent explorers or missionaries who followed him, seem to have troubled themselves about this interesting question. There could have been no difficulty at that time in ascertaining the truth; and indeed, as will be shown, the facts were well known to some at least of those new adventurers. But their minds were absorbed with matters which to them were of more immediate importance, and they did not take the trouble to record events which seemed to them to be of as little consequence as those "battles of the kites and crows," the wars of the ancient Britons and Saxons, appeared to Milton. But as these obscure struggles have lately furnished subjects of much interest to the readers of Freeman, Green and other historians of our day, so the early events of aboriginal history are beginning to assume a new importance in the annals of our continent.

In the time of Champlain, the Indians of the Huron-Iroquois race, nearest to Montreal and Quebec, were the famous "Five Nations" of the Iroquois confederacy. They possessed, as is well known, nearly the whole of Northern New York, their territories extending from Lake Champlain westward to the Genessee River. In another direction, near Lake Huron, in the extreme north-west of what is now the Province of Ontario, dwelt the people who were known to the French as Hurons, and to the English, at a later day, as Wyandots—their proper name being Wăndat, or as the Iroquois now pronounce it Wennat, or Wănat. The Hurons became the allies, and the Iroquois the most formidable enemies of the French colonists. If the people whom Cartier discovered had not been utterly exterminated, it is in one or other of these communities—the Iroquois or the Hurons—that we must look to find the descendants of the former denizens of Hochelaga and Stadaconé.

The evidence of language unfortunately does not help us here. The Huron and Iroquois languages differed considerably, but there was a close family likeness between them. The Iroquois had five dialects and the Hurons at least two, which showed many variations of words and forms. A comparison of the brief vocabularies preserved by Cartier with the words of these various dialects shows a general resemblance, but no clear indications by which we can determine the particular branch of this linguistic family to which this ancient speech belonged. The words are too few and the orthography too uncertain and corrupt to allow of any positive conclusion from this evidence.

The natural inclination of those who have written on this subject has been to find in the Iroquois the descendants of Cartier's Indians. They were the nearest people who spoke a similar language, and they had, as Colden in his "History of the Five Nations" correctly records, a tradition that their ancestors formerly dwelt north of the St. Lawrence, near the site of Montreal.[5] This tradition, however, as is now known, referred to a primitive and long distant period, when the Hurons and the Iroquois formed separate bands of one united people, and possessed the country on the north shore of the St. Lawrence, from Lake Ontario to the Gulf. From this region they both emigrated, at different periods, impelled partly by dissensions which had broken out between them, and partly by the attacks of the fierce Algonkin nomads who surrounded them. The Iroquois took possession of the country south of Lake Ontario, which they had inhabited, as their traditions affirm, for centuries prior to Cartier's visit. At a much later day, and, it would seem, soon after the French explorer had left the St. Lawrence, the Hurons also deserted their ancient seats on the north bank of that river, and retreated to the distant shores of Lake Huron. The impelling cause of their flight was the persistent hostility of the Iroquois, who had lately become much more formidable through their confederation. The retreat of the Hurons to the west gave them a respite of nearly a century, during which their numbers seem to have increased, and their villages along the Georgian Bay, surrounded by well-cultivated fields, acquired the aspect of comfort and homely wealth which delighted the founder of New France when he first beheld it. "To the eye of Champlain," writes Parkman, "accustomed to the desolation he had left behind, it seemed a land of beauty and abundance. There was a broad opening in the forest, fields of maize, with pumpkins ripening in the sun, patches of sunflowers, from the seeds of which the Indians made hair-oil, and in the midst the Huron town of Otouacha. In all essential points it resembled that which Cartier, eighty years before, had seen at Montreal: the same triple palisade of crossed and intersecting trunks, and the same long lodges of bark, each containing many households. Here, within an area of sixty or seventy miles, was the seat of one of the most remarkable savage communities of the continent."[6]

It was mainly to Champlain himself that the destruction of this flourishing community was due. In an evil hour for the Hurons, he formed an alliance with them, and led them on a fruitless expedition against the Iroquois, from whose territories the allies retreated baffled and humiliated. The exasperated confederates retaliated by furious assaults upon the French settlements, and by continual inroads into the country of the Hurons. It was in 1615 that Champlain arrived among them. In 1649 the last of the twenty Huron towns had surrendered to the Iroquois power, and lay in heaps of ruins and ashes. Of the inhabitants who survived the conquest, some joined the conquerors and were adopted among them; others took refuge with theirs French allies at Quebec, near which city their descendants still reside; but the greater number retreated to the far West, and found an asylum among the Ojibways, on the shores and islands of Lakes Superior and Michigan. At one time their principal abode was on the Island of Michilimackinac, and here, apparently, they were residing at the time when the death of their great chief occurred, as related in the following legend. From this retreat they were induced, as recorded in the story, to remove southward and place themselves under the protection of the French forts at Detroit and in northern Ohio. In these new abodes they remained for more than a century, and, in spite of their reduced numbers, played a somewhat important part in the events of western history. In the peculiar Indian system of political relationships their nation ranked as the "grandfather," and head of all the surrounding tribes. Their marked intelligence and force of character gave them a predominant influence among the more loosely organized Algonkin bands. Tenaciously adhering to their French allies, even when the latter had been forced to abandon them, they took a determined part in the war of Pontiac against the English. Finally, about the middle of the present century, the greater portion of the Hurons—now known as the Wyandots—removed to the West, under the auspices of the American government, and found another respite in their wandering existence on reserves which were assigned to them in Kansas and the Indian Territory.

A few families, however, refused to join in this last migration. These families, comprising in all about seventy individuals, clung to the small reservation which had been set apart for them in Canada, on the west bank of the Detroit river, in the township of Anderdon, between Amherstburg and Sandwich. Here they still reside, the last remnant in Canada of the once powerful Indian nation; the last, at least, who speak the language of their people; for the few so-called Hurons of Lorette, near Quebec, are a mongrel community, and have entirely forgotten the speech of their forefathers.

When I visited the Wyandot reservation, in the summer of 1872, the chief of the tribe, an elderly man of fine presence and marked intelligence, who lived in the style of a substantial farmer, gave me much information concerning the history and mythology of his people. He bore in English the name of Joseph White, and in his own language the somewhat singular designation of Mandorong, or "Unwilling." The name, which he owed to the fancy of his parents, did not by any means indicate his disposition, which was particularly frank and genial. He assured me that the traditions of his people represented them as having originally dwelt in the east, near Quebec. He had once journeyed as far as that city, and had then visited the remnant of the Hurons at Lorette. Though they had lost their ancient language, and could only communicate with him in French, they had not forgotten this primitive tradition of their race. They took him, he said, to a mountain, and showed him the opening in its side from which the progenitors of their people emerged, when they first "came out of the ground." The ordinary metaphor by which the Indian tribes, like the ancient Egyptians, declare themselves to be the autochthones of a country, had in this case, as in many others, taken a grossly concrete form. In answer to the inquiry whether his people had any tradition of their migration from the East to their present abode, the chief related the following story, which, strange as some of its incidents may seem, is probably in the main a narrative of events which really occurred:

THE LEGEND OF KING SASTARETSI.

In very ancient times the Hurons (or Wandat) had a great king, or head-chief, named Sastaretsi (or Sastaréché). They were then living in the far East, near Quebec, where their forefathers first came out of the ground. The king told them that they must go to the West, in a certain direction, which he pointed out. He warned them, moreover, that this would not be the end of their wanderings. He instructed them that when he died they should make an oaken image resembling him, should clothe it in his attire, and place it upright at the head of his grave, looking toward the sunrise. When the sunlight should fall upon it, they would see the image turn and look in the direction in which they were to go.

King Sastaretsi went with his people in their westward journey as far as Lake Huron, and died there. But he had time before his death to draw on a strip of birch bark, by way of further guidance, an outline of the course which they were to pursue, to reach the country in which they were finally to dwell. They were to pass southward down Lake Huron, and were to continue on until they came to a place where the water narrowed to a river, and this river then turned and entered another great lake.

When he died they fulfilled his commands. They made an image of oak, exactly resembling their dead king, clothed it in his dress of deerskin, adorned the head with plumes, and painted the face like the face of a chief. They set up this image at the head of the grave, planting it firmly between two strong pieces of timber, its face turned to the east. All the people then stood silently round it in the early dawn. When the rays of the rising sun shone upon it, they saw the image turn with such power that the strong timbers between which it was planted groaned and trembled as it moved. It stayed at length, with its face looking to the south, in the precise direction in which the chief had instructed them to go. Thus his word was fulfilled, and any hesitation which the people had felt about following his injunctions was removed.

A chosen party, comprising about a dozen of their best warriors, was first sent out in canoes, with the birch-bark map, to follow its tracings and examine the country. They pursued their course down Lake Huron, and through the River and Lake St. Clair, till they came to where the stream narrowed, at what is now Detroit; then advancing further they came, after a brief course, to the broad expanse of Lake Erie. Returning to the narrow stream at Detroit, they said: "This is the place which King Sastaretsi meant to be the home of our nation." Then they went back to their people, who, on hearing their report, all embarked together in their canoes and passed southward down the lake, and finally took up their abode in the country about Detroit, which they were to possess as long as they remained a nation. The image of King Sastaretsi was left standing by his grave in the far north, and perhaps it is there to this day.

It will be observed that in this narrative "King Sastaretsi" is described as leading the Hurons in their migration from the east, and as dying just before their return from the northwest to the vicinity of Lake Erie. The time which elapsed between these two events cannot have been less than a century. This portion of the legend, at first perplexing, is explained in a singular and unexpected manner by a passage in the well-known work of the French traveler, Baron La Hontan, whose descriptions of New France in the period between the years 1683 and 1694 contain the results of much inquiry and acute observation. "The leader of the nation of Hurons," he tells us, "is called Sastaretsi. The name (he adds) has been kept up by descent for seven or eight hundred years, and is likely to continue to future ages."[7] This practice of keeping up the name of a chief by succession seems to have been common among the tribes of the Huron-Iroquois stock. The names of the fifty chiefs who formed the Iroquois league have been thus preserved for more than five hundred years.[8] The Sastaretsi who led his people from the St. Lawrence to Lake Huron was the predecessor of his namesake whose dying injunctions induced them, after their overthrow and expulsion by the Iroquois, to take refuge about the French forts at Detroit and in northern Ohio.

It is a curious and noticeable fact, however, that neither the Iroquois nor the French are mentioned in this story, nor is any reason given either for the departure of the Hurons from their original home near Quebec, nor for their return from the northwest to the neighborhood of Detroit. The pride of the Indian character refused to admit that their wanderings were determined by any power beyond their own will and the influence of their chief.

The story of the image is probably true in its main incidents, though tradition has added some marvelous details. It was natural that the French, after they had established their forts in Michigan and Ohio, should desire to have the aid of their Indian allies in defending them against the Iroquois and the English. This project would involve the removal of the Hurons from their asylum in the far north to the perilous vicinity of their powerful and dreaded foes. While the leaders might be persuaded, by the arguments and solicitations of their French friends, to take this risk, the majority of the people may have been unwilling to abandon their secure retreat and their cultivated fields. To overcome this hesitation, it would be natural also for the chief to employ some artifice. Of this species of management, to which the leading men among the Hurons and Iroquois were wont to resort in dealing with their self-willed but credulous people, many curious and amusing examples are related by the early missionaries. In the present instance, it would seem that an appeal was made to the reverence with which the memory of their deceased head chief was regarded. A rude image of him was set up with much formality, and a report was circulated of a death-bed prediction made by him concerning it. Early in the morning after its erection the image was found to have preter-naturally changed its position, and to be gazing in the direction in which the great chief, in his lifetime, had desired that his people should go. This monition from the dead was effectual, and the emigration at once took place. The legend, as told in after times, assumed naturally a more lively and striking cast; but in its leading outlines it is intelligible and credible enough. Its chief interest, however, resides in the fact that it proves beyond question the existence of a belief among the Wyandots of the present day that their ancestors came to the West, at no very distant period, from the vicinity of Quebec.

Two casual references which are made to this subject in the Jesuit "Relations" deserve to be noticed. In general the mission-aries, while describing with much particularity the customs and religious rites of the Indians, and in fact every matter which seemed to have any bearing on the work of their conversion, took no pains to record any facts relating to the early history of the tribes. Only a casual allusion apprizes us that the former residence of the Hurons near the coast was spoken of among them as a well known fact. The Relations for 1636 contain a full and detailed account of the Huron nation by Brebeuf, an ad-mirable work, from which our knowledge of that people in their primitive state is chiefly drawn. In speaking of their festivities he refers to their war-dances in the following remarkable passage:

"Among other songs and dances, there are some in which they take occasion to destroy their enemies as it were in sport. Their most ordinary cries are *hen, hen, or hééééé*, or perhaps *wiiiii*. They refer the origin of all these mysteries to a certain being, rather a giant than a man, whom one of their people wounded in the forehead *at the time when they lived near the sea*, for the offense of not replying by the usual complimentary response of *kwai* to the ordinary salutation. This monster therefore cast the apple of discord among them, as a punishment for the in-jury, and after having taught them their war-dances, the Ononhoroia, and this chorus of *wiiiii*, sank into the earth, and disappeared. Could this indeed," asks the worthy missionary, "have been some infernal spirit?"[9]

The other allusion seems, at the first glance, to bear a different interpretation. It has been quoted by Gallatin and others as affording evidence that the people whom Cartier encountered on the St. Lawrence were Iroquois; but a careful consideration of the facts, in the light of recent information, shows that this inference cannot properly be drawn from it. Father Le Jeune writes from the vicinity of Quebec in 1636: "I have often sailed from Quebec to Three Rivers. The country is fine and very attractive. The Indians showed me some places where the Iroquois formerly cultivated the land."[10] These Indians are of the Algonkin race, and their statement, which we need not question, merely shows that their immediate predecessors in that locality were Iroquois. If, as the Huron traditions affirm, the flight of their ancestors from their eastern abode was caused by the attacks of the Iroquois, we may be certain that the latter did not leave the deserted country vacant. Their first proceeding would be to assume possession of it, and to plant colonies at favorable points. This was their custom in all their conquests. An Iroquois colony was thus established at Shamokin, now Sunbury, in Pennsylvania, after the Delawares were subdued; and other settlements secured the territories which the confederacy acquired in northern Ohio. Thus it would seem probable that, after the flight of the Hurons, the Algonkins held their lands along the northern bank of the St. Lawrence for a considerable time. At length, however, the annoyance and loss from the incessant attacks of the surrounding Algonkins became so intolerable as to make these distant outposts not worth keeping. Their abandonment apparently did not long precede the arrival of Champlain, who, as is well known, found the Hurons and the Algonkins united in strict alliance, and engaged in a deadly warfare with the Iroquois.

We are thus enabled, by the aid of Indian tradition, to clear up some perplexities which have been caused by the seemingly contradictory accounts of the first explorers of our continent.

We gain at the same time a clear conception of the movements among the native tribes which preceded the establishment of European colonies in North America, and which exercised a momentous influence on the fortunes of those colonies.

Notes

1. Abraham Fornander, *An Account of the Polynesian Race; Its Origin and Migrations and the Early History of the Hawaiian People to the Times of Kamehameha I*, 3 volumes (London: Trübner, 1878-1885); and George Gray, *Polynesian Mythology and Ancient Traditional History of the New Zealand Race as Furnished by Their Priests and Chiefs* (London: J. Murray, 1855).

2. For example, see E. G. Squier, "Historical and Mythological Traditions of the Algonquins; with a Translation of the 'Walam-Olum,' or Bark Record of the Linni-Lenape," *American* [Whig] *Review*, 9 (February 1849), 273-293. Reprinted in this collection.

3. Horatio Emmons Hale, *The Iroquois Book of Rites. Library of American Aboriginal Literature No. 2* (Philadelphia: D. G. Brinton, 1883).

4. Francis Parkman, *Pioneers of France in the New World*, 7th edition (Boston: Little, Brown, 1870).

5. Cadwallader Colden, *The History of the Five Indian Nations Depending on the Province of New-York in America* (New York: W. Bradford, 1727).

6. Parkman, p. 367 [Hale's note].

7. Louis La Hontan, *New Voyages to North America. Containing an Account of Several Nations of That Vast Continent* . . . (London: J. Brindley and C. Corbett, 1735), II, 45 [Hales's note].

8. *Iroquois Book of Rites* [Hales's note].

9. Jean de Brebeuf, "Relation de ce qui s'est passé dans le Pays des Hurons en L'année 1636," *Relation de ce qui s'est passé en la Nouvelle France en l'année 1636. Envoyée au v. père provincial de la Compagnie de Jesus en la province de France* (Paris: Sebastien Cramoisy, 1637).

10. de Brebeuf, p. 46. I have somewhat abridged the passage in the translation [Hale's note].

Mythology of the Dakotas

by Stephen Return Riggs

*   *   *   *   *

Stephen Return Riggs (1812–1883) was one of several nineteenth-century Christian missionaries who made genuine efforts to appreciate the cultures of the Native Americans with whom they worked. Because of his aptitude for learning languages, Riggs was sent as a young man of twnety-five to a mission in Minnesota with the assignment to learn the Siouan languages spoken by the mission's Native constituents and to translate devotional and educational literature into it. For over forty years, he pursued this life's work and became a recognized authority on the Siouan languages. His experitse resulted in a number of translations into Dakota: hymns, portions of the Old and New Testaments, The Pilgrim's Progress, *and textbooks are some of the works he rendered into that language. He also made a number of ethnographic contributions to Native Americans studies, the most important being Da-*kota Grammar, Texts, and Ethnography, *which was edited by James*

SOURCE: *American Antiquarian and Oriental Journal*, 5 (1883), 147–149.

Owen Dorsey (another missionary-ethnologist) and appeared in 1893 as volume 9 of the Contributions to North American Ethnology *of the U.S. Geographical and Geological Survey of the Rocky Mountain Region. (This volume was reissued by Ross & Haines in 1973.)*

The short essay reproduced here reveals Riggs's sensitivity to the problems that arose from the methods of studying Native American cultures practiced by many of his contemporaries. His remarks about the necessary rapport between ethnographer and informant remain timely. Less durable are his conclusions about the parallels between Siouan and Roman mythology. Like many other nineteenth-century students of Native American myths, Riggs insisted on seeing correspondences between American and Old World traditions. For many students, this insistence arose from their assumption that Native Americans were incapable of original religious thought and that their elaborate mythological systems were necessarily borrowings from the established mythologies of Europe, Asia, or North Africa. Riggs's notion about how Old World myths reached the New World absolves him somewhat from this racist idea that Native Americans were only borrowers of religious culture. Instead of positing a pre-Columbian pattern of diffusion or suggesting that Native American mythologies developed only after contact with Euro-Americans could have revealed the intricacies of Old World systems to them, he joins such contemporaries as Daniel G. Brinton in hypothesizing that the Siouan (and perhaps other Native American) peoples themselves originated in Europe and brought their Roman-like myths with them as they migrated to North America. Riggs's ideas about "Wākāntänkä" near the end of the essay align him with those students of comparative religion who believed that the "high god" concept was unknown to nonliterate peoples.

For some other speculations about Native American-classical parallels, see Franz Boas, "The Mythologies of the Indians," International Quarterly, *11 (July 1905), 327–342, and 12 (October 1905), 157–173; Jeffrey C. Sobosan, "The Philosopher and the Indian: Correlations Between Plotinus and Black Elk,"* Indian Historian, *7, no. 2 (Spring 1974), 47–48; and Margaret C. Szasz and Ferenc M. Szasz, "The American Indian and the Classical Past,"* Midwest Quarterly, *17, no. 1 (October 1975), 58–70. Also, several works by the French structural anthropologist Claude Lévi-Strauss explore the possible relationships between Native American and classical mythologies. For an example, see "Pythagoras in America," in* Fantasy and Symbol. Studies in Anthropological Interpretation, *ed. R. H. Hook (London: Academic Press, 1979), pp. 33–41.*

* * * * *

Mythology, next to language, affords the most reliable evidence as to the origin or relationship of a people; for peoples have been slow to change their gods. Much of that published in books concerning the mythology of the aborigines is utterly worthless. The writers had no knowledge of the Indian language, and got their information from half-breed interpreters, who, having been taught by their Catholic fathers to detest whatever related to the religion of their mothers, knew next to nothing about it. Not willing to acknowledge themselves ignorant, or to seek information from those who alone could give it, their lively fancy supplied the place of knowledge, and devised a scheme which seems plausible to persons as ignorant of the subject as themselves, and this scheme, which has no foundation in truth, is trusted and received as true.

The mythology of the Dakotas was obtained by my associates in the mission, directly from the Dakotas themselves, partly by direct inquiry of those most capable of giving the information sought. They were much more willing to give such information to us, who were careful not to speak disrespectfully of what they held to be sacred, than to their relatives of mixed blood who generally did so. Our chief and most reliable knowledge of Dakota mythology is, however, from their traditions and tales. When learning the language we always listened to these tales, and wrote out many of them in full, the study of which was very helpful to us in ascertaining the structure or syntax of it. The views they give us of gods and spiritual beings do as truly though not so fully show what the Dakotas believed two hundred years ago, as Homer's Iliad and Odyssey show what the Greeks of his time believed concerning such things. It is probable that the mythology of the Dakotas is nearer to that of the nations of western and northern Europe than to that of the Greeks and Latins, but in the comparison I use the latter because I am more familiar with it. The following account of the Dakota mythology shows a striking resemblance between it and that of the Latins.

I. The Dakotas viewed every object known to them as having a spirit capable of helping or hurting them, and consequently a proper object of worship. Some may doubt as to the Latins worshipping artificial objects, but the writings of Ovid and Horace leave no reason to doubt it. Their principal gods are:

1. Wakingau (Thunder), corresponding to Jupiter.

2. Unktehi (Dreadful Being), the water god, corresponding to Neptune, supposed to have a body much greater than that of any land animal now living, and to whom the bones of the mastodon and other large bones are supposed by the Dakotas to belong.*

3. The War God, corresponding to Mars. He is called Inyän and Tukän, both of which mean stone, and is said by some of the Dakotas to be the greatest of their gods. He is supposed to exist in the numerous boulders scattered over the prairies, and is more worshipped than any of the other Dakota gods.

4. Heyoka, the god of deceit or contrarieties, corresponding with Mercury.

5. and 6. Winyannonpa. Two females, corresponding to Venus and Minerva.

Besides these, they pray to the sun, the earth, the moon, lakes, rivers, trees, plants, snakes, and all kinds of animals and vegetables—many of them say to everything, for they pray to their guns, arrows—to any object, artificial as well as natural, for they suppose every object, artificial as well as natural, has a spirit which may hurt or help, and so is a proper object of worship. This seems to have also been the case with the ancient Greeks and Romans, Gauls and Germans. They also pray to the spirits of their deceased relatives, and believe in transformation, such as are described by Ovid, and think that many of the stars are men and women translated to the heavens. Not only do many of them believe in transmigration of souls, but many of their medicine men profess to tell things which occurred in the bodies previously inhabited for at least half a dozen generations back, and tell of advice given them by their ancestors before white men came among them. It is very difficult to account for such striking similarity between the mythology of the Dakotas, the Hindoos, and the peoples of Europe before the Christian era, without supposing they had a common origin.

There are two other gods not directly connected with their

mythology, some mention of which is necessary to a proper understanding of this subject.

7. Taku Wäkan—a god; the ruler of the world, rewarding the good and punishing the wicked. They usually swore by this god, but never offered sacrifices to him, and seldom worshipped him. This idea of *a god*, the final judge, not connected with mythology and not worshipped, seems to be common to the Dakotas and to our ancestors, but not peculiar to them. Traces of such an idea are probably found among all people, and having an origin in an accusing or excusing conscience.

8. Wäkäntänkä—*great god*. This word is usually incorrectly translated great spirit. Wäkän, in Dakota, as an adjective means incomprehensible, mysterious; as a noun, god, never spirit. This is, according to their understanding, the name of the God of civilized men. Some of them have told me that they learned this expression from white men, and never spoke of Wäkäntänkä till white men came among them. Others have told me that they never pray to Wäkäntänkä except on some special occasion, and then only once for the whole expedition.

In conclusion we would say that tradition, similarity of race, and mythology, shows a very strong case in favor of the Dakotas coming from Europe.

Notes

*Considerable literature has been published about the Native American folklore that seems to deal with prehistoric elephants in North America. For example, see the following: H. C. Mercer, *The Lenape Stone or The Indian and the Mammoth* (New York: Putnam, 1885); W. D. Strong, "North American Indian Traditions Suggesting a Knowledge of the Mammoth," *American Anthropologist*, 36 (1934), 81–88; Horace P. Beck, "The Animal That Cannot Lie Down," *Journal of the Washington Academy of Sciences*, 39 (1939), 294–301; M. F. Ashley Montagu, "An Indian Tradition Relating to the Mastodon," *American Anthropologist*, 46 (1944), 568–571; Loren C. Eiseley, "Myth and Mammoth in Archaeology," *American Antiquity*, 11 (1945), 84–87; Ludwell H. Johnson III, "Men and Elephants in America," *Scientific Monthly*, 75 (October 1952), 215–221; and George E. Lankford, "Pleistocene Animals in Folk Memory," *Journal of American Folklore*, 93 (1980), 293–304.

The Edda Among the Algonquin Indians

by Charles Godfrey Leland

* * * * *

Most of the authors represented in this collection were students of American Indian cultures first and of oral literature only secondarily. For Charles Godfrey Leland (1824–1903), though, Native American studies comprised only one of several folkloric interests in a varied belletristic career. Leland was a native of Philadelphia who spent much of his adult life in Europe, and gained literary fame in the 1850s through "Hans Breitmann," a character in a series of German-American dialect poems he wrote. For more than a decade after Hans Breitmann appeared, Leland worked as a journalist, giving up that profession in 1869 when an inheritance allowed him to begin a ten-year stay in Europe. There his interests in folklore became manifest. He was particularly interestd in the culture of the Gypsies and in 1888 helped to found the Gypsy-Lore Society. He was also a founder or early member of national folklore societies in Italy, Hungary, and England; he represented Great Britain at the First International Folklore Congress in 1888.

SOURCE: *The Atlantic Monthly*, 54 (August 1884), 222–234.

Leland's work with Algonquin-speaking Indian groups in New England occurred during a five-year period (1879–1884) when he returned to the United States with the primary purpose of encouraging industrial arts training as a part of general education. His collecting among the Abnaki, the Micmac, and their linguistic kin resulted in Algonquin Legends of New England *(Boston: Houghton Mifflin, 1884), a book-length assemblage of oral narratives, and* Kuloskap the Master and Other Algonquin Poems *(New York: Funk & Wagnalls, 1902), an attempt to turn stories about an Algonquin culture hero into a verse epic similar to the Finnish* Kalevala. *Yet the work with these Native Americans was only an episode in Leland's folklore career. The varied nature of that career becomes apparent from some representative titles in his bibliography:* Gypsy Sorcery and Fortune Telling *(London: T. F. Unwin, 1891);* Legends of Florence, *First Series (London: David Nutt, 1896);* The Unpublished Legends of Virgil *(London: Eliot Stock, 1901).*

Leland was more a collector of folklore than a theorist about its nature. Nevertheless, the essay presented here reveals some definite theoretical perspectives on Native American oral literature. Like many of his contemporaries—see, for instance, the essays by Stephen Return Riggs, Stephen D. Peet, and William W. Warren in this collection—Leland perceived parallels between Native American folklore and Old World traditions. Yet his discussion of similarities between Algonquin and Scandinavian mythology surpasses most such studies in specificity and detail. His marshalling of evidence is impressive, even if not wholly convincing. Although Leland endorsed the evolutionary scheme of culture history that pervaded ethnological thought during the late nineteenth century, he also showed interest in tracing routes of diffusion that could account for cross-cultural similarities in lore. Thus, he traced Gypsy folklore to India and Algonquin oral narratives through the Eskimo to the Norsemen in Greenland. At the end of his essay, Leland voices the common plaint among students of folklore: that vast treasuries of material that once could have been preserved have become irretrievably lost as time has passed. A field man himself, Leland urges others to join him in collecting what remains.

Leland's focus on Scandinavian analogues to Algonquin folklore reflects the enthusiasm for things Nordic which characterized some aspects of late nineteenth-century American culture. After all, the work of Elias Lonrott in collating Finnish folksongs into the unified epic, the Kalevala, *in the 1840s had been a major influence on Longfellow's* Hiawatha. *Longfellow's poem, "The Skeleton in Armor," as well as books attesting to the Norse discovery of the New World—for example, B. F. De Costa,* The Pre-Columbian Discovery of North America *(Albany: J. Munsell, 1868)—also reflects the Scandinavian interests of the period. The aspect of Scandinavian culture selected for attention by Leland, the Eddic literature, contains the primary sources for Norse mythology. That literature consists of two compilations of Icelandic poetry and prose probably written in the thirteenth century. The Elder (or Poetic) Edda consists of more than thirty individual poems which deal with the activities of Nordic gods and heroes. The Younger (or Prose) Edda, written by Snorri Sturluson c. 1220, seems to be a handbook of Nordic mythology partially derived from the Elder Edda. Leland has drawn his comparative material for Algonquin traditional lore from both Eddas as they were treated in Rasmus B. Anderson,* Norse Mythology; or, The Religion of Our Forefathers, Containing All the Myths of the Eddas, Systematized and Interpreted *(Chicago: S. C. Griggs, 1875). The best modern handbook of Nordic mythology is H. R. Ellis Davidson,* Gods and Myths of Northern Europe *(1964; rpt. Hammondsworth: Penguin, 1974).*

A two-volume biography of Charles Godfrey Leland written by his niece Elizabeth Robins Pennell, is entitled Charles Godfrey Leland: A Biography *(Boston: Houghton Mifflin, 1906). For a shorter account of his career, focusing on the folkloric aspect, see Richard M. Dorson, "American Folklorists in Britain,"* Journal of the Folklore Institute, 7 *(1970), 187–219.*

* * * * *

When Mr. Longfellow declared that the Manobozho legends of the Chippeways formed an Indian Edda, he spoke as a poet, not as an ethnologist.[1] In the same spirit they might with as much justice have been termed an Indian Iliad or Nibelungenlied. But in fact the expression was so inaccurate that even the usually far from careful Schoolcraft hastened to correct it, since in the beginning of his introduction to the Hiawatha Legends he declares, "Of all these foreign analogies of myth lore, the least tangible is that which has been suggested with the Scandinavian mythology. That mythology is of so marked and peculiar a character that it has not been distinctly traced out of the great circle of tribes of the Indo-Germanic family. Odin and his terrific pantheon of war-gods and social deities could only exist in the dreary latitudes of storms and fire which produce a Hecla and a Maelstrom. From such a source the Indian could have derived none of his vague symbols and mental idiosyncrasies, which have left him as he is found to-day, without a government and without a God."[2]

And yet, strangely enough, there was in existence all the time in New England—and at Mr. Longfellow's very door, poetically speaking—an Indian Edda, and there was carefully preserved among the Penobscots and Passamaquoddies of Maine "a myth lore," "the analogies of which with the Scandinavian mythology" were very much closer than those of the Edda with the Kalevala, to which it is so nearly and so incontestably related. In fact, after the most careful perusal and study of every line of the stupendous Finnish epic, I find that where it has one incident or point of resemblance with the Edda, or with other Norse poems, the Indian legends of New England and New Brunswick have a score. Rasmus B. Anderson, in the notes to his translation of the Younger Edda,[3] declares that as regards the origin of the Asa system, that is of the Norse mythology, it is chiefly composed of Finnish elements. But all that there is to be found of the Finn in the Edda is feeble and faint compared to what there is of the Edda in the legends of the Wabanaki Indians.

The Algonquin subdivision of the six or seven stocks of American Indians includes, as J. H. Trumbull has shown,[4] forty principal tribes, speaking as many different dialects of what was once a common or root language. Of these the Wabanaki, or Abenaki, deriving their name from *Wa-be-yu, white* or *light*, are to us the nearest and most interesting. The word *light* is applied to them as living to the east. The St. Francis Indians, who call themselves specially *the* Abenaki, and who all speak French, translate their generic name as *point du jour*. They embrace in addition to the St. Francis tribe the Micmacs of New Brunswick; the Passamaquoddies, chiefly resident at Pleasant Point, or Sebayk near Eastport, Maine; and the Penobscots of Oldtown, in the same State. The last two tribes can converse together, but it is almost or quite impossible for them to understand Micmac. Yet all of them have in common a mythology and legends which as a whole are in every respect far superior to those of the Chippeways, or, so far as I know them, to those of any of our Western tribes.

I have collected directly from the Indians themselves more than one hundred of these legends. The Rev. S. T. Rand,[5] of Hantsport, New Brunswick, the original discoverer of Glooskap,—"the Hiawatha of the North," but a creation inconceivably superior to Hiawatha,—has very kindly lent to me eighty-five Micmac tales, forming a folio volume of one thousand pages. In addition to these I am indebted to Mrs. W. Wallace Brown[6] for a small but extremely valuable collection of stories from the Indians living near Calais. I have also two curious Anglo-Indian manuscripts: one a collection of tales, with a treatise on Superstitions in Indian and English; the other a Story of Glooskap, a singular narrative of the adventures of the great hero of the North, composed in Indian-English of the obscurest kind. Mr. Jack,[7] of Fredericton, N.B., has very kindly communicated to me legends and folk-lore, Malisete and Micmac, while I am specially obliged to Miss Abby Alger,[8] of Boston, for aid of every kind, including a small collection of tales of the St. Francis tribe. Some idea of the immense extent of this literature may be inferred from the fact that, while I have duplicates of almost every story, I never received one which did not in some important respect amend the others. All of these tribes in their oral or wampum records tell of Glooskap, a superior heroic demigod. I say demigod, since there is no proof of the existence among our Indians of a belief in a Great Spirit or in an infinite God before the coming of the whites. Glooskap was, however, more than a Hercules or a Manco Capac, for he created man and animals before teaching agriculture, hunting, and language. He was a truly grand hero; his life was never soiled with the disgraceful, puerile, and devilish caprices of the Manobozho, whose more creditable deeds were picked out and attributed by Mr. Longfellow to the Iroquois Hiawatha. A singular admixture of grandeur, benevolence, and quiet, pleasant humor characterize Glooskap, who of all beings of all mythologies most resembles Odin and Thor in the battlefield, and Pantagruel at home.

Glooskap was born of the Turtle *gens*, "since it is on the Turtle that all rests." He had a twin brother, Malsum the Wolf. Before birth the pair conferred as to how they would enter the world. Glooskap preferred to be born as others, but the Wolf in his wicked pride tore through his mother's armpit and killed her. In the Iroquois version of this tale, the two are called the Good Being and the Evil One. The Wolf is therefore the type of evil, or the destroyer.

Malsum asked Glooskap (who subsequently appears distinctly as the sun god) what would kill him. He replied that of all created things the bulrush alone could take his life. So Malsum tried to kill him with it; but the bulrush would take his life only *for an instant*. So, recovering, he slew the Wolf. The resemblance between the bulrush, cattail, or, as one version says, "a ball of soft down," and the mistletoe, the softest of all plants, which kills Balder in the Edda, is here apparent enough. The same tale is told, but in a broken and abbreviated form, among the Hiawatha Legends.

Glooskap proceeded to create the dwarfs or fairies, and then man. He made him from an ash-tree. Man was in the ash-tree as a principle or as a being, but lifeless. First the dwarfs were created from the bark, and then mankind from the wood. Glooskap shot his magical life-giving arrows into the tree, and men came forth. In the Edda man existed as the ash; the elm was added as woman; but as in the Indian tale man was without consciousness till the three gods

> "Found on Earth
> Ask and Embla,
> Nearly powerless,
> void of destiny.
> Spirit they possessed not,
> Sense they had not,
> blood nor motive powers,
> nor goodly color.
> Spirit gave Odin,
> Sense gave Hoenir,

Blood gave Lodur,
and goodly color."[9]

In the Edda, the first created on earth are two giants, born from their mother's armpit. Their father, who is an evil Jötun, has feet male and female. The next beings created are the dwarfs, and then man from the ash-tree. Every one of these details corresponds step by step with the Wabanaki mythology, except that in the latter it is Lox, the evil principle of fire, who has feet male and female. This Lox, the Indian devil, is no specific man or animal, but he is like Loki in every respect.

That the ash alone was the primitive tree of life or of man appears from the account of Yggdrasil in the next verse.[10] To hunt and draw his sled Glooskap took the Loons. But they were too often absent. So he had, like Odin, two attendant wolves, one black and one white. There can be no doubt of the accuracy of this statement, for the Indian is still living who actually met Glooskap a few years ago, "very far north," and ferried him over a bay. His black and white wolf dogs were at the landing before them, when all mysteriously vanished. In the Edda two wolves also follow, one the sun, another (Manogarm) the moon.

In one legend Glooskap is described as directing and guiding the course of the seasons. He has always by him a being named Kool-pe-jo-tei, meaning in Micmac "rolled over by handspikes." Hi lies on the ground; he has not a bone in his body. He rests under the heaven all the year. He is rolled over with wooden handspikes in the spring and autumn. This was very clearly explained by the Indian narrator as referring to the course of the seasons. Glooskap's sledge is drawn by wolves. In the Elder Edda Odin is described as riding a wolf. Odin has, however, two pet wolves, Gere and Freke, whom, like Glooskap, he feeds from his own hands. To recapitulate, Odin and Glooskap have each two attendant wolves. They use wolves as steeds; those of Glooskap are black and white, corresponding to the day and night, or sun and moon wolves of the Edda, termed Skol and Hate.

Gylfe, the great sorcerer,[11] when he went to Asgard to see if the gods were really so mighty as he had heard, disguised himself as an old man. Glooskap, going with a similar intention to

135

see the wicked giant magicians, who dwelt by North Conway, N.H., or in the Intervale, also went as an old man, but made himself so like the father of these monsters that the sons could not tell one from the other. If it should ever be definitely proved that there was a common source for the Wabanaki tales and the Norse, we shall find much that has been lost from the latter in the former. It has often seemed to me that these Indian traditions contained incidents wanting in their Norse counterparts.

Glooskap has a canoe which is, when he wishes it to be large, capable of carrying an army, but which also contracts to the smallest size. At times it is made into an ordinary birch *akevédun*, but when not in use it is a rocky island, covered with trees. Odin, or Frey,[12] has a ship, Skidbladnir, so large that all the Asas can find room in it, "but which, when not wanted for a voyage, may be folded by Frey like a napkin and carried in the pocket."

Glooskap has a belt which gives supernatural strength. This belt is often mentioned. Thor possesses the *meginjarder*, or belt of strength,[13] which doubles his might when he puts it on. The little old woman who typifies old age in the Indian tales puts on a similar magic girdle when she wrestles with the Micmac Hercules. This belt has passed into all fairy lore, but in the Wabanaki legends it is still distinctly mythical or heroic.

The gods in Valhalla feed on the boar Sahrimnir, which is inexhaustible. "It is boiled every day, and is whole again in the evening."[14] Glooskap sets before his guests a small dish, in which there is very little food. But however hungry they may be, the dish is always full.

As all these coincidences cannot be given within the limits of an article like this, I would say that the tale of Idun and her apples does not contain a single incident which does not occur in unmistakably ancient form in the Wabanaki legends. The only part which I have believed came in from Canadian French or modern European influence is the apples themselves. There is an Indian tale of such magic apples (Micmac); but then the fruit did not grow of old in this country, and the story cannot therefore be pre-Columbian.

There is a very ancient Wabanaki legend, originally a poem, and which, like most of these narratives, has been transmitted for generations, word by word. The Rev. S. T. Rand has recorded his astonishment at finding that the Indians would always readily resume the narrative which had been discontinued, at the very word where they had left off. I made the same discovery when I observed that my friend Tomaqu'hah would often pause to recover the word which led the sentence. I mention this because in this tale there are not only incidents but verbal passages almost identical with some in the Elder Edda. In it Glooskap went with his host Kitpooseagunow (Micmac), a mighty giant, to fish for whales. The guest carried the canoe to the water, and asked, "Who shall sit in the stern and paddle, and who will take the spear?" (that is, who will fish?) Kitpooseagunow said, "That will I." So Glooskap paddled, and his host soon caught a great whale. In the Edda[15] Thor asks,

> " 'Wilt thou do
>   half the work with me:
>   either the whales
>   homewards carry,
>   or the boat
>   fast bind?'
>   Thor went,
>   grasped the prow
>   quickly with its hold-water,
>   lifted the boat
>   together with its oars
>   and scoop,
>   and bore them to the dwelling.
>   The mighty Hymir
>   he alone
>   two whales drew up."[16]

In both the Edda and the Indian tale stress is laid on the fact that the guest rowed. The Norse Hymir grudgingly admits that Thor does this well, but declares that he wishes to see further proof of his abilities. Then, going home, Hymir and Thor have a great mutual trial of strength and endurance; that is to see if Thor can break a cup against Hymir, the ice giant's icy head. The two Indian Titans try to see which can freeze the other to death. If we go to the direct meaning of the Norse myth, this after-contest amounts to the same thing in each case. In both the Norse and Indian myths, the heart or the head of an ice giant is represented as being made of "ice harder than the hardest stone," to express the intense coldness of his nature. In each it is a contest with cold.

The Wabanaki as well as the Chippeways and others, call the Milky Way the spirits' road or the ghosts' highway. In the Edda, Bifrost the rainbow is the bridge over which the gods pass; but Mr. Keary[17] has shown that in many old Norse and German tales the Milky Way is the spirits' path, while in the Vedas both rainbow and Via Lactea are described as roads or bridges for supernatural beings.

In Norse mythology, Jötunheim, inhabited by giants of ice and stone, lies far in the North Atlantic. Its stone giants dwell in Stony-town. They are all sorcerers. Hrungnir with the flint heart is their chief. In the Wabanaki tales the same North Atlantic has the same land of precisely the same inhabitants. Hence came "the stonish giants" of the Iroquois, which Mr. Schoolcraft avowed his inability to explain,[18] but which are explained in minute and remarkable detail by the Wabanaki. Hrungnir with the flint heart is the counterpart of the cannibal giant Chenoo of the Micmacs, and Keeawahqu' of the more southern Wabanaki, who has a heart of "ice, harder than the hardest stone." It is the principal business of Glooskap to fight these beings, which are identical with Jötuns and Trolls.

Once Glooskap sent a great sorcerer (*megŭmawĕssū*) to this land of the Boöin. (Micmac, *powwow*, a sorcerer). They made him run a race with one of them. But it was not a man, but the Northern Lights disguised as a man. Yet the giants were deceived, for he who visited them was the Lightning, and he conquered. In the Edda, Thiasse is made to race, on a precisely similar visit to the same people, with Thought (Huge) disguised as a man. In the Edda, Thor wrestles with a little old woman (Elle), the foster mother of the giant Ganglere. In the Micmac and the Passamaquoddy story of the Culloo, a man of miraculous strength, an Indian Hercules, wrestles with a little, feeble-looking old woman, who has previously defeated all the strong men of the world. He, it is true, overcomes her. But the point lies in this: that old age (Elle) is incarnate among the Indians as a little old woman. In the very wild Passamaquoddy tale of the Dance of Old Age, a young sorceress in an Indian waltz grows a year older at every turn, and at the hundredth falls dead as a small, shriveled, wrinkled old squaw.

When Glooskap's envoy visited the giant sorcerers, he was required by his host to kill a dragon as a task. The American Wabanaki had the dragon long ere the whites told them of it. It was a being like a monstrous wingless serpent, with horns and scales like shining copper, or a kind of brown-golden gleaming fish. The Micmacs call it *che-pitch-calm*, the Passamaquoddies *wee-wil-l-mecqu'*. The Indian killed it by putting a log across its hole, and when it was half out chopped it in two. In the Edda, Sigurd, visiting Regin, was instigated by his host—also as a task—to kill the dragon Fafnir. He dug a pit, and when the monster crawled over it thrust his sword up and slew him.[19] The Norse dragon left a treasure which brought ruin to all who received it. The invaluable horns of the dragon (described as such in other legends) were brought to the host by the victor, but they proved to be his bane or death, for the dragon was his *téomul* (Micmac; in Passamaquoddy, *pou-he-gan*; in Norse, *ham*); that is, his tutelary beast or guardian angel. When this dies, the *protégé* also perishes. This narrative is as Norse in its general tone as in the details. Like most of the older tales, it has evidently been a poem. The death of Fafnir also caused the death of Regin. In every important part the two stories are the same. I have only one entire long legend which is as yet all a real song. But nearly all have passages from which the gilding of metre (if I may so call it) or *euphony* has not entirely disappeared, or in which verses still remain.

The Edda tells us that the wind is caused by a giant clad in eagle's plumes, and when he flaps his wings the wind blows:—

> "Hraesvelg he is called
> Who sits at heaven's end,
> A giant in eagle plumes,
> from his wings comes
> All the wind."

This is in every detail identical with the account of the Wabanaki, who say that the wind is raised by a giant, who is also an eagle, who sits at the extreme north on a high rock. In Passamaquoddy he is called *Wut-chow-sen*, or the Wind-Blower. With the Western tribes there is a thunder bird; but as in all the cases which I have met of coincidences between Indian and Norse myths, that of the Wabanaki is most like the latter. Once the wind blew so terribly that Glooskap tied the Wind-Blower's wings. Then there was no air for months; the sea grew stagnant. He untied one wing: then there was a wind, but since then there have been no tornadoes like those of the olden time. I have a vague recollection of a Northern myth in which Thor, or some strong god, conquers Hraesvelgar, but cannot speak with certainty of it. I have long and detailed accounts of this legend from both Micmac and Passamaquoddy Indians.

Glooskap left the world, promising to return, but did not. From an old squaw, who could not speak a word of English, Mrs. W. Wallace Brown recently obtained the following, to which I add a few details gathered from other sources:—

"Glooskap is alive. He lives in an immense lodge. He is making arrows. One side of the lodge is now piled full of them. They are as close together as that:" here she put her fingers closely together. "When the lodge shall be full, then he will come out and make war, and all will be killed. Then he will come in his canoe; then he will meet the great wolf, and all the stone and ice and other giants, the sorcerers, the goblins and elves, and all will be burned up; the water will all boil away from the fire."

This is not from any Christian source. It is simply the account of Ragnarok, when Odin is to come and fight the Fenris wolf, or the destroying type of evil, and all be consumed. But the Indian woman, when closely questioned, drew a sharp distinction between the Wabanaki Day of Judgment and the account of it in the Bible. And after much experience of these legends and traditions, I cannot help believing or feeling that one acquires an almost unerring *flair* or faculty of perceiving in them what is Eskimo, what Norse, what Indian, and what is French Canadian fairy tale. Add to these a few of Aesop's fables, very strangely

Indianized, and we have almost all there is in them. The Eskimo element, which is very important, is simply indubitable. The French Canadian stories are apparent enough, with their coaches and horses, kings and swords, gunpowder, God, and the devil.

The next character to be considered is Lox, the "Indian devil." The word Lox is not, I believe, Indian. This character includes the wolverine, badger, and raccoon, though strangely enough not the fox. Collectively he forms a character,—a man who is so much like Loki of the Edda that I have often been amazed at the likeness. There is not a Wabanaki Indian who would not recognize the latter as an old friend. Yet, although the incidents of the lives of Lox and Loki are so much alike the real resemblance lies in their characters, style of tricks, and language; in their mutual infinite blackguardism and impudence, and their greed for devilish mischief, for mere fun's sake.

Loki is fire, and Lox, as it appears from many instances, is a fire spirit; both are distinctly described as the fathers of the wolves. Lox dies by cold and water, but when dead is revived by heat. In the Edda, Loki is carried about and grievously punished by a giant in the form of an eagle. Lox is treated in the same way, for having played the following trick. Entering a house, he was rather coolly treated by a woman; the slight to his vanity was of the most trifling kind, but he revenged it by cutting her head off and putting it into the pot with the rest of the dinner to boil, to give the family a surprise on returning. All of this is related in one of Dasent's Norse tales.[20] The head of the family was a Culloo, a kind of giant eagle or roc, and he punished Lox by carrying him up to the top of the sky and letting him drop.

In the Edda there is a scene between Thor and Harbard, the ferryman, in which Thor is sadly chaffed and abused. How it is that any critic could have mistaken Harbard for Odin, or for any one but Loki, is really incomprehensible. That the name could have been assumed does not occur to any one. In an Indian tale Lox satirizes and insults the crane—the ferryman—so effectually that the latter drowns him when pretending to pass him over. This legend has manifestly been a poem.

Lox is a fire spirit. Mr. Keary, in his work on the Norse Mythology, has asserted that in many old German and Norse legends fire is typified by thorns, prickles, nettles, stings, and the like. In one Indian tale, Lox, "the Indian devil," is thrown on a bed of thorns, falls into a mass of briers, steps into a wasp's or hornet's nest, and is rolled on sharp flints; while in another, in consequence of eating itch berries, he scratches himself almost to death.

On one occasion, the Indian devil, after cruelly burning two old women in jest, dies of delight, and being then in the form of a raccoon is put into a pot to boil. The touch of scalding water gives him life again, and he springs out of the pot. But at the very instant of revival his sense of mischief awakens, and as he leaps from the kettle he gives it a kick; the hot water falls into the ashes; the ashes fly up and blind an old woman. Compare with this a passage in the Finnish Kalevala, the elder sister of the Edda. When, by evil magic, a stag or elk was created for mischief, the first thing the creature did on coming to life was to run at full speed. But it had hardly started ere it went by a Lapland hut, and as it ran it kicked over a kettle, so that the meat in it fell in the ashes, and the soup was dashed over the hearth. Surely this never came to the Indians through a French fairy tale. Once, when the Indian devil is drowned and is then revived by his brother, he says, "It seems to me that I have been asleep." In the Kalevala, likewise, the completely drowned Lemmekäinen, brought to life by his mother, makes the same remark. In a Samoyede tale a dead man's bones are picked up by a *half man*, with one leg and one arm. Of these *unipeds* I shall speak anon. He burns the bones; his wife sleeps on them; the dead man comes to life, and makes the same remark. As we go on it begins to seem as if there were some world-old Shamanic root for half the Norse tales, and all the Finnish, Samoyede, Eskimo, and Indian. No one has raised the veil of the mystery as yet, but it will be lifted.

In a Micmac story the Indian devil runs a race with a stone giant; that is, an immense rock. Loki is chased by the stone giant Thiasse, but as an eagle, both having wings. In another Indian legend an evil sorcerer, who is evidently a form of the Indian devil, flies in a race with another man, who is, for the nonce, a hawk.

It came to Lox's mind to change himself to a woman, to make mischief. Loki did the same thing in Fensal. The Indian devil's trick got him into trouble, and he took refuge in a waterfall, where, through being over cunning, he perished. Loki's tricks of killing Balder, which are incidentally like the Indian as to the mistletoe, led to his being chased to *Franangurs fors*, "the bright and glistening cataract," where he was caught and came to his ruin. Finally, Loki in this waterfall turns himself into a salmon, and also catches a salmon and an otter before his capture. In another Indian story Lox the devil perishes just as he catches a salmon. And in another Passamaquoddy tale, an evil sorcerer, who is the veritable devil of a village and perfectly identified with Loki and Lox by certain sinful tricks, dies in consequence of catching an otter; this otter being, exactly like the otter of the Norse tale, not a mere animal, but a goblin, a human otter, or, as the story expressly declares, a *pou-he-gan* (Norse *ham*). In this same story two girls go to sleep in a cabin. A man's neck bone lies by the door. The younger, being told not to touch it, gives it a kick. All night long the bone abuses her. In a Norse tale an old woman brings home a human bone, and till morning it disturbs her by talking and howling. The Indian story is unquestionably a very old one.

A passage in the Edda which has been a stumbling-block to all commentators, of which Grimm could make nothing, and Benjamin Thorpe[21] said, "I believe the difficulty is beyond help," is this:—

> "Loki, scorched up
> In his heart,
> Found a woman's
> Half-burnt thought-stone.
> Loki became guileful
> From that wicked woman;
> Thence in the world
> Are all giantesses come."

In Norse this is, "Loki of hiarta lyndi brendu fann hann halfs vithinn hugstein Kona." In the Indian tales, a man may become a misanthrope, and then a Chenoo, a being at once ghoul, cannibal, and sorcerer. Then he acquires incredible swiftness, and may grow up to be a giant at will. His heart now turns to ice, harder than any stone. But he still does not become utterly devilish until he overcomes in battle a female Chenoo, and swallows her heart. The Indians, when they kill a Chenoo, take great pains to burn the heart. Should they leave it half burned, another Chenoo would find and swallow this "thought-stone," and become twice as terrible as before. This story explains of itself that the heart, not the head, is supposed to be the seat of the thought or intellect. All of these details I found originally in the tale of the Chenoo: first, from the Micmac, by Rev. S. T. Rand; and again, in a much more detailed form, from the Passamaquoddy, told me by an Indian. In the latter, the heart is said to be a miniature human figure of the owner.

Loki is the father of the wolves, and Lox is represented as the same. On one occasion they give him a charm by which he can make three fires,—one for each night of a three days' journey. But in his impatience to be warm he burns them all out the first morning, and then freezes to death. What can this typify if not fire,—its raging impatience and the manner in which it dies by its own indulgence?

At another time Lox found many women making bags of fine fur. "You have a very slow way of doing that," he observed. "In our country the women manage it much more rapidly." "And how, then?" inquired the good-wives. "Thus," replied Lox; and taking a fine piece of fur he buried it beneath the ashes, and then heaped on coals, after which, with great style, he drew from under it all a very fine bag. Having done this he ran out of town. Whereupon the women put all their furs under ashes and coals, but when they took them out, what remained was ruined. This is a fire trick, again.

It is true that the fire test is not infallible as an indication of the devil; for once Odin himself was obliged by his host Geirrod to sit eight days and nights between fires, roasting. The atrociously wicked sorcerer Porcupine obliged Glooskap in like manner to sit in a cave full of fire. But as he had far greater power of resistance, it was the host who perished, as he does, indeed, in the Norse tale, though not by fire. But the whole of this Indian legend sings like an Icelandic tale. In it the hero is obliged to pass on a roaring rapid through a sunless cave, in midnight blackness, till he emerges on a broad, quiet river in a lovely land. As this is repeated in different narratives of different heroes, it appears to be a regular ordeal or ceremony of initiation.

The Cold is a distinct personage in Northern Indian tales. But he is with the Wabanaki much more like the Pakkaren, or Cold incarnate of the Finns and of the Kalevala than that of the Western tribes. In the same epic there is a supernatural being who cuts down a tree at a single blow with an axe. Among the Passamaquoddies, Atwakenikess, the Spirit of the Woods, always does the same thing. When a tree is heard to fall afar in the wilderness the Indian says, "There is Atwakenikess!"

But it is not from the Indians alone that we learn their myths. Among the Wabanaki, as well as among the Eskimo, there are strange tales of half men, lengthwise. These were also known to the Eskimo of the European side; that is, to the Samoyedes and Lapps. The Norsemen seem to have regarded them as American. "In 1009 Karlsefne went around Cape Cod, and sailed along the coast, until off Boston he 'raised' the Blue Hills, when he returned to the settlement in Rhode Island, appearing unwilling to venture up the coast of New Hampshire and Maine on account of the unipeds, or one-footed men fabled to live there."[22] Karlsefne, as it would seem from the story, picked up his information as to unipeds in Boston. It would be interesting to be able to prove that Boston had begun at so early a date to influence the religious opinions and philosophy of its visitors. One of Karlsefne's men was killed by a uniped, and they made up a song on it. Charlevoix[23] assures us that the celebrated chief Donnaconna told him that he had seen these one-legged people, and that an Eskimo girl brought to Labrador, or Canada, in 1717 declared they were well known in Greenland. While writing this paper, I have received from Mr. S. T. Rand a long story entitled Esluman the Half Man. The Abbé Morellet,[24] in his work on the Eskimo, cites from the Sagas an account of a Norse sea-rover, a great hero, who, having been wrecked on the icy coast of Greenland, was attacked by two ravenous giantesses, but conquered them, and returned to tell the tale at home. It is said that two giantesses were the last of the race left in Scandinavia.[25] These monstrous women cannibals are the female Kiawaqu' or Chenoo of the Micmacs. They form the subject of many tales. They belong to the post-Jötuns.

Though the story of the Swan or Sea-Gull maiden, who, having laid her wings aside, was caught by a youth, is known all over Europe, it is for all that probably of Norse origin. The Northern races are more familiar with such birds than the men of the South. In the story the girl lives with her husband until finding one day her wings, she flies away with her children. This legend occurs not once, but many times, among the Wabanaki, and it did not come to them through the Canadian French. It is imbedded as an essential part in their oldest myths. It begins the tale of Pulowech, which is evidently one of the earliest, most serious, and most thoroughly Indian of all the legends of New England and Canada.

I have gathered in conversation from several Indians, and I have it recorded in several written-out tales, that it is a very ancient belief that beings which correspond exactly to the Trolls of the Edda often attack brave men by night. If the latter can only prolong the fight till the sun shines on the fiend, it turns to stone or a dead tree immediately, *and all its strength and wisdom pass into the conquerer.* In the Edda,[26] where a dwarf or Troll contends in argument with Thor, the wily hero prolongs the contest until daybreak, when the dwarf is petrified by the light.

> "By great wiles thou hast,
> I tell thee, been deluded;
> Though art above ground,
> Dwarf, at dawn!
> Already in the hall
> The sun is shining!"

The same is said in the Helgakvida, where Atli tells the giantess Hrimgera, "It is now day; you have been detained to your destruction. It will be a laughable mark in the harbor, where you will stand as a stone image." At the corner of Friar's Bay, Campobello, is the ridiculously so called "Friar," a rock thirty feet high, which the Indians in one tradition say is a petrified woman. It is certainly both a petrified Troll and a harbor mark.

Dead men made to live again by sorcery are very common in Wabanaki, Eskimo, Finnish, and Samoyede tales. They occur in the Norse, but are by no means frequent. A study of Shamanism in all its phases from the Accadian or Turanian Babylonian, through the Tartar or Lapland, the Eskimo, and so on to the American Indian, must result in the conviction that there has been a regular "historical" transmission of culture from a very ancient common source through all of these.

It is to be remarked that when the Wabanaki kill a bear they always beg his pardon, and in fact many other Indians address long speeches of apology or of excuse to the dead Bruin. When the Laplanders do the same they sing to him:—

> "Kittulis pourra, kittulis iiskada!
> Soubi jalla zaiti
> Iii paha talki oggio
> Ii paha talki pharonis!"

> "We thank thee for coming hither,
> That thou didst not harm us,
> Nor break the clubs and spears
> Wherewith we killed thee.
> We pray thee do not raise tempests
> Or do any other harm
> To those who slew thee!"[27]

But in the Kalevala an entire *runot* is devoted to the songs of apology and ceremonies incident to killing a bear. The French translator Le Duc[28] loses himself in bewildered conjectures as to the meaning of it all. It is fully explained in three of my Passamaquoddy stories. The she-bear was the grandmother or foster-mother of both Glooskap and Manobozho. This was as sacred a relation as that of mother. The she-bear as the mother of their god, and when her son leaves her she exacts that a bear shall never be slain without certain ceremonies or under certain conditions. There is a Norse story which is identical in minute detail with an Indian one of a girl marrying a white bear and of a boy reared by bears.

There is one Indian legend which is throughout so Norse, so full both of the Icelandic folk tale and the Edda, that if no other link of union existed between the Wabanaki and Europe this would almost establish it. It is the one already alluded to as a Micmac song, communicated by Mrs. W. Wallace Brown, of Calais. It is a tale of Three Strong Men. In it a starved-looking little elf eats the food of three men, and fights all day long with a man of incredible strength, the son of a white bear. In an entirely Norse tale, a very small elf fights a white bear all night long ere he is conquered. The wife of the hero invokes the Wind-Blower or Giant Eagle to send a wind. When her husband leaves her, she, fearing a rival sorceress, warns him that if, when he approaches his place of destination, a small whelp should lick his hand he will forget her. In the Edda, to dream of whelps is the most evil of all Atli's many bad dreams.[29] In the Atlamal in Groenlenzku, Högui is warned against going,[30] and he takes a potion which causes oblivion. Broken and bewildering as this is, there is at every step in both the Indian tale and this particular part of the Gudrun song something which recalls in one the other. We are told in the Norse that to dream of a white bear means a great storm; that is, a startling event. It rarely occurs in a Wabanaki tale that the white bear's skin is brought in unless there is at hand some startling magic transformation. I had observed this long before any connection between Indian and Norse stories suggested itself.

In the Edda, Odin takes Mimir's head, and prepares it by magic, so that it answers all his questions and gives him advice. In three Indian stories the head of a magician does the same thing, and, as in the Edda, it is constantly kept as an oracle. But in the Wabanaki it is eventually reunited to its body, and the man thus formed runs *amok*, killing every one he meets. It may be conjectured that in the old Norse tale, now lost, Mimir will, at the last day, regain his head, and fight madly. Without this the Edda is at present manifestly defective, since in it Mimir, the source of all Odin's wisdom, that is of all wisdom, has no share in the final revival.

There are not in the Chippeway or any other Indian tales known to me such indications of culture as are found among the legends of the Wabanaki. Regarded as literature, the latter are marvelously accommodated to the European style and standard. There is a large-hearted, genial spirit of strength, health, and humor in them which is, one may say, Norse, and nothing else,—the spirit of Rabelais and of Shakespeare. Glooskap, the Lord of Men and Beasts, the sublime American Thor and Odin, who towers above Hiawatha and Manobozho like a colossus above pigmies, the master of the mighty mountains, has still a wonderfully tender heart. He has one ever-repeated joke,—his canoe, which he lends, always saying, "I have often lent it, and everybody has promised to bring it back, but I have always been obliged to go after it myself." It is his umbrella. He often sends certain friends to the land of the giant sorcerers. There they have terrible adventures; they slay giants and serpents. One invariable and dreadful trial awaits them at the last station, returning. A giant skunk, big as St. Paul's, standing on the shore, opens on them his battery. Of course the monster is triumphantly slain by the hero. But this skunk forms no part of the devices of the enemy. It is a little private trick of Glooskap's own,—a genial potent delusion, a joke.

It may naturally be inquired how it came to pass that there is so much in common to the Wabanaki and Norse. The latter were in Greenland for three centuries. They left there the ruins of fourscore churches and monasteries. In their time the Eskimo are believed to have ranged as far south as New York. The Wabanaki or Algonquin live to-day in Labrador. When I wrote recently to the Rev. S. T. Rand to know if the Micmacs ever visited the Eskimo, he did but go to his next Indian neighbor, a woman, who told him that her husband had passed seven winters with Eskimo,—four among the "tame," and three among the heathen. The Indians do not appear anywhere or at any time to have told stories to the Iglesmani,—that is, English or Americans,—or to have listened to any of theirs. The ordinary American, as for instance Thoreau,[31] listens to their tales only to ridicule them. He immediately proceeds to demonstrate to the Indian the "folly" of his belief; that is, his own moral supremacy. This was not the case with the French Canadians, who emptied out on the Indians in full faith all their *contes des fées*. With the Eskimo and half-pagan Norsemen there was an even greater sympathy. The Indian had his *téomul*, his *pou-he-gan*, his animal fate or spirit; the Norseman had his *ham*, or *fylgia*, which was precisely the same thing.

It has been objected to me that these Greenland Norsemen were all Christians. So are the Indians, every one good Catholics. Once there was one Sunday morning (I am assured that this is really true) a small church full of Christian Wabanaki Indians. They were all at prayers. The church was surrounded by their enemies, the Megwech or Mohawks. They were marched out to die. But there was among the Christians a *K'chee medéoulin*, a great sorcerer. He asked the Mohawk chief if he might, ere he was slain, walk thrice round the church. This is an old Norse magical formula.[32] The request was granted. He walked and sang. He invoked the tempest. It came, and the lightning killed all the wicked heathen Mohawks, who were at once scalped by the good Christian Micmacs. Doubtless the Norsemen were equally pious. It was only a few years before Karlsefne visited Boston that Thangbrand, the pirate bishop, converted so many to Christianity in Iceland by splitting with a cross the heads of the heathen who would *not* believe,—*pour encourager les autres.*

There has been as yet very little study of the Shamanic mythology, folklore, and poetry of the early world. The commentators on the Edda should study more closely the races with the magic drum. There is some mighty mystery behind it all, as yet unsolved. I cannot admit of our Indian legends that popular tales are the same the world over. Were this apparent Norse element not in those of the Wabanaki, what remains would be French or Eskimo fairy stories, every one easy to recognize. I would add to this a conviction that the Chippewas drew their legends from the East. Thus, for instance, the Toad Woman of Schoolcraft and many others are imperfect and distorted, compared to the versions of the same stories as told in the East. *The Iroquois Book of Rites*, edited by H. Hale,[33] and the early accounts of that race indicate that it was gifted with a high sense of justice, that it had men of great genius, that while savage it developed elements of culture such as we cannot at all understand as coexistent with barbarity. This appears to have been to a striking degree the case with the Algonquin or Wabanaki, whose culture, however, while not inferior to that of the Iroquois, was very different from it. It was a little more Eskimo, and very much more Norse. I have here given only the minority of the proofs of resemblance. The majority consists of the genial, hearty, and vigorous Norse feelings which inspire these wonderful and beautiful legends, and the ever-continued evidence that in some utterly strange way both drew their life from the same source.

The Lay of Grotti, or the Mill-Song of the Edda, which tells how the sea became salt, is also known to the Indians. As they give it with the same additions which appear in the common fairy tale, I do not cite this as proving that it came from old Norse narration. But it is remarkable that in all cases the Indian tales and incidents incline to the Eddaic, and that they have much more of it than of modern stories.

The best of these legends have utterly perished. What I have recovered has been from old squaws, from old men, or here and there a clever Indian. The great chroniclers are all dead. But I learn every day that the work of collection should have begun, especially in New England, at least a century ago.

I have recovered, thus far, twenty-seven legends or sagas relative to Glooskap, forming a connected series, and many more of Lox, the rabbit, etc. All of the old Indians can remember when these were sung, and declare that till within fifty years they were preserved with sacred care. I believe that the most ancient and important myths still exist among the Algonquin of the *far* north, and that our historical societies or the government would do well to employ a scholar to collect them. Such as I have been able to get together are now in press, and will soon appear in a volume entitled The Algonquin Legends of New England.[34] Unfortunately, there is perhaps no subject of so little general interest to the American as the Indian,—unless it be, indeed, the art of extirpating him. There was a time when every rock and river, hill and headland, had its legends,—legends stranger, wilder, and sweeter than those of the Rhine or Italy,— and we have suffered them to perish. Indians have made a fairy-land for me of certain places in New England; and there is not a square mile in the country which was not such to them. When the last Indian shall be in his grave, scholars will wonder at the indifference of the "learned" men of these times to such trea-sures as they have allowed to perish. What the world wants is not people to write about what others have gathered as to the Indi-ans, but men to collect directly from them. We want, not theo-ries, but material. *Après nous la théorie.* There are four hundred books on the gypsies, but in all not more than ten which tell us anything new or true about them. There will be speculators in abundance, and better than any now living, through all the ages, but then there will be no Indians.

Notes

1. The influence of Scandinavian traditional literature on Longfellow is developed in Ernest J. Moyne, *Hiawatha and Kalevala. A Study of the Rela-tionship Between Longfellow's "Indian Edda" and the Finnish Epic. Folklore Fellows Communication No. 192* (1963).

2. Henry Rowe Schoolcraft, *The Myth of Hiawatha, and Other Oral Leg-ends, Mythologic and Allegoric, of the North American Indians* (Philadelphia: Lippincott, 1856), p. xvi.

3. Rasmus B. Anderson, *Norse Mythology; or, The Religion of Our Forefa-thers, Containing All the Myths of the Eddas, Systematized and Interpreted* (Chicago: S. C. Griggs, 1875).

4. James Hammond Trumbull (1821-1897) published a number of works on Algonquin languages, especially names.

5. The Rev. S. T. Rand, of Hantsport, New Brunswick, is a Baptist missionary to the Micmac Indians. This gentleman can write twelve languages. Great

credit is due to him for his incredible industry as a scholar in collecting Indian lore, and in recording the Micmac and Malisete languages, as well as for his earnest work as a clergyman. He has now in MS. grammars and dictionaries of these tongues (Leland's note).

6. Mrs. W. Wallace Brown contributed articles dealing with the cultures of Algonquin-speakers in the Northeast to a number of periodicals in the 1890s.

7. Leland probably refers to David Russell Jack, who published a history of St. John, New Brunswick, in 1883.

8. Among Abby L. Alger's several publications on folklore topics is *In Indian Tents: Stories Told by Penobscot, Passamaquoddy, and Micmac Indians* (Boston: Houghton Mifflin, 1897).

9. *Völuspa*, 17, 18 [Leland's note]. The Elder Edda consists of thirty-nine poems. The first is *Völuspa* (The Vala's Prophecy), wherein a prophetess summarizes the history of the universe, as perceived in Norse mythology. The Arabic numerals refer to stanzas in the poem.

10. *Völuspa*, 19 [Leland's note].

11. Younger Edda, chapter ii [Leland's note].

12. Younger Edda, chapter xiii [Leland's note].

13. Younger Edda, chapter viii [Leland's note].

14. Younger Edda, chapter xii [Leland's note].

15. *Hymiskriđa*, 25 [Leland's note]. This is the seventh poem in the Elder Edda, which includes an account of one of the adventures of the hero-god Thor.

16. *Hymiskriđa*, 21 [Leland's note].

17. *Northern Mythology* [Leland's note]. The reference is probably to one of these works by Charles F. Keary: *The Dawn of History: An Introduction to Pre-Historic Study* (New York: Scribners, 1879); or *Outlines of Primitive Belief Among the Indo-European Races* (New York: Scribners, 1882).

18. Henry Rowe Schoolcraft, *Historical and Statistical Information, Respecting the History, Condition and Prospects of the Indian Tribes of the United States: Collected and Prepared Under the Direction of the Bureau of Indian Affairs per Act of Congress of March 3d, 1847* (Philadelphia: Lippincott, 1851–1857), vol. 1 (Leland's note).

19. *Fafnismal*, 1 [Leland's note]. This is the twentieth poem in the Elder Edda, which recounts how the hero Sigurd slew a dragon.

20. George Webbe Dasent, *Popular Tales from the Norse* (New York: D. Appleton, 1859).

21. Benjamin Thorpe, *Yule-Tide Stories. A Collection of Scandinavian and North German Popular Tales and Traditions, from the Swedish, Danish, and German* (London: G. Bell, 1853).

22. B. F. Costa, *The Northmen in Maine: A Critical Examination of Views Expressed in Connection with the Subject* . . . (Albany: J. Munsell, 1870) (Leland's note).

23. Pierre F. X. de Charlevoix, *Histoire et description generale de la Nouvelle France, avec le Journal historique d'un voyage fait par ordre du roi*

dans l'Amérique Septentrionnale (Paris: Chez Pierre-François Giffart, 1744).

24. André Morellet (1727-1819), economist, *philosophe*, and general man of letters, translated into French several works which dealt with North America and its natives, including Thomas Jefferson's *Notes on Virginia*.

25. See Thorpe [Leland's note].

26. *Alvissmal*, 36 [Leland's note]. The tenth poem in the Elder Edda, this recounts how Thor tricked a dwarf.

27. Johannes Scheffer, *The History of Lapland, Wherein Are Shewed the Original Manners, Habits, Marriages, Conjurations, &c. of That People* (Oxford: At the Theatre, 1674) (Leland's note).

28. L. Leouzen Le Duc's translation of the Finnish epic appeared in 1867.

29. *Gudrun II*, 41 [Leland's note]. This is the twenty-sixth poem in the Elder Edda.

30. *Gudrun II*, 24 [Leland's note].

31. For the transcendentalist's ideas regarding Native Americans, see Robert F. Sayre, *Thoreau and the American Indians* (Princeton: Princeton University Press, 1977).

32. See Thorpe, (Leland's note).

33. Horatio Hale, *The Iroquois Book of Rites. Library of Aboriginal American Literature No. 2* (1883).

34. Charles Godfrey Leland, *Algonquin Legends of New England* (Boston: Houghton Mifflin, 1884).

An Evening in Camp Among the Omahas

by Alice Cunningham Fletcher

* * * * *

Although she had demonstrated a philanthropic concern for Native American welfare in her youth, Alice Cunningham Fletcher (1838–1923) was over forty years old before she began to study the Plains and Midwest Indians. In 1881, she paid the first of several visits to the Omaha, Winnebago, Ponca, and Rosebud Sioux of the Central Plains and was introduced to the La Flesche family, highly acculturated Omahas. Her friendship with Bright Eyes La Flesche Tibbles and her brother Francis became instrumental in the ethnographic fieldwork that Fletcher engaged in for the rest of her life. Francis La Flesche, whom she adopted as a son, served as Fletcher's collaborator on many of the papers on Native American culture which she contributed to such series as the Archaeological and Ethnological Papers of the Peabody Museum *and the* Annual Reports of the Bureau of American Ethnology. *In addition to a major monograph on Omaha culture, which appeared in the latter series in 1911, Fletcher and La Flesche produced pioneer-*

SOURCE: *Science,* 6 (31 July 1885), 88–90.

ing studies of Native American music and some extremely thorough descriptions of the ceremonials of the Omaha and neighboring groups. Fletcher's interest in folklore resulted in her being chosen as president of the American Folklore Society for 1905. She was also instrumental in establishing Santa Fe's School of American Research, devoted to the study of the archeology and ethnology of the American Southwest.

Fletcher's access to even the most sacred oral traditions of the people she studied stemmed not only from her close association with the La Flesches, but also from a continuing philanthropic interest in Native Americans. She was especially concerned with the tenuous federal treaties which guaranteed land rights to the Omaha. This accounts for her contributions to formulating the Omaha Allotment Act of 1882, which replaced group ownership of large tracts of tribal land with individual ownership of smaller acreages. Motivated by an enlightened appreciation for the Native American capacity to become "civilized" and by a not-so-enlightened notion that in order to do so Euro-American patterns of property ownership had to be adopted, Fletcher was instrumental in creating a program that had unexpectedly negative consequences. For within a generation after the new land legislation went into effect, most of the individual land allotments had fallen into Euro-American hands. Moreover, the 1882 legislation served as a model for the Dawes Severalty Act of 1887, which extended the program to Native American groups besides the Omaha. During the time of her fieldwork, though, neither Fletcher nor the affected Indians foresaw the results of her misguided beneficence. She was genuinely trusted, more so than many other fieldworkers have been, and was able to document aspects of the traditional cultures that few Euro-Americans had access to.

Her description of a companionable evening among the Omaha, reproduced here, reveals Fletcher's intimacy with the Native Americans, for she appears to be an accepted member of the group. In recording in her description the conversational context for storytelling, Fletcher anticipates the emphasis on context that has characterized folklore studies in the late twentieth century. She also recognizes the significance of narrative forms less glamorous than the myths that fascinated most of her contemporaries in Native American studies. She provides the reader with a slice of narrative life among the Omaha in this record of personal narratives about practical jokes and marvelous animals. Her subjects become human beings, not just repositories of exotic folklore waiting to be tapped by ethnographers.

Material on Fletcher's career is available in Nancy Oestreich Lurie, "Women in Early American Anthropology," in Pioneers of American Anthropology. The Uses of Biography, *ed. June Helm (Seattle: University of Washington Press, 1966), pp. 31–81; and Joan Mark,* Four Anthropologists. An American Science in Its Early Years *(New York: Science History Publications, 1980), pp. 62–95. For a discussion of Fletcher's involvement with the land allotment programs, see Nancy Oestreich Lurie, "The Lady from Boston and the Omaha Indians,"* American West, *3, no. 4 (Fall 1966), 31–33, 80–85. American folklore from various ethnic groups abounds in accounts of remarkable animals. A recently published work on some of these traditions is Richard M. Dorson,* Man and Beast in American Comic Legend *(Bloomington: Indiana University Press, 1982).*

* * * * *

We had just finished out supper in the long conical shadow of the tent; and, the dishes being disposed of, we settled ourselves for the evening chat. While Ma-wa-da-ne was filling his pipe, the other four men disposed themselves comfortably preparatory to the enjoyment of the smoke. Te-me-ha, with her usual industry, had spread upon her lap the brilliant-colored porcupine-quills with which she was embroidering a pair of moccasons, while old Me-pe sat rocking to and fro, and dividing her attentions between the gay-colored quills and the fringe of my wrap. After the ceremonial round of the pipe, I said to the men,—

"You do your share in this embroidery, since you capture the porcupine. Tell me about hunting them."

After a few moments of silence, a smile that broadened into a quiet laugh stole over Ma-wa-da-ne's face; then tightening his blanket about his bent knees, and giving a little shake of the shoulders to settle himself, he began,—

"The porcupine is a great digger, and makes a hole large enough for a man to crawl in. He likes best to live on the brow of a sandy hill, where there are no hollow trees. We hunt them with a long crotched stick. This we thrust into the hole until it strikes the animal; then we twist it to snarl it in the quills and fur. When we think the stick is well caught, we begin to pull gently to draw the animal out. Sometimes the stick loosens, and only the fur comes; then we have to try again, and get a better hold. When the animal is successfully brought to the opening, we look for his head, and give it a sharp, hard stroke with a stick which we carry for the purpose, and so kill him. We then have to skin him, and the women take what they want of the quills."

The smile had faded during this practical talk, but it returned as Ma-wa-da-ne resumed,—

"There were two Poncas who married sisters. The wives were fond of embroidery, and used so many porcupine-quills that it was hard to keep them supplied. One day they were at work, when they discovered they would very soon be out of quills, and each wife began to tease her husband to go hunting for porcupine. The young men were newly married, and wanted to please their wives: so, after enjoying the teasing a while, the men started, each going his own way toward the sand-hills. As one of them sped along, he noted near the top of a hill the large hole of a porcupine. As he approached the opening, he saw that the hole ran through to the opposite side of the hill. He thrust in his stick to search for the lateral burrows, hoping to find the animal. Creeping into the opening himself, while he was thus engaged, the entrance from the opposite side of the hill slowly darkened, and he discerned, to his consternation, the figure of a man. Not knowing whether this apparition might be friend or foe, he concluded to keep perfectly still. While thus watching, he felt a stick gently strike his breast; then, with more force, it began to be twisted. He seized it in his hands, holding it firmly, when the holder of the stick began to pull. The man in the hole allowed his arms to be stretched forward a little, and then dropped the stick. By repeating this operation, the outside hunter's enthusiasm was aroused, and he exclaimed, 'He must be a big fellow!'

"The man in the hole recognized the voice of his brother-in-law, and fear gave place to the desire to play a trick. After baffling the hunter for a while longer, the man crept slowly toward the opening, keeping tight hold of the stick as he advanced, while the hunter kept twisting to make sure of his game. The entrance reached, the make-believe porcupine plunged suddenly forth, exclaiming, 'What do you want?'

"The terror-stricken hunter dropped his stick, his excitement being too great to recognize his relative, and ran crying, 'Grandfather, have mercy on me!' A shout of laughter from the 'grandfather' made the hunter turn, and he, too, joined in the laugh."

When the merriment over the story had subsided, Sin-da-ha-ha remarked,—

"We catch rabbits and raccoons and skunks in the same way. The skunk hears the hunter advancing; and the animal will sometimes come near the entrance of his hole, and pound with his feet, making quite a loud noise, hoping to scare us. When we have thrust in our stick, and twisted it well in the tail, we draw the skunk near the entrance; then we put our arm in the hole, and grasp him tightly around the hind-quarters, pressing the tail firmly against the body; we then draw him out, striking the head quickly to prevent the animal biting. Sometimes we find eight or ten skunks in a single hole, each one of whom will try his charm of drumming on us. Young men like to wear gaiters made of the skunk-skin," turning, as he said this, to the youngest member of the party, to whom I said,—

"You tell me a story now."

In a few moments the young man began,—

"When I was young [here the old men shouted, but the young man with a merry twinkle in his eye went on], "I was very observing. One day I was looking about me, near the slough back of father's, when I noticed a frog hopping very fast. Suddenly he stopped, and picked up a stick three or four inches long, and turned, holding it firmly in his mouth. I saw he was being closely chased by a water-snake who tried to swallow the frog, but the stick in the frog's mouth caught in the jaws of the snake. Several times the snake withdrew, and tried to attack the frog from the rear; but he would jump around, and immediately face the snake again. This happened several times; and at last the snake got tired, and slipped off in the bushes, leaving the frog victorious."

"Pretty good," said Wa-ja-pa. "I'll tell you something. Once late in the fall, Badger and I went hunting along the Loup River. We were afoot. We started up several elk, ran them down, and killed one. While I was butchering, Badger returned to camp for a pony to bring in the meat. After I had skinned the animal, and piled the cuts of meat on the skin, I lay down near by in the tall grass, and fell asleep. I was awakened by the sound of footsteps. Rising cautiously, I saw a large gray wolf standing near the meat. When he espied me, he began to growl, showed his teeth, and all the hair on his back stood up. Taking my gun, I levelled it at him, and shot. He was a fine fellow, and, as he fell, I determined to have his skin at once. It was the work of a few moments to flay him. As I threw his skin to one side, the legs of the wolf began to twitch, and the blood to trickle. In a moment the wolf was on his feet, and walking off without his skin.

"I never have believed in dreams, or the wonderful animals they tell about; but, when I saw that wolf walking away, I felt uncomfortable, but I made up my mind to shoot again. I did so, and he fell, and walked no more."

"When I got there with the pony," put in Badger, "I saw the place where the wolf was skinned, and tracked his steps by his blood to where he lay dead from the second shot."

"I remember hearing," said the young man, "Ou-zu-ga-hae and his brother tell that once, when they were flaying a buffalo-bull they had just shot." Then, turning to me, he said, "You remember, we first cut the skin of a bull down the centre of the back, and take off one-half at a time. Well, when the men had one-half the hide off, up got the buffalo-bull, shaking his head and staggering forward. The frightened brothers ran away as fast as their legs could carry them. The bull went but a little distance, fell, and died. It was some time, however, before the brothers could make up their mind to go back and skin the other side of that animal."

Old Me-pe gave a twitch at my wrap, and said,—

"Can't you tell a story?"

"Yes," I replied, "I will tell you about a black hen I once had. A friend sent me a present of a pair of guinea-fowl. By and by the guinea-hen began to lay; and, as I wanted to be sure to raise some fowl, I put ten of her eggs under a little black hen. She sat patiently for three weeks (the time it takes chickens to hatch), but she had to wait another week for the guinea-chicks. When they came out,—little sleek brown things with yellow legs,—the hen was very happy. But she was soon a troubled hen; for, when she clucked and bustled and scratched for them, they all darted away and hid. In her astonishment, as she stood silently looking for them, they would gradually creep back. Then she would cluck and scratch again, desiring to give them something good to eat; but away would dart the chicks, leaving the hen alone. After several such experiences, the hen evidently thought it was the clucking that scared them: so, as she walked along with her brood, she would scratch, but make no sound. Still, every time she scratched, the chicks shot off and hid. Then she thought a second time, and determined to cluck and call them, but not to scratch. This suited the little guineas, and ever after that the black hen and her ten guineas walked among my flowers and vegetable-garden, doing no damage."

"I have heard white men say hens have no sense," said Wa-ja-pa; "but your hen knew something. Of all the animals, I like the beaver best. He is most like a man. He plans and works and builds."

"You wanted to see an artichoke; there is one," said the young man, tossing the little brown root into my lap. "Yesterday evening I found a field-mouse's nest, and he had stored many artichokes. I went back to-day to get you some; but the mouse had been busy all night, transferring his stores to a secret place. Although I tracked him, it was too bad to rob the little fellow: so I only took one for you." I dropped the root into my purse, where it lies to the present day.

Some Deities and Demons of the Navajos

by Washington Matthews

* * * * *

The first serious student of Navajo culture, Washington Matthews (1843–1905) was already a seasoned ethnologist when he was transferred to the Southwest by the army in the 1880s. Born in Ireland and educated in medicine at the University of Iowa, Matthews had served as post surgeon at Fort Berthold in the Dakota Territory for six years. There he had maintained regular contact with the Hidatsa and published several works on their language and culture, the most important being Ethnography and Philology of the Hidatsa Indians, *which was issued as Miscellaneous Publication No. 7 of the United States Geological and Geographical Survey in 1877. But for the last twenty-five years of his life, Matthews concentrated on the Navajo, laying the foundation for the vast literature about the group that has since accumulated.*

Matthews was especially concerned with the verbal art and religion of the Navajo and was the first to record and present some of their important myth-

SOURCE: *The American Naturalist,* 20 (October 1886), 841–850.

ritual complexes. For example, his presentation of the Mountain Chant *appeared in the* Annual Report of the Bureau of American Ethnology *for 1883–1884, and his treatment of the* Night Chant *was included in the sixth* Memoir of the American Museum of Natural History *in 1902. A translator whose renderings of Navajo oral literature are still well regarded, Matthews also presented a major collection of Navajo narrative folklore in* Navaho Legends, *published in 1897 as the fifth* Memoir of the American Folklore Society. *(This volume provided the basis for Franz Boas's exercise in comparative folklore, included in this anthology.) Matthews was president of the American Folklore Society in 1895.*

The essay by Matthews reproduced here is primarily descriptive. As he retells Navajo myths and details the group's supernaturalism, he provides a running commentary on the material's significance. Although primarily a cultural evolutionist, Matthews exhibits some eclecticism here, for his commentary draws upon the perspectives of several mythographic and anthropological theories of the late nineteenth century. The influence of the cultural evolutionism of Lewis Henry Morgan as refracted through John Wesley Powell is evident in Matthews's identification of Navajo zoolatry as representing a stage in religion universal to all cultures. But his equation of the benevolent goddess Estsanatlehi with Mother Nature recalls the allegorization of comparative mythologists such as Max Müller. His frequent references to analogies between Navajo and various European mythologies are in line with the practice of many of his contemporaries, though Matthews' use of the analogies is for clarification only and not to suggest genetic relationships. In sum, though this essay offers no theoretical innovations, Matthews's thorough description and willingness to employ ideas from various schools of thought represent a healthy trend in his work. He thus emerges as one of the more "scientific" of the "amateur" ethnologists of the period.

A brief note, "Washington Matthews: His Contribution to Plains Anthropology" by Waldo R. Wedel, appears in Plains Anthropologist, 14 *(1969), 175–176. Matthews' work of translation is discussed extensively in Paul G. Zolbrod, "From Performance to Print: Preface to a Native American Text,"* Georgia Review, 35 *(1981), 465–509. Accompanying the essay (on pp. 473–488) are copies of some of Matthews' previously unpublished field notes on the Navajo. Zolbrod's treatment of Matthews precedes his own translated excerpts of the Navajo creation narrative (pp. 510–533).*

* * * * *

The great dry-paintings of the Navajo priests, which I described in a previous number of this journal (October, 1885),[1] illustrate, as I then explained, the visions of the prophets. But the prophets saw the gods in their visions, hence the paintings contain pictures of the gods with all their hieratic belongings. The characters which perform in the great dances conducted by the priests, are representatives of the gods. In the ancient creation-myth of the tribe some descriptions of the gods are incidentally given. In the later myths, recounting the acts of the prophets, more exact descriptions are to be found. It is from such material as this—these oral traditions, these paintings, these ceremonies, with their hundreds of songs and elaborate unchangeable rituals, handed down from generation to generation by word of mouth and by example only—that the student must evolve the nature and scope of their worship.

In one of the great ceremonies, that of the *Kledji Hathal*, or *Gaybechy*, there are, according to the circumstances, from twelve to sixteen different supernatural characters represented. Some of these, like the *gaybaäd*, being a numerous race of divine ones, are represented by many dancers—men masked, dressed and painted to represent gods, bearing sacred wands and talismans and symbolizing in every act and motion something in the lives of their prototypes; living and breathing idols to whom the suppliant prays and offers his sacrifices, well knowing that he addresses with reverent prayers only his own brother or uncle masquerading in the panoply of divinity.

They begin their cosmogony with an already existing world. It is a dim world; there is light, but as yet no sun, moon or stars. It is inhabited, however, by animals or animal gods with the gift of speech and other human attributes, and by some vague gods, probably meteorological personifications, possessing more of the human than the animal character. Just when mortal man first appears on the stage it is difficult or impossible to determine. True there is a first man and a first woman, as there seem to be in nearly all Indian myths; but they do not appear as the progenitors of the race. The time of their beginning is not told, they are coeval with the universe, and they still live in distant lands, but not in the nether world where dead Navajos go; in short, they are immortal and eternal—they are gods. Perhaps we have in them but an extension of the zoölatry of the Indian; as the lower animals have their ancient divine prototypes, so man must have his. With a strange suggestion of the existence of a primeval Darwin, we find in the legend the animals assuming more and more the human character, until the lower worlds which were once peopled only by flying animals are later inhabited by creatures who are spoken of as men. All the beings in the first world are able to fly away on wings from the rising waters of the flood; while in the third and fourth worlds they are obliged to seek protection in the hollow of a great reed, which grows as fast as the rising waters advance and bears the fugitives upward out of danger.

Arrived on this, the fifth, world, men increased and multiplied; but soon various enemies to the human race arose, demons and giants who devoured men, until after a while the race became nearly or quite extinct. Then came the great hero-god *Nagaynezgani,* to whom I will refer later, and killed the demons. After this, by special acts of creation, new men and women were made. Possibly the first of these creations is to be regarded as the first appearance of the true mortal Indian on the earth.

The Navajo has no faith in monogenesis, he believes in several special creations even for his own tribe. The process by which their rude gods made men in the old days was quite an elaborate one, and the Navajo shaman, in relating the myth, does full justice to all the difficulties. A full recital of all the symbolic mummeries that the divine beings thought it necessary to perform in this creative act, would be at best but tedious reading. A brief sketch of their toils must suffice here. They took two ears of corn, one yellow and one white, the former was to become the female of the new couple and the latter the male, and it is in memory of this event, they say, that white corn is called male corn and yellow corn is called female corn to this day among the Navajos. The gods laid these ears on a large dish of pure turquoise, and covered them with embroidered blankets of different colors, and with sacred buckskins, *i.e.,* the skins of deer not slain by weapons but pursued to exhaustion and then, smothered. They were laid with their points towards the east; but before they were laid down they were handed round from one god to another and each god turned them in a different direction, and this is the reason the Navajos to-day never dwell in one locality long, but wander from place to place.

From time to time the benevolent god *Has-chay'-el-thee* peeped under the covering to see how the incubation progressed, and when the ears of corn had assumed the shape of man, the wind-god entered under the blankets to give them life. He went in at the mouth and came out at the tips of the fingers. "Do you not believe this?" said an old shaman to me. "Look then at the tips of your fingers and there you will see *Niyol Bithín*, the trail of the wind." A double helical line is with the Navajos and other tribes a symbol of the whirlwind, and this symbol is impressed on the palmar aspect of the terminal joint of every human finger—satisfactory evidence to the Navajo philosopher that the wind-god, when he gave the breath of life to man, made his exit through the finger-tips. It was the gods of the white rock crystal, who live in Jemez mountain, that furnished these new beings with mind, and the goddess of the grasshoppers gave them voices. Then they rose, but at this moment a dark cloud descended from the heavens and covered them as a garment.

This pair became the ancestors of the *Tsedjinkini*, or people of the dark cliff house, the oldest gens of the present Navajo nation. The story tellers say that they are thus called because the ears of corn of which they were made were taken by the gods from certain dark cliffs. But the archaeologists will be more inclined perhaps to think that the myth refers to some remnants of the ancient inhabitants of the cliff houses of Arizona, enslaved or otherwise adopted by the conquering Navajos.[2] The myths contain several other accounts of the making of men, sometimes the human forms are molded of moistened corn meal, while different ceremonies are performed and by different gods. But always Indian corn, in some form, is the substance used. As this has been from time immemorial the staple food of the Indian, it is not without reason that his gods have chosen it as the proper substance for making men. All Indian flesh is largely derived from maize.

It is a difficult task to determine which one of their gods is the most potent. Religion with them, as with many other peoples, reflects their own social conditions. Their government is a strict democracy. Chiefs are at best but elders, men of temporary and ill-defined influence, whom the youngest men in the tribe may contradict and defy. There is no highest chief of the tribe. Hence their gods, as their men, stand much on a level of equality. But, as you hear the myths recited, you gain the idea that at the present day the sun–god is the most potent, though very far from being omnipotent. In the earlier days of the world, and in the lower worlds, First-man and First-woman, the Coyote and the wind-gods, and, above all, the sea-monster, appear as personages of greater importance.

When the race came up from the fourth world to this, to escape the last flood, two very popular and much beloved persons were chosen to carry the sun and the moon, and all were deeply grieved when they departed for their distant homes beside the great eastern ocean. The sun-god dwells there now in a beautiful house built of turquoise. The sun is a bright shield which the god carries on his arm. The creation myth in one place describes with much exactness how he comes home after his day's work, how he hangs his shining shield on the wall, how it lights up the inside of the vast edifice, how it dangles and sways on the wall, going "tla, tla, tla" until at last the vibration stops and the noise ceases.

But, although they attribute great power to *Chohanoai*, the sun-god, it is not to him that they pray the most. It is not he who takes the greatest interest in human affairs and lends his ear most readily to human supplication. Is it because they naturally suppose the most active sympathy to dwell in the breast of a woman that they have found in a goddess their most beneficent deity? It may be so, but perhaps there are other reasons equally strong, which will presently appear, why *Estsanatlehi*, the goddess of the west, is their most honored divinity. Various accounts are given of her origin. Some versions of the myth declare that she was found by First-man and First-woman; others add that they found her at the foot of a rainbow; but the version which I regard as the most ancient and purest gives an elaborate account of a special creation, by the gods, of two divine women, one of whom was made of a piece of blue turquoise and the other of a piece of white shell, precious substances highly valued among the Navajos. The former, she of the turquoise, was *Estsanatlehi*, the latter, called her sister, was *Yolkai-estsan*, or White-Shell Woman, who figures as a less important character in the myths. This *Estsanatlehi* afterwards became the wife of the sun-god, who like a true savage god is a polygamist. He has a wife in the east and another in the west; but *Estsanatlehi*, the goddess of the west, is beloved. She embodies attributes of various queens of heaven, of various wives of the highest deities which appear in a hundred mythologies. She has, however, none of the low jealousy and petty spite of her sister Juno; she reminds one more of the Scandinavian Frigga. If one's opinions of the Indian is based on the popular accounts of their excessive cruelty, he will marvel that such an embodiment of benevolence can have a place in their mythology. If his estimate of the social status of the Indian woman is the one most common in current literature—for she is usually represented as the over-worked slave of a pitiless master—he will marvel that to a female should be assigned such a high place among the gods. But an intimate observance of this people demonstrates that she may fairly represent the Navajo matron at her best.

The name *Estsanatlehi* signifies the woman who changes or rejuvenates, and it is said of her that she never remains in one state, but that she grows to be an old woman, and in the course of time, at will, she becomes a young girl again, and so passes on through an endless cycle of lives, changing but never dying. In the light of this narration we see her as none other than our own Mother Nature, the goddess of the changing year, with its youth of spring, its middle age of summer, its senility of autumn, growing old only to become young again. The deity of fruitful nature is, it will be admitted, fitly a goddess, and fitly also the wife of the sun, to whose potent influence she owes her fertility. Our Aryan forefathers never conceived a more consistent myth than this. But why is she the goddess of the west? Let it be remembered that the Navajo land lies to the west of the continental divide, and slopes toward the setting sun. The Pacific, not the Atlantic, is the reservoir from which it draws its scanty moisture. From the west, not from the east, come the storm-clouds of the summer and the soft thawing breezes of the spring. Hence naturally this beneficent goddess, who loves her Navajo children so well, dwells in the western ocean, and from there dispenses her bounty. While she still lived in the Navajo land, and long before she journeyed to the west, she was blessed with a child whose father was the sun, at the same time her sister bore a child whose father was a water-fall, or, as some versions make it, a rain-storm. These boys were *Nagaynezgani* and *Thóbadji-scheni*. One version of the myth says they were both children of *Estsanatlehi* and the sun. They are called brothers throughout the myth; but according to the Indian system of relationship their mothers being sisters constitutes them brethren as well if they were children of one mother.

These are the sacred brothers, the Dioscuri, who figure in the myths and legends of so many races not only of this continent but of the old world as well. Comparative mythologists usually regard the sacred brothers as myths of night and day, of light and darkness. Max Müller regards this as the proper interpretation of the Asvinau of India, but Mr. Talboys Wheeler, in his History of India, says they are "apparently a personification of light and moisture," and this I believe to be the true explanation of the Navajo myth, for the name *Thobajischeni* signifies Kinsman of the Waters, and the portion of the myth which refers to his paternity strengthens this theory.[3]

Both of the brothers receive homage as gods of battle, but *Nagaynezgani* is regarded as the more potent of the two. It is to these that men offer their sacrifices and prayers when they are about to go on the war-path. The sacrifices may be offered anywhere, but their special shrine is at *Tho-yet'-li*, a place at the junction of two rivers in the valley of the San Juan, somewhere in what is now the Territory of Utah. Hither it is said they went to dwell when their mission on this earth was done, when they had slain all the more powerful demons and left man with no worse enemy in the world than his own kind. Here it is said they still dwell, and here their reflection is still to be seen on the waters of the San Juan river. This part of the myth doubtless refers to some natural phenomenon observable at this point, but I know not what it is, for I have never visited *Thoyetli*. If the Navajo would have special fortune in some war, he must make a pilgrimage to the far *Thoyetli* and lay there the sacred cigarettes for the gods to smoke.

Nagaynezgani is distinctly an Indian war-god, and the god of an especially shrewd and crafty tribe even among Indians. Like Thor he is the terror of evil spirits, but unlike Thor the evil spirits never outwit him. He too has the thunder-bolts for weapons, but he has not an unlimited supply of them. He must husband them, even as the Indian husbands his well-made arrows. His chief weapon is a great stone knife; but he depends not so much on his weapons as on his presence of mind, his craftiness, his powers of dissimulation and, above all, on his "medicine." He is no coward, no vacillator, once sped on his journey he never returns unsuccessful; but in accomplishing his purpose he exhibits more the character of the cunning Ulysses than of the bold Hercules.

It is not, however, the warriors alone who pray to him, he is appealed to by all classes of suppliants as well, and there are songs in his honor in all the rituals that I have yet learned. Here is one of the songs taken from the great rite of the *Zilyidji Hathal* or Mountain Chant.[4] It is a literal translation. I have only chosen such English forms and phrases as would represent, to some extent, the excellent rhythm of the original Navajo song, which is a monologue on the part of the god:

> I am the slayer of the alien gods,
> > I walk afar;
> From out the hole that passes through the sky,
> > I walk afar;
> My enemies assail me, but in vain,
> > I walk afar;
> My foes of all sorts stand in fear of me,
> > I walk afar;
> I go on errands of a dangerous kind,
> > I walk afar;
> Upon the highest of the mountain peaks,
> > I walk afar.

In the Navajo language all not of their own or cognate tribe are called *ana*, or *na*, *i.e.*, foreigners or aliens. The minor gods or genii are called *yay* or *gay*. Hence *anagay*, or alien gods, is a term applied to all those supernatural beings who once devoured and harassed mankind. *Nezga* means to kill by violence, to slay, and thus we have *Nagaynezgani*, Slayer of the Alien Gods, a name which has its very close analogue in that of Jack the Giant Killer. His mission in life was to destroy these alien gods, which he did with a few exceptions, notable among which were the gods of cold, hunger and old age. These creatures pleaded so well for their lives, and demonstrated so well to the hero that they were not unmixed evils, that they were spared to still torment man. As a specimen of the Navajo way of reasoning, I will relate his adventure with *Sakaz'-estsan'*, the Cold-woman:

When he returned from his adventure with Old-age, he said to his mother, "Tell me where the Cold-woman dwells," she did not answer him; four times he repeated the question, when she replied, "You have done enough, my son. Seek to slay no more." But the wind-god whispered in his ear, "She dwells on the summit of *Depentsa*" (the San Juan mountains). So he set forth and traveled to the north and wandered around over the highest peaks of the mountains until he, at length, encountered a wrinkled old woman sitting nearly naked on a bed of snow. She had neither food, fire nor shelter, her eyes streamed tears, she shivered constantly and her teeth chattered so that she could scarcely talk. He knew at once that she was *Sakaz-estsan*. A vast crowd of snow-buntings flitted around her. These were the couriers whom she was accustomed to send forth to announce the coming of storms. They were the spies who told her what was going on in the outer world. As he approached her he said, "I have come on a cruel errand. I have come to kill you that man may suffer no more torture from you, or die at your hands." "You may kill me if you will," she chattered, "but man will be worse off when I am dead than he is now; for when I die it will be always hot, and the land will dry up, and the springs will cease to flow, and men will die of heat and thirst. You will do better if you let me live." So he lowered the arm he had raised to kill her, and reflected a moment. "Grandmother, you speak the truth," he said at last; "you shall live," and he returned to his mother's dwelling without a trophy.

His journeys in which he failed to listen to the voice of mercy are, however, much more numerous than those in which he relented, and, had I space to relate them, the reader would hear of many myths with which he is already familiar in tales of our own antiquity and in the folk-lore of modern Europeans. Many characters with whom he has become acquainted in the pages of Grimm he would meet again, but dressed in buckskin and disguised in paint and feathers.

The ancestral prairie wolf, the apotheosized coyote, is an important figure in their mythology, as he is in the mythologies of all our aborigines to whom the coyote was known, and in their earlier fabulous ages, particularly when the Navajos dwelt in the lower worlds, he was a potent god. Closely allied to the fox in nature, he has so many mythic similarities to the reynard of European folk-lore, that we can not but suspect that our own distant ancestors once worshipped the fox-god. In Arizona, as in Europe, he always appears as a cunning, deceitful mischief-maker.

It was the Coyote who brought about the expulsion of the people from the lower world. He stole the young of *Ticholtsodi*, the sea-monster, and the latter in revenge, or in order to rescue the lost ones, caused the great floods which drove all up to the surface of this earth. It is Coyote who is responsible for the present irregular position of the stars. He usually had the laugh on his side as the result of his trickeries, but he was not always so fortunate.

Once he went out hunting with his father-in-law, and they rested at night on the top of a rugged mountain where they lit their camp-fire and cooked some meat for supper. As they were lying down to sleep Coyote said to his companion, "This hill is called the Hill of the Burned Moccasins." As the old man had never heard of this extraordinary name before, he could not help wondering at it until the wind-god whispered in his ear, "Change your moccasins;" so before he fell asleep he took the Coyote's moccasins and put them under his own head, while he put his moccasins in place of the Coyote's. Late in the night the Coyote rose softly, took the moccasins from under the old man's head and buried them in the hot embers. When they woke in the morning the old man pretended to look in vain for his lost moccasins, "Ah!" said Coyote, "You have forgotten that this is the Hill of the Burned Moccasins." "Oh! there they are under your head," said the elder; "I thank you, my son-in-law, for taking such good care of them." "Yes," said Coyote, "I have taken care of them for you; but the ground is so nice and soft on this mountain I think I shall prefer to go barefoot to-day."

Not only is the prairie-wolf a god, but nearly every animal in the Navajo land has its own apotheosized prototype, its generic ancestral god. All of these gods have their special place in the mythology of this people. Many of them have to this day special sacrifices proper to them which are prepared in the medicine lodge and offered according to established ritual. The Navajos then are zoölaters; that is, in common with all the still pagan aboriginal races of our continent, they worship the lower animals; or perhaps it would be more proper to say they worship zoömorphic gods. A degraded form of worship no doubt many of my readers deem it; but it should be remembered that zoölatry was common to all the races of antiquity, and that a marked remnant of it is our own heritage to this day.

Besides all these gods, the Navajos have a host of local divinities so numerous that I never hope to get a complete list of them. The Navajo land is, or was, bounded by four great mountains, Jemez on the east, San Mateo on the south, San Francisco on the west and San Juan on the north. The resident deities of these great peaks seem to receive more honor than any other place-gods, but the presiding genii of other mountains, rocks and cañons are not neglected by the devout. No people are more ingenious than our American aborigines in framing fanciful stories of locality. The Navajos particularly delight in this form of myth. Their land abounds in strange geologic formations, in rocks fancifully sculptured by the elements, and it abounds equally in myths accounting for these features.

Some recent writers have stated that our American Indians as a rule offer prayer and sacrifice only to evil spirits, believing that time is wasted in endeavoring to gain the favor of beings who are always benevolent. Among the Navajos, at least, I can venture to assert that such is not the case. The gods seem to receive worship in proportion to their reputation for good-will towards men. Indeed, according to the Navajo's mythology, the evil gods have nearly all been destroyed, and his worst conceptions of malevolence are altogether things of the past.

Notes

1. "Mythic Dry Paintings of the Navajos," *The American Naturalist*, 19 (October 1885), 931-939.
2. Cf. the Paiute traditions about previous inhabitants of their territory, shown to have some historical value in David M. Pendergast and Clement W. Meighan, "Folk Traditions as Historical Fact: A Paiute Example," *Journal of American Folklore*, 72 (1959), 128-133.
3. I have been unable to identify the work by Talboys Wheeler to which Matthews refers.
4. Matthews was apparently the first to record and publish this important myth-ritual complex of the Navajo. See "The Mountain Chant. A Navajo Ceremony" in the *Annual Report of the Bureau of Ethnology* for 1883-1884.

The Borrowed Myths of America

by Stephen D. Peet

* * * * *

When Stephen Denison Peet (1831–1914) began publication of the Ameri-can Antiquarian and Oriental Journal *in 1878, he launched what be-came this country's first successful ethnological periodical. Trained at Yale Divinity School and Andover Theological Seminary, Peet had been ordained as a Congregational minister in 1855, and managed to combine an active career in the clergy with abiding interests in North American ethnology. He was primarily interested in the archeology of the Moundbuilders of the Ohio and Mississippi Valleys and of Central America, but his speculations touched on many aspects of Native American studies, including oral litera-ture. He contributed many essays to his own journal and produced a monu-mental five-volume study,* Prehistoric America *(Chicago: Office of the American Antiquarian, 1890–1905). Peet showed a particular interest in the*

SOURCE: *American Antiquarian and Oriental Journal,* 14 (1892), 336–343. I have silently corrected a number of what are obviously typographical errors in this essay.

symbolism of Native American artifacts and advocated the theory of diffusion to explain cross-cultural similarities in these symbols. Thus he was much less committed to cultural evolutionism, which usually explains such similarities by positing independent origins, than were many of his contemporaries. However, his diffusionist ideas often seem to rely on data as tenuous as that used to support the evolutionists' notion that cultures went through identical stages as they progressed from primitivism to civilization.

Peet's major achievement was his journal. Most of the major figures in Native American studies of the era contributed to it, and it served as the first continuing forum for the exchange of their ideas. Although it was eventually superseded by the American Anthropologist *and the* Journal American Folklore, *both of which began publication a decade later, the* American Antiquarian and Oriental Journal *did not cease publication until the death of its founder.*

In the essay reproduced here, Peet applies his diffusionist perspective to the deluge myth in the New World. He plays upon a familiar theme in all of his writings about Native American mythology: the similarity of American Indian sacred oral narratives to those of European and Asian cultures, a situation which could indicate pre-Columbian contact. As a proponent of diffusionism, Peet was more grandiose in his conclusions and less meticulous in his methodology than like-minded anthropologists such as Franz Boas, but his perspective represents a refreshing departure from the evolutionary emphasis that dominated his times.

* * * * *

We have spoken in a previous number of the prevalence of the "deluge myth" in various parts of America,[1] and have intimated that the wide distribution of this tradition is proof that it had come in some way from another continent, and is in itself an indication of pre-Columbian contact. Prof. E. B. Tylor, however, takes the ground that all such deluge myths can be ascribed to the influence of the missionaries, and that they were all post-Columbian in their origin. He maintains that many of them are owing to the misinterpretation of the picture writings and other traditions of the natives. To illustrate: The migration myth of the Aztecs has been preserved in a kind of picture writing. In part of this picture there may be seen a curved mountain, which arises from a lake; on either side of the mountain crowned heads; beneath it is a boat; above it a tree. In the tree a bird; from the mouth of the bird issue a number of symbols, resembling "commas," which might be taken for tongues. Fifteen human forms are in front of the bird, each one with a totem above his head. This part of the picture has been interpreted as representing the Ark, Noah and his wife, and Mt. Ararat, the confusion of tongues and the dispersion of the races. This interpretation Dr. Tylor thinks entirely gratuitous, and maintains that the picture contains no reference to traditions which prevailed among the civilized races, but in reality represents the history of the immigration of the Aztecs. It was the popular tradition among the Aztecs that their starting place was an island in a lake, and that the voice of a bird started them on their wanderings; so a bird with the usual symbols of speech was drawn above the mountain.[2]

Mr. H. H. Bancroft also says that not one of the earliest writers on Mexican mythology, those who were familiar with the old traditions at the time of the conquest, seem to have known this tradition. "A careful comparison of the passages (in the later writers) will show that the escape of the Ancon and his wife by a boat from the deluge, and of the distribution by a bird of different languages to their descendants, rest upon the interpretation of the Aztec paintings."[3] He intimates that the tradition which connects the great divinity of the Toltecs—the white god, who was called Quetzalcoatl—with the pyramid at Cholula, came from the same source. The story about the departure of this god belongs to the ancient Toltec period, which preceded the Aztec, and the person that represented the national god of the Toltecs, who had, like all the national gods of the Americans, a personified nature worship as a basis, but the historical tradition fastened itself upon the pyramid because of the resemblance of the divinity to the ancient Noah.

There is a plausibility about this view which becomes more apparent as we examine the myths of the civilized races. In these myths we find allusions, not only to "the mountain," "the boat," "the bird," "the gift of tongues," and other events of the "flood," but we find also many allusions to the "creation," with the same figures which are used in the Scriptures. To illustrate: from the fragments of the Chimalpopoca manuscript we learn that the Creator produced his work in successive epochs under one sign (Tochtli) the earth was created, in another (Acalt) the firmament, in the third (Tecpatl) the animals; on the seventh (Checatl) man was made out of ashes or dust, by that mysterious personage or divinity (Quetzalcoatl). This manuscript is supposed to be prehistoric, although, according to Bancroft, it shows traces of Christian influence and is by him ascribed to the Toltec School.[4] Still it is regarded as "one of the most authentic accounts of such matters, extant." There is also the tradition of giants upon the earth. We are told by Boturini[5] that the first age or sun was called the "Sun of the water;" it was ended by a tremendous flood, in which every living thing perished except a man and woman of the "great race." The second age was called the "Sun of the earth"—giants or Quinames were the only inhabitants of the world. The third age, the "Sun of the air," was ended by tempests and hurricanes. The fourth age is the present, and belongs to the "Sun of fire." It is to be ended by conflagration. Another Mexican version is that, in the "age of water the great flood occurred, and the inhabitants were turned into fishes and only one man and woman escaped." The man's name was Coxcox. They saved themselves in the hollow trunk of a bald cypress. They grounded their "ark" on the peak of Colhuacan, the "Ararat" of Mexico. Their children were born dumb, but a "dove" came and gave them tongues. A Michoachan tradition has the name of Tezpi as a substitute for Noah. When the waters began to subside he sent out a vulture, but the vulture fed upon carcasses. Then Tezpi sent out other birds, and among them a humming bird. The humming bird found the earth covered with new verdure and returned to its old refuge bearing green leaves. There is another version which fastens upon the pyramid of Cholula. According to this the world was inhabited by giants; some of these were changed to fishes, but seven brothers enclosed themselves in seven caves. When the waters were assuaged one of these, surnamed the "Architect," began to build an artificial mountain, but the anger of the "gods" was aroused. As the pyramid slowly rose toward the clouds they launched their fire upon the builders and the work was stopped. The half finished pyramid still remains, dedicated to Quetzalcoatl, the god of the sun. According to another extract of this Chimalpopaca manuscript, the god Titlacahuan warned the man, Nata and his wife Nena, saying hollow out for yourselves a great cypress in which you shall enter and he "shut them in." The Miztecs have a legend which they were accustomed to depict in their primitive scrolls. In the year and in the days of obscurity and darkness before the days of the years were, when the world was in great darkness and chaos when the earth was covered with water, and there was nothing but mud and slime on the face of the earth, behold, a god became visible named the deer, and surnamed the "lion snake," and a beautiful goddess also called the deer and surnamed the "tiger snake." The palace of the gods was on a mountain, in the province of Mizteca Alta. It was called the "palace of Heaven." Two sons were born to them, very handsome and learned. The brothers made to themselves a "garden," in which they put many trees, flowers, roses and odorous herbs. They fixed themselves in this garden to dress it and to keep it, watering the trees and the plants and the odorous herbs, multiplying them, and burning incense in censors of clay, to the "gods"—their father and mother. But there came a great deluge afterward, wherein perished many sons and daughters that had been born to the gods, but when the deluge had passed the human race was restored as at first. In Nicaragua it was believed that ages ago the world was destroyed by a flood and that the most of mankind perished. In the Papago country, lying south of the Gila, there is a tradition that the "Great Spirit" made the earth and all other things, but when he came to make man he descended from heaven and took clay, such as the potters use, from which he made the hero god, Montezuma, and afterward the Indian tribes in their order. He made them all brethren; men and beasts talked together in common language, but a great flood destroyed all flesh, Montezuma and his friend, the Coyote, alone escaping. This Montezuma afterward hardened his heart and set about building a house that should "reach up to heaven." Already it had attained a great height, when the Great Spirit launched his thunder and laid its glory in ruins. This legend accounts for the connection of the name of Montezuma with ancient buildings in the mythology of the Gila Valley, and perhaps, also for the connection of the same name with the various ruins in Arizona and New Mexico. The legendary adventures of this hero are narrated by the natives in all this region.[6]

We have thus given nearly all the deluge myths which have been presented by the Mexicans, and would ask whether there was not a good reason for the interpreting, the "picture writing" of the Aztecs, as having reference to the same event. The picture refers to an event which had occurred at the very earliest date of history, the place where it is located being often the starting point for the tribe or nation. May it not be that the picture itself embodied this tradition, and that it represented the starting point of the Aztecs, exactly as their traditions represent the starting point of other tribes? So we maintain that the correspondence between the verbal traditions of the wild tribes and the written or recorded traditions of the civilized peoples proves that the deluge myth was at the bottom of both.

Let us look at some of the traditions. Mount Shasta, with the wigwam of the great divinity. The smoke was formerly seen curling above it. The Great Spirit stepped from cloud to cloud down the great ice pile, and planted the first trees near the edge. He blew upon the leaves and the leaves became birds. He broke sticks in pieces and they became fishes and animals. The sun melted the ice and they became rivers. The daughter of the Great Spirit looked out of the wigwam and was so curious at the sight that she flew away to the earth, and mingled with the great bears, and became Eve, the mother of the human race. The Papagoes have the tradition that a great flood destroyed all flesh, but Montezuma and a Coyote escaped. Montezuma was forewarned and kept his canoe ready on the topmost summit of Santa Rosa. The Coyote prepared an ark out of cane, and the two sailed over the waters and repopulated the world. In Northern California the tradition of the flood is connected with Tahoe. Lake Tahoe was caused by an earthquake. A great wave swept over the land; the Sierra Mountains were formed; the inhabitants fled to a temple tower, which rose like a dome above the lake; but the divinity thrust them like pebbles into a cave and keeps them there until another earthquake shall occur.

The Californians tell of a great flood which covered the earth, with the exception of Mount Diablo and Reed Peak. The Coyote escaped to the peak and survived the flood. At that time the Sacramento and San Joaquin began to find their way to the Pacific. Thus we see that the myth is localized in connection with nearly every mountain, river and lake. The springs on the Pacific coast are also localized among the former tribes of the Atlantic coast. Now the inquiry arises, would a tradition which had been introduced by the missionaries at different times, and received by the converts to Christianity, and so altogether modern, have been likely to spread so extensively among the pagan tribes and to have been so thoroughly adopted by them as an integral part of their history. It is to be noticed that the tradition, as localized by the pagan tribes, always refers to an event which occurred at the very earliest date of history and has reference to the starting point or original home of the tribes. The only exception to this is the one that relates to the pyramid of Cholula, this having been the last place of refuge, rather than the starting point of the Toltec race. In the picture writing of the Aztecs, the starting point is like that of other tribes. It is represented as a mountain beside a lake. After the departure from the mountain to the various points of the immigration route the same symbol of the mountain and the tree continues. This correspondence between the verbal and the written, or in other words, the traditionary and recorded, proves that the story must have existed in pre-Columbian times, and perhaps was known by the Aztec before they commenced their wanderings.

It is to be noticed further that the imagery which is used by the pagan tribes wherever any is used in repeating the story of the deluge is always such as would be natural to them. The wild hunters of the north used the figure of the canoe, the island and the lake; the semi-civilized, in the interior, used the figure of the cave, the mountain, the auroya; the civilized tribes of the southwest used the figure of the boat, the curved mountain, the symbol of speech, the temple and the pyramid. This might have occurred if the tradition was modern, for the story, when filtered through the native minds, would naturally receive the tinge of their own thoughts and would vary acccording to different habits, conceptions and surroundings of the people. We must remember, however, that while there is a great difference between the versions of the story, yet the same elements remain—the boat, the mountain, the ancient divinity who was the first ancestor, the flood, the survival from the flood and the repeopling of the land.

These elements or images seem to have spread as far as the story of the deluge itself. They are evidently prehistoric in their character and are associated with the prehistoric cultus. They have been regarded as autochthonous, but taken in connection with the deluge story, they furnish an additional evidence of contact with historic countries. There are also symbols of the cross, the suastika, the serpent, the horse-shoe, the hand, the eye, the spectacle ornament, the loop, the turreted figure, the bird, the Nile key. These symbols are the most prevalent in Oriental countries, and the most widespread in this country. These symbols are, indeed, associated with the various forms of nature worship and are rarely with the tradition of the deluge. In this we recognize a contrast. The water cult in this country was, like that of Great Britain, a pre-historic system. It always was localized at some spring and was preserved by the spring into historic times. There are many springs in America which were regarded as sacred by the people in pre-historic times. They are found in the Mound-builders' territory, in the regions of the Pueblos, among the wild tribes and among the civilized races.

The largest number of symbolic works were placed near streams and fountains, indicating that the use of waters was essential to religious ceremony. The traditions linger about many of these springs, some of which are interesting and very suggestive. No animal may partake of the sacred waters of the spring. The most ancient vessels were kept on the wall of the spring. The frog, the rattlesnake and tortoise were depicted upon these and were sacred to the patron of the spring. The Shoshones have a spring whose origin they explain as follows:

Wankanaga was the father of the Shoshones and the Comanches. He arose from a cloud as a white-haired Indian, with his ponderous club in his hand and with his totem on his breast and struck a rock with his club and caused it to burst forth with bubbling water. In Sitka they had a light and fire, but no fresh water, as Kanuph kept it all in his well. Yehl, the great divinity, visited this personage and managed to steal the water and scattered it in drops over the land, and each one became a spring.

The question arises, how came these symbolic works to be so connected with springs and with water courses. Shall we say that the symbols of nature worship originated in this country and that they are associated with the springs according to the law of parallel development. In England sacred springs are regarded as proving that the water cult was introduced, and localized, and afterwards perpetuated into historic times. M. Lawrence Gomme has treated of this in his book, called "Ethnology in Folk Lore."[7] He maintains that the localizing of such myths as relate to the water cult, stone worship and demons, preceded the tribal myths, and that they were pre-historic or pre-Aryan in their origin; that the pin wells, rag wells, and other sacred springs were the same as those that were haunted by the rain gods and water divinities. The appearance of river gods, sea serpents, hill deities and well worship was nearly universal, which was contemporaneous with the area of the megalithic monument.

In this country the localizing of the myth and the water cult may also have preceded the tribal myth, though the presence of symbols near the spring would show that the cult was transmitted. The "rain gods" and the "nature powers" were associated with the springs, and there were offerings to the water divinities exactly as in Great Britain during pre-Aryan times. The association of the story of the deluge with some of these springs may be merely accidental, yet the presence of the symbols known in historic countries, near some of the springs, would render it probable that the water cult and the deluge myth were introduced, perhaps, at the same time, and perhaps in the same countries.

The story of the deluge prevailed among the eastern tribes of Indians, the Algonkins, the Sioux, the Athabascans, the Crees, and the Cherokees. In these the mountain and tree, the lake, the raft or canoe, are prominent, and the ancient Noah appears as a divinity, under different figures and names. There is generally an animal, either a muskrat, a loon, a diver duck, or otter, which serves the behests of the chief divinity, in bringing up the soil from below and making a new earth. The story has been localized. A rock at the Mackinaw, another on the Ottawa River, a beach at Grand Traverse Bay, and a mountain on Thunder Bay are selected as the spot where the event occurred. The falls of Sault St. Marie are the scene of another tradition—that of the Great Beaver, who opened the dams and let out the water,—a tradition which reminds us of one which is common in Great Britain, which is contained in Faber's History of Idolatry.[8]

Ewbank[9] speaks of the High Priest of the Zuni, whose special duty was to officiate before the water deities. He seeks for some sacred spot where he plants sticks in a circle adorned with feathers and threads, and dedicates them to the divinities of water, such as frogs, snakes and turtles; these embody his invocation for rain. They are, in fact, snares for the spirit of the "water divinity". Near these "sacred circles" there are wooden columns covered with such symbols as the crescent, the Nile key and the suastika. These symbols remind us of the nations of the east, but the custom is peculiar to the Zunis, among whom there is a tradition in reference to the Montezuma as having been the divinity of the springs and the preserver of the people. The myth bearer is contained in the legendary rock . . . . This rock perpetuates the tradition of the flood and the pair which was sacrificed to appease the water divinity. The ruins of an ancient town upon a high mesa are said to be the place to which the Zuni escaped. A horizontal vein in the rocks marks the line of high water.

Both the Moquis and Zunis have a custom of bringing water from a sacred lake to their pueblo before they commenced their rain-dance.[10] They have one who represents a "fire-god" during these rain-dances. There is another singular custom which reminds us of the one described by Catlin as common among the Mandans.[11] A man comes from the west and approaches the pueblo and finally enters the estufa, while he remains. Food is handed down to him. He may represent the ancient man, possibly the Noah of the Zunis. There is a rock spring near Williams River, within which is a pool of water and a crystal stream flowing from it. The rock is covered with pictographs. There are figures cut upon the rock near Arch spring near Zuni. There seems to be a similarity between them and the inscriptions near Rocky Dell Creek. There is a story which is told of the sudden deluge which swept over the country, destroying all men and beasts. The ruins of an ancient town upon a high mesa are said to be the place to which the Zuni escaped, and a yellowish horizontal vein mark the line of high water. The Zunis have pottery vessels in the shape of the Rocky mountain goat or sheep, and rude statuettes made from pottery which may be called idols. Thus we see that the worship of fountains or well-worship was as common as in the Eastern hemisphere.

Notes

1. Stephen D. Peet, "Water Cult and the Deluge Myth," *American Antiquarian and Oriental Journal*, 13 (1891), 352–360.

2. Sir Edward Burnett Tylor (1832–1917), often considered the founding father of modern anthropological theory, influenced many of the students of American Indian folklore during the late nineteenth century, including several represented in this antholoy.

3. See *The Works of Hubert Howe Bancroft. The Native Races*, 5 volumes (San Francisco: History Company, 1886). I have been unable to identify precisely where this passage may be found in these volumes.

4. See Bancroft's *Native Races*, Vol. II, p. 547; Vol. II, p. 69 [Peet's note].

5. Lorenzo Benaducci Boturini (c. 1702–1750) wrote *Idea de Una Nueva Historia General de la America Septentrional* (Madrid: J. de Zuñiga, 1746).

6. For an interesting perspective on this folk figure, see Adolph F. Bandelier, "The 'Montezuma' of the Pueblo Indians," *American Anthropologist*, o. s. 5 (1892), 318–326 (reprinted in this collection).

7. George Laurence Gomme, *Ethnology in Folklore* (New York: D. Appleton, 1892).

8. Presumably, the reference is to George Stanley Faber, *The Origin of Pagan Idolatry Ascertained from Historical Testimony and Circumstantial Evidence* (London: F. and C. Rivingtons, 1816).

9. Most likely, Peet means Thomas Ewbank (1792–1870), an inventor of some note, who was one of the founders of the American Ethnological Society. He had done some work on Native American pictographs and petroglyphs.

10. See *Studies of the Ceremonies of the Moquis*, by Walter Fewkes [Peet's note]. Jesse Walter Fewkes (1850–1930), who became fourth director of the Bureau of American Ethnology in 1918, published over forty articles on the ethnology and archeology of the Hopi.

11. George Catlin, *O-Kee-Pa: A Religious Ceremony; and Other Customs of the Mandans* (London: Trübner, 1867).

Development of a Pawnee Myth

by George Bird Grinnell

* * * * *

One of the leading conservationists in American history, George Bird Grinnell (1849–1938) accumulated an impressive record in the still continuing campaign to preserve North America's wildlife and other natural resources. After graduation from Yale in 1870, he made his first trip to the West on a fossil-hunting expedition. He then served as naturalist for General George A. Custer's survey of the South Dakota Black Hills in 1874 and studied the mammals and birds of Yellowstone Park in 1875. He received his Ph.D. from Yale in 1880 and became editor and principal owner of Forest and Stream, *a sportsmen's periodical. Grinnell was instrumental in founding the Audubon Society in 1886 and helped to plan the New York Zoological Gardens. An avid supporter of the National Park system, he was largely responsible for the establishment of Glacier National Park.*

Beginning with his first trip to the West, Grinnell developed an interest in the Native American groups of the plains. Through years of interaction with

SOURCE: *Journal of American Folklore*, 5 (1892), 127–134.

them, he became an authority on the Pawnee, Blackfoot, and Cheyenne and published many books and articles, primarily descriptive, about their cultures. He advised Presidents Grover Cleveland and Theodore Roosevelt on American Indian affairs and was a dedicated spokesman for Indian causes. His published work on Native Americans deals with many facets of their cultures, including three important collections of oral narratives: Pawnee Hero Stories and Folk-Tales with Notes on the Origin, Customs and Character of the Pawnee People *(New York: Forest and Stream, 1889);* Blackfoot Lodge Tales. The Story of a Prairie People *(New York: Scribners, 1892); and* By Cheyenne Campfires *(New Haven: Yale University Press, 1926). Since he saw himself not as a scholar but as a recorder of Indian cultural traditions that were fast disappearing, Grinnell's books present myths, legends, and folktales unadorned by theoretical apparatus. Dee Brown has edited selections from the three collections in* Pawnee, Blackfoot, and Cheyenee. History and Folklore of the Plains from the Writings of George Bird Grinnell *(New York: Scribners, 1961).*

In the article reprinted here Grinnell's speculations about the origin of a Pawnee myth draw upon several schools of folklore theory. As with many other students of Native American cultures during the late 1800s, Grinnell's ideas were shaped by cultural evolutionism, which posited that folklore was a "survival" from earlier stages in a culture's development. Consequently, Grinnell suggests that the story of Ti-Kē-Wá-Kūsh *describes a cultural practice long abandoned by the Pawnee but more recently employed by the Blackfoot, their more primitive neighbors to the north. Grinnell's analysis, though, also seems to have been influenced by the "mirror-of-culture" approach to oral literature developed by Henry Rink in his studies of the Greenland Eskimo— see* Tales and Traditions of the Eskimo with a Sketch of Their Habits, Religion, Language and Other Peculiarities, *ed. Robert Brown (Edinburgh: William Blackwood, 1875)—and utilized by Franz Boas in* Tsimshian Mythology, *which appeared in the* Annual Report of the Bureau of American Ethnology *for 1909–1910, and in* Kwakiutl Culture as Reflected in Mythology, *the twenty-eighth* Memoir of the American Folklore Society *(1935). Their approach avers that the analyst can reconstruct a culture based upon knowledge obtained through its myths and legends. In a sense, Grinnell seems to accept the basic assumption of the approach, that folklore reflects culture, bur realizes that such reflection becomes distorted when the cultural forms are no longer current among the people who tell about them.*

Another apparent influence on Grinnell's thinking is euhemerism, perhaps the oldest interpretive approach to the study of mythology. Named for a Sicilian mythographer of the second century B. C. who thought that the classical gods were real historical personages who had become deified over the passage of centuries since they had actually lived, euhemerism, simply stated, assumes that myths have a historical basis which has been buried beneath the imaginative fantasies of storytellers. The idea has pervaded mythographic study since the time of Euhemerus. For example, the early twentieth-century literary historians Hector and Nora Chadwick suggested that the hero myths of various Eurasian cultures (such as that of Odysseus among the Greeks, of Romulus among the Romans, of Siegfried among the Germanic peoples, and of Cuchulain among the Irish Celts) were actually magnifications of charac-teristic types who really lived during a transitional phase in those cultures' histories. Another twentieth-century euhemerist is Dorothy Vitaliano, who claims that a number of Near Eastern myths—including that of Atlantis and the Old Testament account of the plagues of Egypt—are but imaginative byproducts of a historical event, a volcanic eruption that occurred in the east-ern Mediterranean c. 1500 B. C. Grinnell's euhemerism becomes apparent when he explains the supernatural elements in the Pawnee narrative as an accretion onto a fundamentally historical account of a supplanted hunting practice.

The relevant euhemeristic work by the Chadwicks is The Growth of Literature *(Cambridge: Cambridge University Press, 1932–40). Vitalia-no's theory is presented in* Legends of the Earth. Their Volcanic Ori-gins *(Bloomington: Indiana University Press, 1973).*

* * * * *

Among the Pawnees two or three stories are current which tell how in ancient times men who had strong dream power, or had been especially helped by the *Nahúrac*—the animals—or by *Atius,* called the buffalo to the camp in a time of starvation, and so gave life to the tribe when it was about to perish with hunger. One of these tales belongs to the *Kit-ka-háh-ki* tribe, and the Skidi have a similar story of something which happened to them many years ago. I give this *Kit-ka-háh-ki* tale as I have told it in my "Pawnee Hero Stories,"* and will endeavor to trace this myth

189

to its origin, to show how the story came to be told and believed:—

TI-KĒ-WÁ-KŪSH.
THE MAN WHO CALLED THE BUFFALO.

This happened in the olden time before we had met the white people. Then the different bands lived in separate villages. The lodges were made of dirt. The Kit-ka-hahk'-i band went off on a winter hunt, roaming over the country, as they used to do, after buffalo. At this time they did not find the buffalo near. They scouted in all directions, but could discover no signs of them. It was a hard time of starvation. The children cried and the women cried; they had nothing at all to eat.

There was a person who looked at the children crying for something to eat, and it touched his heart. They were very poor, and he felt sorry for them. He said to the head chief: "Tell the chiefs and other head men to do what I tell them. My heart is sick on account of the suffering of the people. It may be that I can help them. Let a new lodge be set up outside the village for us to meet in. I will see if I can do anything to relieve the tribe." The chief said that it was well to do this, and he gave orders for it.

While they were preparing to build this lodge they would miss this man in the night. He would disappear like a wind, and go off a long way, and just as daylight came he would be there again. Sometimes, while sitting in his own lodge during the day, he would reach behind him, and bring out a small piece of buffalo meat, fat and lean, and would give it to some one, saying, "When you have had enough, save what is left, and give it to some one else." When he would give this small piece of meat to any one, the person would think, "This is not enough to satisfy my hunger;" but after eating until he was full, there was always enough left to give to some other person.

In those days it was the custom for the head chief of the tribe, once in a while, to mount his horse, and ride about through the village, talking to the people, and giving them good advice, and telling them that they ought to do what was right by each other. At this time the chief spoke to the people, and explained that this man was going to try to benefit the tribe. So the people made him many fine presents, otter skins and eagle feathers, and when they gave him these things each one said: "I give you this. It is for yourself. Try to help us." He thanked them for these presents, and

190

when they were all gathered together he said: "Now you chiefs and head men of the tribe, and you people, you have done well to give me these things. I shall give them to that person who gives me that power, and who has taken pity on me. I shall let you starve yet four days. Then help will come."

During these four days, every day and night he disappeared, but would come back the same night. He would say to the people that he had been far off, where it would take a person three or four days to go, but he was always back the same night. When he got back on the fourth night, he told the people that the buffalo were near, that the next morning they would be but a little way off. He went up on the hill near the camp, and sacrificed some eagle feathers, and some blue beads, and some Indian tobacco, and then returned to the camp. Then he said to the people, "When that object comes to that place of sacrifice, do not interfere with it; do not turn it back. Let it go by. Just watch and see."

The next morning at daylight, all the people came out of their lodges to watch this hill, and the place where he had sacrificed. While they were looking, they saw a great buffalo bull come up over the hill to the place. He stood there for a short time and looked about, and then he walked on down the hill, and went galloping off past the village. Then this man spoke to the people and said, "There. That is what I meant. That is the leader of the buffalo; where he went the whole herd will follow."

He sent his servant to the chiefs to tell them to choose four boys, and let them go to the top of the hill where the bull had come over, and to look beyond it. The boys were sent, and ran to the top of the hill, and when they looked over beyond it they stopped, and then turned and came back running. They went to the chiefs' lodge and said to the chiefs, sitting there, "Beyond that place of sacrifice there is coming a whole herd of buffalo; many, many, crowding and pushing each other."

Then, as it used to be in the old times, as soon as the young men had told the chief that the buffalo were coming, the chief rode about the village, and told every one to get ready to chase them. He said to them besides: "Do not leave anything on the killing ground. Bring into the camp not only the meat and hides, but the heads and legs and all parts. Bring the best portions in first, and take them over to the new lodge, so that we may have a feast there." For so the man had directed.

Presently the buffalo came over the hill, and the people were ready, and they made a surround, and killed all that they could, and brought them home. Each man brought in his ribs and his young buffalo, and left them there at that lodge. The other parts they brought into the village, as he had directed. After they had brought in this meat, they went to the lodge, and stayed there four days and four nights, and had a great feast, roasting these ribs. The man told them that they would make four surrounds like this, and to get all the meat that they could. "But, he said, "in surrounding these buffalo you must see that all the meat is saved. *Ti-rá-wa* does not like the people to waste the buffalo, and for that reason I advise you to make good use of all you kill." During the four nights they feasted, this man used to disappear each night.

On the night of the fourth day he said to the people: "Tomorrow the buffalo will come again, and you will make another surround. Be careful not to kill a yellow calf—a little one—that you will see with the herd, nor its mother." This was in winter, and yet the calf was the same color as a young calf born in the spring. They made the surround, and let the yellow calf and its mother go.

A good many men in the tribe saw that this man was great, and that he had done great things for the tribe, and they made him many presents, the best horses that they had. He thanked them, but he did not want to accept the presents. The tribes believed that he had done this wonderful thing,—had brought them buffalo,—and all the people wanted to do just what he told them to.

In the first two surrounds they killed many buffalo, and made much dried meat. All their sacks were full, and the dried meat was piled up out of doors. After the second surround, they feasted as before.

After four days, as they were going out to surround the buffalo the third time, the wind changed, and, before the people got near them, the buffalo smelled them and stampeded. While they were galloping away, the man ran up on to the top of the hill, to the place of sacrifice, carrying a pole, on which was tied the skin of a kit fox; and when he saw the buffalo running, and that the people could not catch them, he waved his pole, and called out *Ska-a-a-a*! and the buffalo turned right about, and charged back right through the people, and they killed many of them. He wished to show the people that he had the power over the buffalo.

After the third surround they had a great deal of meat, and he called the chiefs together and said, "Now, my chiefs, are you satisfied?" They said, "Yes, we are satisfied, and we are thankful to you for taking pity on us and helping us. It is through your power that the tribe has been saved from starving to death." He said: "You are to make one more surround, and that will be the end. I want you to get all you can. Kill as many as possible, for this will be the last of the buffalo this winter. Those presents that you have made to me, and that I did not wish to take, I give them back to you." Some of the people would not take back the presents, but insisted that he should keep them, and at last he said he would do so.

The fourth surround was made, and the people killed many buffalo and saved the meat. The night after this last surround he disappeared and drove the buffalo back. The next morning he told the people to look about, and tell him if they saw anything. They did so, but they could not see any buffalo.

The next day they moved camp, and went east toward their home. They had so much dried meat that they could not take it all at once, but had to come back and make two trips for it. When they moved below, going east, they saw no fresh meat, only dried meat; but sometimes, when this man would come in from his journeys, he would bring a piece of meat,—a little piece,—and he would divide it up among the people, and they would put it into the kettles and boil it, and everybody would eat, but they could not eat it all up. There would always be some left over. This man was so wonderful that he could change even the buffalo chips that you see on the prairie into meat. He would cover them up with his robe, and when he would take it off again, you would see there pounded buffalo meat and tallow (pemmican), *tŭp-o-har'ŭs*.

The man was not married; he was a young man, and by this time the people thought that he was one of the greatest men in the tribe, and they wanted him to marry. They went to one of the chiefs, and told him that they wanted him to be this man's father-in-law, for they wanted him to raise children, thinking that they might do something to benefit the tribe. They did not want that race to die out. The old people say that it would have been good if he had had children, but he had none. If he had, perhaps they would have had the same power as their father.

That person called the buffalo twice, and twice saved the tribe from a famine. The second time the suffering was great, and they held a council to ask him to help the tribe. They filled up the pipe, and held it out to him, asking him to take pity on the tribe. He took the pipe, and lighted it and smoked. He did it in the same way as the first time, and they made four surrounds, and got much meat.

When this man died, all the people mourned for him a long time. The chief would ride around the village and call out: "Now I am poor in mind on account of the death of this man, because he took pity on us and saved the tribe. Now he is gone and there is no one left like him."

This is a true and sacred story that belongs to the Kit-ka-hahk'-i band. It happened once long ago, and has been handed down from father to son in this band. The Skidi had a man who once called the buffalo, causing them to return when stampeded, as was done in this story.

NOTE.—Big Knife, a Skidi, who died only recently, said that the man was alive in his time. *Kuru' ks-u le-sharu* (Bear Chief), a Skidi, says that he knew the man. His name was Carrying Mother.

So far as can be gathered from this narrative, the calling of the buffalo is the direct result of the supernatural powers of the hero, but I shall endeavor to show that the main event here related—the calling of the buffalo—was at one time a commonplace occurrence among the Pawnees; that by the introduction of new elements into the life of the tribe this custom became obsolete; and that all the circumstances connected with it, except the one central fact that men once brought buffalo within the reach of the people, long ago passed from the memory of the tribe.

A study of some of the recent customs of more primitive plain tribes will, I hope, make this clear.

Far to the north of the home of the Pawnees live a people who have had much less intercourse than they with the whites, who have not had horses nearly so long, and who up to within ten or twelve years had to a great extent preserved their primitive habits. These are the Blackfeet.

Up to the time when they obtained horses, the only way in which the Blackfeet secured buffalo was by means of *piskuns*. These were inclosures, built usually at the foot of a precipice, the cut bank forming one of the walls, and the fence on the other side being made of logs, rocks, brush, and so on, built up to a height of six or eight feet. From a point on the edge of the precipice above this inclosure two diverging lines of stone heaps, or of clumps of brush, ran out for a long distance on to the prairie, so that their farther ends were widely separated, forming a >-shaped chute. When meat was needed, the people went up on to the prairie, and concealed themselves behind the stone heaps or the brush, and a man especially selected for the purpose was sent out toward the feeding herd of buffalo to bring them within the arms of the >. This man, who had prepared himself for the task by praying and fasting, advanced pretty close to the buffalo, and then, by calling and by alternately showing himself and disappearing, attracted their attention. Sometimes the man wore a robe and a bull's head, at others he was naked, without any disguise. At first a few of the buffalo would raise their heads and look at him, but it was not long before all had stopped feeding and were staring at him. After a little, they would begin to walk toward him, and as they approached, he would move away. If they began to trot, he would increase his speed so as to equal theirs. They followed, and in this way he induced them to come after him within the arms of the >. After they had passed within the arms of the chute, the Indians behind the outer rock piles would spring into sight, and shout and wave their robes. This frightened the buffalo, who now ran away from the enemy in the rear, and the man who was leading them soon slipped out of sight, and either hid himself, or climbed down the precipice toward which the buffalo were running. As a rule, the wings of the chute kept the buffalo travelling in the desired direction, that is, toward the angle of the >, where they would reach the precipice, and fall over it into the corral below. But sometimes in winter, when snow was on the ground, a method was adopted to make this doubly sure. A line of buffalo chips, each one supported on three small sticks, so that it stood a few inches above the snow, was carried from the angle of the > straight toward the prairie. The chips were about thirty feet apart, and ran midway between the wings of the chute. This line was of course conspicuous against the white snow, and when the buffalo were running down the chute they always followed it, never turning to the right nor to the left. No doubt they thought it a trail which other buffalo had followed.

In the latter days of the *pískun*, the man who led the buffalo was often mounted on a white horse. He rode near the herd, and then began to zigzag from side to side in front of it. As he approached, the buffalo began to raise their heads and look at him. Pretty soon they walked toward him, and then began to go a little faster, until at last they were running, the rider, of course, always retreating from them. When he had led them into the chute, the people rose up from behind the rock piles and drove them on. The Blackfeet also practised the surround, by which the buffalo were led into a circle of people or lodges, as described in my "Pawnee Hero-Stories." *Pískuns* were in use among the Blackfeet within thirty years, and very likely to within a more recent time.

It may be assumed that the motive which led the buffalo to follow this moving and (to them) remarkable object was curiosity. They saw something they did not recognize, and approached it for the purpose of identifying it. Other animals are known to act in a like manner under similar circumstances. The old practice of alluring the prong-horned antelope within shot by showing a red flag, or even a white handkerchief on the end of a ramrod, is familiar to us all. I myself have had antelope, which ran away startled before they had seen me distinctly, come back from the distance of a mile, and trot up within forty or fifty yards, in the effort to make out just what I was. Of course this is more commonly done by young animals than by those older and more experienced. Elk, too, will often walk toward an object which they do not recognize as dangerous, in the endeavor to determine for themselves just what it is. In the same way, ducks used commonly to be "toled" within gunshot, on the shores of Chesapeake Bay, by a little dog trained to run up and down the beach; and within a few years I have been told by a well-known ornithologist that he has seen this practised with success.

I am satisfied that, before the Indians of the northern plains obtained horses, they all of them secured most of their buffalo by means of traps and surrounds, and that the leading of buffalo into the inclosure or into the ring of people was universally practised by them. Among the tribes who used to surround the buffalo, my own inquiries have given me the names of the following: Cheyennes, Arapahoes, Pawnees, Omahas, Otoes, Poncas, some bands of the Dakotas, Arikaras, Mandans, Snakes, Crees, Gros Ventres of the Village, Crows, Blackfeet, Sarcees, and Gros Ventres of the Prairie. In primitive times the only weapons which these people had to use against the buffalo were stone-headed arrows, and it must be apparent to any one who has given any attention to the subject that these would be ineffective against this animal.

Very likely the Pawnees never built *pískuns*, or anything exactly corresponding to them, for their country was not adapted to this mode of capture, but there is no doubt that they did decoy the buffalo into a circle of people, just as we have positive testimony that the Blackfeet and the Rees used to do. No people are keener observers than Indians, and no people are better acquainted with the habits of animals, especially of those animals on which they depend for food. It is not to be supposed that any one of the plains tribes was ignorant of the fact that buffalo could thus be brought by an appeal to their curiosity.

Now it is to be remembered that horses came to the plains Indians from the south, and that as soon as they obtained horses, and learned to ride, the primitive methods of taking the buffalo began to be supplanted by the more effective, easy, and exciting one of running. As the buffalo in later times was always rushed at and put to flight, was known to have keen powers of scent and easily to take the alarm if the wind blew from the hunter toward the game, it would gradually come to be forgotten that it could readily be decoyed by an appeal to its curiosity; but the fact would be remembered that in ancient days the buffalo used to be called up close to the people, and the only way to account for this would be to attribute to the man who called them powers which were supernatural. The tribes who had earliest obtained horses would be the first to abandon their primitive methods of taking the buffalo. Those who had longest given up their original customs would have most completely forgotten them; but about the one remembered fact that the buffalo were called, there would gradually grow up many details, supplied by successive narrators, which would add to the interest of the story, and would tend to make the performances of the man who accomplished this wonderful act appear more and more marvellous.

The Pawnees have had horses for more than two hundred years, and, since they obtained them, have always chased the buffalo. That they used commonly to decoy the game to its death has long been forgotten, but that the buffalo came when they were called has not been forgotten; and so around the memory of this single fact has grown up among the tribe the miraculous story of *Ti-kah-we-kush*, the man who called the buffalo.

If my conclusions are just, the memory of this old custom of decoying the buffalo should have passed away from the tribes of the south earlier than it did from those of the north, and such appears to have been the case.

Confirmation of this explanation of the myth may be found in a similar story related to me by the Arikaras. This tale has not had so much time in which to grow as has the Pawnee story, and the powers attributed to the hero are not nearly so noteworthy.

The Arikaras belong to the Pawnee family. They live farther north than the true Pawnees, have had less intercourse with the whites, and are more primitive in their ways than their more southern relatives. These people also tell of a man who called the buffalo. This man's name was Chief Bear. As is readily seen by the way in which the people now speak of them, his feats were less surprising than those of the Pawnee or Skidi hero, and he does not appear to have called the buffalo in response to any special needs of the tribe. It is not told that he did it under any great stress of circumstances, nor that the tribe was in danger of starvation, or was even in great want. The act seems to have been performed as an ordinary matter, and yet Chief Bear's powers are regarded as peculiar. He is singled out for special mention, and is compared by the Rees with the Pawnee hero who did the same thing.

The story told by the Rees is as follows: The Rees also had a man who called the buffalo. The people would go out on the prairie, and would hide themselves so as to form a big circle, open at one side. Then Chief Bear would go off over to where the buffalo were, and would bring them into the circle, and the people would close up the gap, so that the buffalo would be surrounded. They would run round and round within the circle, and the people would keep closing in on them, and would prevent them from breaking through the line by yelling and tossing their robes in the air, and finally the buffalo would get tired out and it was easy to kill them.

Finally, as has been said, when we get up north among the Blackfeet, the calling of the buffalo becomes an every-day matter, and was practised certainly as late as the year 1862 among the Pikúni tribe of the Blackfeet; while, among the *Sík-si-kau* tribe and the plains Crees, *piskuns* were used down to much later times.

A hundred years ago the Pawnees had probably forgotten that the buffalo were once commonly called up to the people, but among the Blackfeet there are still living many men who time and again have seen this done.

Notes

Pawnee Hero Stories and Folk-Tales with Notes on the Origin, Customs and Character of the Pawnee People (1889; rpt. Lincoln: University of Nebraska Press, 1961). The text of this narrative appears on pp. 132–141.

The "Montezuma" of the Pueblo Indians

by Adolph F. Bandelier

* * * * *

*Adolph Francis Bandelier (1840–1914) assumed a truly interdisciplinary
stance in his studies of traditional cultures in South America, Mexico, and the
American Southwest. A native of Switzerland, he came to the United States
when he was eight years old. Bandelier's father, a businessman who left
Switzerland in response to unfavorable political developments, eventually
settled in Highland, a Swiss community in central Illinois, where he helped to
establish a bank. The younger Bandelier, after studying geology at the University of Berne, returned to the United States and became involved in his
father's banking and other business enterprises. However, the influence of
cultural evolutionist Lewis Henry Morgan turned Bandelier's interests toward ethnological research.*

SOURCE: *American Anthropologist*, o. s. 5 (1892), 319–326. At the end of the
essay that periodical's editor has appended the following: "The above article
was written by Professor Bandelier while on board the steamship *San Juan*,
off the coast of Tehuantepec, en route to Bolivia, his new field of investigation."

Bandelier was particularly interested in the cultures of ancient Mexico and learned Spanish to further his studies of those cultures. In 1880 he began a decade of field research in Arizona and New Mexico, surveying the region's archeology, living among the Pueblos as participant observer, and delving into the Spanish archival resources at Santa Fe. The result of his researches was a spate of publications in the 1890s which revealed a sensitive combination of the archeologist's interpretation of prehistoric artifacts, the ethnographer's keen eye for cultural detail, the historian's evaluative judgment of archival documents, and the folklorist's appreciation of oral literature. Most of these publications appeared in technical journals, but Bandelier also produced material on American Indians with broader appeal, especially The Delight Makers (New York: Dodd, Mead, 1890), a novel, and The Gilded Man (El Dorado) and Other Pictures of the Spanish Occupancy of America (New York: D. Appleton, 1893). The 1890s saw Bandelier shift his research emphasis to Bolivia and Peru, where he continued archeological, ethnographic, and archival work until 1903. During the last decade of his life, he worked for the American Museum of Natural History, Columbia University, and the Hispanic Society of America.

Perhaps the first recorded instance of the propagandistic creation and manipulation of folklore occurs in Plato's Republic. There the Greek philosopher suggests that in order to maintain social stability the aristocratic elite of his projected utopian state should promulgate "the myth of the metals," by which the lower classes would be convinced of the justness of their position. In the following essay, Bandelier posits that the Mexican government similarly manipulated folklore for political ends during its war with the United States in the 1840s. Expanding upon already extant oral traditions, the Mexicans tried to convince the Pueblos of the legitimacy of their claims to the territory now included in the American Southwest. What Bandelier describes is the creation of what Richard M. Dorson has called "fakelore"—that is, stories, songs, and the like composed with the express purpose of passing them off as real folklore. Dorson's most familiar example of "fakelore" in twentieth-century America is the stories about Paul Bunyan, which were not part of lumbermen's oral tradition but created for an advertising campaign by a California lumber company in the 1910s. As Dorson and others have shown, Paul Bunyan never existed in oral tradition to any extent but was made the center of an artificial folklore by popular writers and advertisers. Modern folklorists have noted other examples of manipulation of folklore by governments or political groups, similar to that reported by Bandelier, including its *use for propaganda purposes in Nazi Germany and by the governments of the Soviet Union and China.*

Among sources on Bandelier's career are F. W. Hodge, "Biographical Sketch and Bibliography of Adolphe Francis Alphonse Bandelier," New Mexico Historical Review, *7, no. 4 (1932), 353–370; and C. H. Lange, "Adolph Bandelier as a Pueblo Ethnologist,"* Kiva, *29, no. 1 (1963), 28–34. Dorson's concept of "fakelore" as well as some material on the political use of folklore appears in* American Folklore and the Historian *(Chicago: University of Chicago Press, 1971). For a thorough study of Paul Bunyan, see Daniel G. Hoffman,* Paul Bunyan, Last of the Frontier Demigods *(Philadelphia: University of Pennsylvania Press, 1966). For the propagandistic use of folklore in Nazi Germany, see Christa Kamenetsky, "Folklore as a Political Tool in Nazi Germany,"* Journal of American Folklore, *85 (1972), 221–235. The manipulation of folklore by communist-oriented thinkers is illustrated in Y. M. Sokolov,* Russian Folklore, *trans. Catherine Ruth Smith (New York: Macmillan, 1950).*

✳ ✳ ✳ ✳ ✳

There is no need of proving that the name of the Mexican "Chief of Men" (Tláca-tecuhtli) who perished while in the custody of the Spaniards under Hernando Cortés in 1520 was Mo-tecuh-zoma, literally "Our Wrathy Chieftain." Bernal Diez del Castillo,[1] an eye-witness and the much-prejudiced author of the "True History" of the Conquest, is responsible for the corruption into Montezuma, which has since become popular and most widely known. It is interesting how that misspelling has taken hold of the public mind, how it has completely supplanted the original true orthography and meaning. Meaning even is out of place here, for, while *Motecuhzoma* is a legitimate Nahuatl word with a very plain signification, and also a typical Indian personal name, *Montezuma* has no signification whatever; and yet, in Mexico, even the Nahuatl Indians—those who speak the Nahuatl language daily—know only Montezuma and would hardly recognize the original name as applicable to him, whom they have been taught to call an "emperor."

Still, it is not so very strange when we consider that at Cozcatlan, in the State of Puebla, at least two hundred miles from the

City of Mexico, the Indians gravely tell the traveler that the ruins of an ancient Indian town in that vicinity are those of the "Palace of Montezuma," where that "emperor" was "born" and whence he started out to "conquer the city of Mexico." It cannot surprise us to hear of perversions of names only. The folk-tale of the Indians of Cozcatlan (a modern tale, of course) shows how easily facts are distorted in the minds of primitive people when they do not originally belong to the circle of their own historical tradition.

In the story of Cozcatlan we have a conquest of Mexico by Montezuma from the *southeast*. In New Mexico the present century has evolved the story of the conquest of Mexico by Montezuma from the *north*. It is necessary, however, before we examine that story and its origin to investigate how the name of Montezuma crept as far north as the southwest of the United States, through what vehicles, and how far it extended its fame.

No mention is made of Montezuma in Spanish documents on the Southwest of an earlier date than 1664, when, speaking of the (then recently discovered) ruins of Casas Grandes, in northwestern Chihuahua, Francisco de Gorraez Beaumont and Antonio de Oca Sarmiento speak of those buildings as the old "houses of Montezuma." Such an utterance, coming from Spanish officers of high rank, shows that already then the name Montezuma had become, in the minds of the Spaniards themselves, confounded with migration-tales of Indian tribes of a very ancient date, and that those tales apply, not to the unfortunate war-chief of the time of Cortés, but to one of his predecessors in office, Motecuhzoma Ilhuicamina, who commanded the forces of the Mexicans in the early part of the fifteenth century, according to the still doubtful chronology of the ancient Mexicans. The confusion between those two personages had already been procreative of a mythical Montezuma in the minds of the educated people. Is it to be wondered at if that mythical figure took a still stronger hold on the conceptions of the simple Indian?

Genuine folk-tales of the Chihuahua Indians are reported at an early date by Captain Gaspar Perez de Villagran, one of the officers of Juan de Oñate, when the latter colonized New Mexico in 1598. The metrical chronicle of Villagran was printed in 1610, and it mentions the tradition of a migration of tribes from the north, during which migration they divided into two bands. But no mention is made of the name of Montezuma as connected with Indian folklore of northern Mexico; nor do the Jesuit Fathers, who studied the Indians of all the States north of Jalisco as early as the latter part of the sixteenth and the beginning of the seventeenth centuries, and who consequently enjoyed the advantage of holding intercourse with those natives while the latter were still in their primitive condition, make any mention of a Montezuma lore. Ribas,[2] whose classical work on Sonora and Sinaloa appeared in 1645, is absolutely silent on that subject, although he makes frequent and detailed mention of the creeds, beliefs, rites, and traditions of nearly all the tribes that inhabited those two states of the present Mexican republic. In none of the reports on the New Mexican Pueblos, as far as we have them previous to 1680, does the name of Montezuma appear in connection with those aborigines. Hence it may safely be assumed that the Montezuma story is, in the North American southwest, as much of an importation from the south and subsequent transformation, as it is clearly an importation and transformation, though imported thither from the northwest at the village of Cozcatlan.

Every Spanish expedition that penetrated to the northward had in its company Indian followers as servants and sometimes as interpreters, since dialects of the Nahuatl tongue prevailed as far north along the Pacific coast as Sinaloa. Among natives from the interior of Mexico the name Montezuma was, of course, a household word already in the second generation, for the fame of the war chief and of his tragical end increased in proportion to distance from the time as well as from the scene of his career. In that second generation Motecuhzoma was already practically forgotten, and Montezuma remained in the mouths of the people as a hero. An Indian hero very soon becomes a mythical personage, and what with confuse reports of old traditions and folk-tales current among nearly every tribe, Montezuma could not fail to become a figure which, in course of time, shone among the folk-lore of nearly every tribe. It may be asserted that the New Mexican Montezuma is probably the latest of these numerous local adaptations and infiltrations into the mythical history of the Mexican and Southwestern aborigines.

At an early date confuse notions of the geography even of central Mexico took root among the inhabitants of the New Mexican pueblos. When Coronado evacuated New Mexico in 1542, some Indians from the valley of Mexico remained behind at one of the villages of Zuñi. Forty-two years later Antonio de Espejo visited the Zuñis and found three of these Indians still alive. He also heard of a great lake on the shores of which were important settlements of sedentary Indians, all of which were rich in gold and precious stones. That lake was said to be at least several moons distant from Zuñi. It is easy to recognize in those wild statements a distorted picture of the home of the Mexican Indians. Combining it with the name and fame of Montezuma, we obtain a basis upon which a well conceived Indian folk-story might be established.

The Montezuma story circulated slowly among the New Mexican tribes. During the interrogatories of Indian prisoners taken before Governor Don Antonio de Otermin in the autumn of 1681, when the latter made his unsuccessful expedition into New Mexico as far north as Cochiti, quite detailed information was elicited as to the original causes of the great Insurrection of the Pueblos. The witnesses examined were Indians who had not been in almost daily contact with the Spaniards and their Mexican Indian servants, and not one of them spoke of Montezuma, whereas the names of specific Pueblo deities, such as Caudi, Heume, and Tilim, were mentioned as those of gods appearing to Popé[3] in the estufa of Taos. Only the Indians from the pueblos around Sante Fé spoke of Montezuma, connecting his name with that of Pose-yemo (Pedro Lezumu in the defective copy of the journal of the siege of Sante Fé of 1680, which copy was made in the last century by order of the Spanish crown), a historical personage of Tehua folk-lore, also called Pose-ueve, and known to the Keresan or Queres tribes of New Mexico under the name of Push-ay-a, to the Zuñis as Pó-shai-an-k'ya, and to the Jemez as Pest-ia-sod-e. The prisoners on the 20th of August, 1680, treated of Pose-yemo and Montezuma as of two distinct personages though related. In this century they have gradually become confounded.

Hardly anything is heard of Montezuma in New Mexico during the last century; in fact, until the time of the Mexican war of 1846. Farther south, however, it became customary to attribute the origin of every notable ruin, about the past of which nothing was known, to Montezuma and to the hosts which he was said to have led to the south. Casa Grande, on the Gila river, escaped from this fate. Already Father Kuehne (Kino) heard from the Pimas that the erection of that building and of the cluster of houses surrounding it was due to a chief named Siva, who came from the north, and although Father Sedelmair in 1746 incidentally refers to the Montezuma story in connection with Casa Grande, there is a decided inclination toward attributing the construction of those edifices to some fraction of the Moki[4] tribe rather than to the Nahuatl of Mexico. It may be noticed here without impropriety and without any danger of misinterpretation that it is a singular coincidence to find early explorers mentioning the Moki as the possible founders of settlements so similar in architectural type to Casas Grandes in Chihuahua as the Casa Grande is, when subsequent investigation tends to prove that the Moki belong to the same linguistic stock as the Nahuatl, the Pima, and the Opata of Sonora. I mention this merely as a coincidence, not as a historical indication.

At the present day, when one inquires of the Indians at El Paso del Norte about "ruinas," they fail to understand him and reply that there are none; but if he asks concerning "Montezumas," they will at once point to the spots where mounds covered with pottery denote the former existence of permanent aboriginal buildings. The same is the case along the course of the Casas Grandes river from the Hacienda of San Diego to Ascension. Every mound, every ancient wall, is not a "ruin" but a "Montezuma" in the mouths of the people. The tribes who inhabited that section at the time it was first discovered, the Sumas, also roamed about El Paso, and were even located thereabout by the Spaniards during the last century. It is, therefore, likely that through them the original Spanish mistake of attributing the erection of Casas Grandes to a mythical Montezuma (in the absence of any other aboriginal tradition or folk-lore touching their origin) became circulated, and that thus the personal name was transformed into a designation for a certain class of ancient vestiges.

We now come to the time when the Montezuma story assumed a prominent position among the New Mexican Pueblos. The manner in which this happened is not devoid of interest.

In the year 1846, when war between the United States and Mexico was imminent, a singular document was concocted (according to its tenor, at least) in the City of Mexico. It is written in Spanish and was, to my knowledge, never printed, but exists in several manuscript copies in New Mexico. It purports to be a "History of Montezuma." Beginning with the folk-tale current among the Tehuas about their hero god Pose-yemo or Pose-ueve, it applies that part of the story relating to the latter's childhood to the childhood of Montezuma, and then goes on to relate the career of the latter, of his sister and mother, etc., until it makes of him a conqueror of Mexico. There Montezuma becomes connected with the Malinche. What the Malinche was is well known. The name itself is a corruption of the Spanish name Marina by the Nahuatl, who, not having the letter "r" in their alphabet, substituted always the letter "l," thus making "Malina" out of "Marina." Marina was the interpreter *en chef* of Cortés during his conquest of Mexico. The document cited makes of the Malinche a daughter of Montezuma, and, after bringing in Cortés and his conquest and victory over Montezuma, concludes by marrying the Malinche to Cortés, and by representing New Mexico as a part of the dower which the Indian maiden brought to her Spanish husband. Such a document, manufactured at a time when an American invasion of New Mexico was apprehended, written at the City of Mexico and circulated in every New Mexican pueblo that could be reached, is plainly what may be called a "campaign document," conceived in view of strengthening the claims of Mexico upon New Mexico in the eyes of the Pueblo Indians and refuting anything to the contrary that might be anticipated from the side of the United States. It is written in a style peculiarly within the grasp of the Indian, it being Spanish after the fashion in which the Pueblo Indian uses that language in conversation. Whether written in New Mexico and only dated from the capital, or written at that capital, it is certain that the author deserves great credit for the shrewdness with which he has adapted both story and style to the imagination and power of understanding of the aborigines. Since the circulation of that document the story of Montezuma has become stereotyped in the mouths of many Pueblo Indians, and when interrogated by tourists and ethnological volunteers they repeat it with greater or less precision.

On the surface it would appear that the "History of Montezuma" just spoken of cannot have been written anywhere else than at the City of Mexico, since it seems to have been plainly a political instrument in view of an impending invasion. Still, it is not impossible that it was a product of New Mexican ingenuity. There was material for it in one of the pueblos of that territory, that of Jemez.

For many years past it has been known that the Indians of Jemez had in their possession a printed book, which they carefully concealed and of which it was stated that it contained a "History of the Pueblos," profusely illustrated. I never succeeded in seeing it, but the Most Reverend Archbishop of Santa Fé, during one of his official visits to Jemez, obtained permission to peruse the mysterious volume. It proved to be, as we ascertained by comparing it with a copy in my possession, a copy of the Letters (*Cartas*) of Cortés edited by Lorenzana[5] and illustrated with pictures of Mexican costumes, etc. From this book, the existence of which was known to all the Pueblos and about the contents of which they had been partially informed, it would have been easy to gather material for the "History of Montezuma" of 1846, and it is not unlikely that it has been the source of the latter, except of the introductory portions, which embody a genuine tradition of the Tehua Indians, which was easy to obtain from any one of the more communicative members of that or of any neighboring tribe.

The Montezuma of New Mexico is, therefore, in its present form a modern creation. The Indian—that is, the Indian of higher standing in his tribe, the wizard, for example—discriminates between the modern imaginary figure and the historic gods of his own, and, while he may repeat the Montezuma tale to an unsophisticated listener, fresh from the outside world, with the greatest apparent sincerity, he inwardly thanks that modern story for the service it renders him in screening his own sacred traditions from pryers into secrets which the Indian considers as his own and no one's else. Younger people may repeat the Montezuma tale in all candor, simply because they do not yet know better; but, as it is, it stands as an importation first, a modern fabrication or compilation next, without the slightest connection whatever with original mythology and traditional history of the North American southwest and northern Mexico.

Among the many vehicles that contributed to popularize the name of Montezuma in these regions the dance of the "Matachines" should be mentioned. It was introduced among the Indians of central Mexico in the sixteenth century as a part of the semi-religious theatrical performances, by means of which the Franciscans gradually superseded the idolatrous dances of Indian paganism. In it appear two prominent characters—the "Monarch" (*el Monarca*) and, as solo-dancer, the Malinche. With the idea of the Monarch the recollection of Montezuma became intimately connected. When the Matachines were introduced into New Mexico I am unable to tell, but certainly, at latest, during the 18th century. The relations, which in that dance are indicated as between the Malinche and the Monarch, bear a striking analogy to those represented in the "History of Montezuma" above mentioned.

It is also to be noticed that several villages—above all, that of Pecos—have been represented in this century as the birthplace of Montezuma. This seems to give color to the assumption that Montezuma was indeed a real character of New Mexican aboriginal tradition. If we compare, however, the genuine tradition of

Pose-yemo among the Tehuas with the Montezuma tale, we see at a glance that the latter is only an adaptation, spun out to much greater length and carrying the career of Pose-yemo into lands with which no New Mexican Indians had the least intercourse previous to the coming of the Spaniards. According to the folk-tale of Pose-yemo, the latter was a great wizard, born at the now ruined village of Pose-uing-ge, above the hot spring of the Hon. Antonio Joseph, in northern New Mexico. He performed the usual wonderful tricks attributed to a powerful Indian shaman, and, after rendering his people very prosperous and powerful, disappeared at his native place "in the course of human events." In regard to the statement that Montezuma was born at Pecos, it must be remembered that the Pecos were a branch of the Jemez, and the existence of the book spoken of at the latter village, coupled with the intimate relations between the two tribes, contributed to create and foster the notion that Montezuma had been a wonder-child of the Pecos pueblo.

Notes

1. Bernal Diaz [Bandelier's spelling is incorrect] del Castillo, *Historia verdada de la conquista de la Nueva Espāna por Fernando Cortez, y de la cosas acouncidas desde el año 1518, hasta la en muerte en el año 1547, y despues hasta el 1550* . . . (Madrid: Emprenta del Reyno, 1632).

2. Andres-Perez de Ribas, *Historia de los Triumphos de Nuestra Santa Fee entre Gentres las mas Barbaras, y fieras del nuevo Orbe* . . . (Madrid: Por Aloso de Paredes, 1645).

3. Popé (?-1690) was a spiritual leader from San Juan Pueblo who led the successful uprising against Spanish imperialism in 1680.

4. Also spelled "Moqui." This is a name given to the Hopi by their traditional enemies the Navajo.

5. Hernando Cortes, *Historia de Nueva-España, escrita por su esclareido conquistador Hernan Cortes, aumentada con otros documentos, y notas, por el ilustrissimo Señor Don Francisco Antonio Lorenzana, Arzobispo de Mexico* . . . (Mexico City: en la Imprenta del Superior Gobierno, 1770).

The Sioux Mythology

by Charles A. Eastman

* * * * *

*The life of Ohiyesa, as Charles Alexander Eastman (1858–1939) was
known during his boyhood among the Santee Sioux, seems to exemplify the
process of successful acculturation. He spent his first fifteen years as a typical
Indian boy, but in 1873 his father, returning to the Santee after a period of
captivity among Euro-Americans, introduced the young man to white society. After some formal schooling in Nebraska, Eastman attended Beloit
College, Knox College, Dartmouth College, and finally the Boston University School of Medicine. He was working as a government physician at the
Pine Ridge Indian Agency in South Dakota at the time of the Wounded Knee
massacre and later practiced medicine in Minnesota and at the Crow Creek
Agency, also in South Dakota. Eastman's varied life included serving as a
Y.M.C.A. representative, helping to establish the Boy Scouts and the
Campfire Girls, teaching at the Carlisle Indian School in Pennsylvania, and
participating on federal committees investigating Indian policy.*

SOURCE: *The Popular Science Monthly*, 46 (November 1894), 88–91.

Although his extensive writings include some collections of Native American folktales, Eastman's most important literary contributions were two volumes of autobiography: Indian Boyhood *(Boston: Little, Brown, 1902), which covers his life until the age of fifteen, and* From the Deep Woods to Civilization. Chapters in the Autobiography of an Indian *(Boston: Little, Brown, 1916), which continues the narrative through his graduation from medical school. Eastman's writing is informed by a cultural evolutionist perspective, for he viewed his own life as a microcosm of a culture's progress from savagery to civilization. This perspective did not alienate him from his Native American origins; as he wanted to emphasize the American Indians' potential for progress, and consequently dwelt upon features of their cultures which seemed to foreshadow civilized development.*

Despite its title, Eastman's essay included here does not focus on the sacred oral literature of his tribal heritage. Instead, it offers a cursory survey of several aspects of the entire religious system, in which mythology played an important role. He shows that the Sioux religion, which he erroneously ascribes to other Native American groups as well, was ripe for evolutionary development. The religion of the Sioux contained the germinal ideas which would lead inevitably to a "higher" religion such as Christianity. On the religious level, Eastman shows, the Sioux were well prepared to rise from the deep woods to civilization.

Two biographies of Eastman are available: Marion W. Copeland, Charles Alexander Eastman (Ohiyesa), *Boise State University Western Writers Series No. 33 (Boise, Idaho, 1978); and* Raymond Wilson, Ohiyesa: Charles Eastman, Santee Sioux *(Urbana: University of Illinois Press, 1983).*

* * * * *

The tendency of the uncivilized and untutored mind is to recognize the Deity through some visible medium. The soul has an inborn consciousness of the highest good or *God*. The aborigines of our country illustrate this truth. I wish to write of the mythology of the Sioux nation, more particularly that portion of the tribe dwelling east of the Missouri River, with which I am very familiar, although the others are not distinctively different in their religious customs.

The human mind, equipped with all its faculties, is capable even in an uncultured state of a logical process of reasoning. Freed from the burdensome theories of science and theology, it is impressed powerfully by God's omnipresence, omniscience, and omnipotence. Alexander Pope's worn-out lines—

"Lo, the poor Indian! whose untutored mind
Sees God in clouds and hears him in the wind"—*

are true, in that the Indian recognized a power behind every natural force. He saw God, not only in the sky, but in every creation. All Nature sang his praises—birds, waterfalls, tree tops—everything whispered the name of the mysterious God.

The Indian did not trouble himself concerning the nature of the Creator. He was satisfied that there was a God, whose laws all must obey, and whom he blindly or instinctively worshiped as the "Great Mystery."

The relation between God and man he conceived from the analogy of Nature. His God is a gracious yet an exacting parent. He punishes both the disobedient and the evil-doer, and forgives and helps the penitent and the good. He hears prayers. He is called *Wakantanka*, or the Great Mystery. The word *wakan* means mystery or holy, and *tanka* means great, mighty, or supreme. Neither of the two words signifies *spirit*; however, it may imply that. The word *wakan* may also mean reverenced or sacred.

Before the coming of the missionaries the Sioux never prayed or gave any offering direct to God, except at a great feast once a year. It was believed that he was too great to be approached directly, but that a prayer or a gift through some of his attributes would reach him. The legend is that God occasionally descends to earth in the shape of some animal, or envelops himself in a great wind. If any person beholds his face he dies instantly, although the same person may be born again as a child and become a great "medicine man."

Before the advent of the white man these people believed that the earth was flat, with a circular form, and was suspended in a dark space, and sheltered by the heaven or sky in the shape of a hollow hemisphere. The sun was regarded as the father and the earth the mother of all things that live and grow; but as they had been married a long time and had become the parents of many generations, they were called the great-grandparents. As far as I can judge, the moon seemed to be their servant; at least, she was required to watch, together with her brothers, the stars, over the sleeping universe, while the sun came down to rest with his family.

In the thunder-bird they believed God had a warrior who presided over the most powerful elements—the storm and the fearful cyclone. This symbolic creature is depicted as an impatient and wrathy god of war, at whose appearance even the ever-smiling grandfather, the sun, hides his face. In the realms of water the whale is the symbolized chief of the finny tribes. In every great lake the Sioux imagines a huge fish as ruler of its waters.

Yet none of these possess the power of speech. The Great Mystery had shown them some truths denied to man, but he did not trust them fully, therefore he made them dumb. They can only show to man some supernatural things by signs or in dreams; as, for instance, to foretell future events or explain the use of certain powerful remedies. The savage holds that the key of heaven is vested in the visible phenomena of the universe. All creatures, save man, are assigned to a peculiar paradise, in which there is a forbidden fruit—namely, the apple of speech and reasoning. Hence the animals and inanimate things are exempted from sin. Thus it is that rocks, trees, and rivers are surrounded with an atmosphere of grandeur, beauty, and mystery. Nature is the interpreter of the Great Mystery, and through her man is convinced of truth.

The root-eating animals were believed to be intrusted with the mysteries of medicine. They were the medicine-givers. The sun and the thunder-bird also possessed efficacious treatments, but without the use of roots and herbs. On account of these beliefs the practices of no two medicine men among the Sioux are exactly the same. Each claims that his knowledge of medicine was obtained from some particular animal, of whom

214

the bear, beaver, etc., are first in the profession. Those who found their treatment upon the power of the sun or the thunder-bird do not use any medicine. There was but one general organization among the Sioux, and this was based upon medicine and religion combined. It was called the "Holy Medicine Lodges." There were many of these lodges, each one different in its medicines and medicine songs, but alike in all other respects. They had a common form of initiation. It was effected publicly at a union meeting of all the lodges. Whenever a member of one of the lodges died, a candidate was introduced, and he was instructed by a select committee of experienced and pure men, according to the savage notion.

The novice must bear in mind that purity and feast making are the foundations of the lodge, and pleasing to the Great Mystery. "Thou shalt often make a holy feast or a lodge feast to the God. Thou shalt not spill the blood of any of thy tribe. Thou shalt not steal what belongs to another. Thou shalt always remember that the choicest part of thy provision belongs to God." These were some of their commandments. It is a peculiar fact, already mentioned, that the Great Mystery was never directly approached except upon special and extraordinary occasions, such as the union meeting and dance of the "medicine lodges" once a year. Then a chosen priest usually made a prayer to the Supreme Being. The material rewards of a godly life were looked for in the immediate future; and yet there was a feeling of satisfaction in the savage bosom that God was pleased with his efforts.

The spirits of the departed Sioux were, it was supposed, admitted at once into the mysteries of God, except those of the very wicked, who were returned to this world in the form of one of the lower animals. This was their punishment. Yet such a spirit might retrieve its misfortune by good behavior, and thus be promoted to its former shape.

In man there were believed to be three souls. One of these, as I have said, immediately enters heaven by the "spirits' path"—the milky way—escorted by the stars. The second remains where the body is placed, as guardian of the grave; while the third lives and travels with its relatives. On this account the natives believe that everything said of the departed is heard by them. I do not know just how this triune conception originated. No doubt it had a reasonable explanation somewhere in the early life of the race, but the legend connected with it is lost.

There is a strong implication that the Great Mystery has made man after himself, and that he is in shape like a man, but with a few modifications. For instance, he is supposed to have horns, symbolic of command; and his eyes are like the sun—no one can gaze into them. The Sioux formerly believed that every created thing can hear what is said of the Creator. Therefore, an Indian fears to take God's name in vain, and there is no profane word in their language. Whenever God's name is used it is done with reverence. In this connection I may be permitted to add that when the Indian found that his white brothers used the name of God indiscriminately and irreverently he was shocked.

It was further observed by him that, inasmuch as there are pairs or opposites in all things, there is a good and an evil spirit; yet both of these are appointed and controlled by the Great Mystery. There were no angels in the Indian's theology. As there is a spirit of antagonism among animals, so also the Indian believed that the elements do often wage war upon each other, and sometimes upon the animals. For instance, it was supposed that the thunder-bird often goes upon the warpath, traveling over vast tracts of country and chastising both animate and inanimate things.

Notes

*The lines come from Alexander Pope's *An Essay on Man*, Epistle I, ll. 99-100. They were quoted so frequently—particularly the first four words—that some wags in the late nineteenth and early twentieth century came to refer to the typical American Indian as "Lo."

Northern Elements in the Mythology of the Navaho

by Franz Boas

* * * * *

Franz Boas (1858–1942), one of the most important figures in the history of anthropology, received his academic training in physics and psychology at several major universities in his native Germany. However, it was principally the influence of some training in cultural geography that led to his interest in the ethnographic study of the Natives of the northwest coast of North America. In 1883 Boas had tried to apply Friedrich Ratzel's theory that the nature of a culture was determined by its geographical milieu to the lifeways of the Cumberland Sound Eskimo. When he returned from this field trip to Germany, Boas joined the staff of Berlin's Museum of Ethnology, where he worked until the lure of fieldwork tempted him to return to the New World. In 1886 he formally began his career as a fully committed anthropologist by investigating Indian groups in western Canada. The following year he settled permanently in the United States. Boas taught at Clark University in

SOURCE: *American Anthropologist*, o.s. 10 (1897), 371–376.

Worchester, Massachusetts, from 1889 to 1892 and in 1896 joined the faculty of Columbia University, where he served until 1936. He also worked for Chicago's Field Museum and for the American Museum of Natural History.

As an anthropologist, Boas was interested in all aspects of the cultures he studied, but throughout his career a primary focus of his attention was folklore, especially oral narratives. In fact, he was president of the American Folklore Society in 1900. He collected folklore from the Canadian Eskimo as early as 1883, and his ethnographies of Arctic and Northwest Coast groups contain folk–narrative texts. In 1894 his first volume devoted to oral narratives, Chinook Texts, *was issued as* Bulletin No. 20 *by the Bureau of American Ethnology. In this work Boas helped to set the style that came to characterize presentations of folklore by anthropologists during most of the twentieth century: accurate renderings of the texts in the native language, interlinear translations to accompany several of these texts, free translations or summaries of all the material, and a minimum of commentary. This approach to presenting American Indian folklore was used by many of Boas's anthropology students as well as in the periodicals he edited:* Publications of the American Ethnological Society, International Journal of American Linguistics *and* Journal of American Folklore.

Boas saw folklore primarily as a tool for obtaining data on native languages and cultures. Hence, he was more interested in the collection of folklore texts than in thier analysis. In part, his position constituted a reaction against the speculative theorizing that had dominated nineteenth-century folklore studies. But it also reflected his view of folklore as a device for data retrieval rather than as a product of oral literary artistry. Nevertheless, Boas did develop two concepts about folklore that influenced his contemporaries and successors. One of these was the idea, borrowed from the student of Eskimo traditions Henry Rink, that folklore mirrored other aspects of culture and could serve as a means for gathering information about a culture that an anthropologist had not encountered first-hand. Boas presented this idea most fully in Tsimshian Mythology, *which appeared in the* Annual Report of the Bureau of American Ethnology *for 1909–1910, though it had been suggested in his earlier work.*

Boas's other theoretical stance, suggested in the article reproduced here, involved the idea that the occurence of the same or similar folk narratives in various cultures resulted from diffusion. This notion placed him at variance with those nineteenth-century theorists who explained this phenomenon by asserting that since man possessed psychic unity and cultures always developed along the same evolutionary lines, cross-cultural similarities could exist despite independent origins. Boas believed that whenever a number of narrative elements existed in similar combination in several different places, the most logical explanation was that this combination had originated in one place and spread from storyteller to storyteller. Therefore, parallels between Navajo narratives and those of other Native American groups stemmed from monogenesis and diffusion, not polygenesis. Virtually the same idea about the dissemination of folklore was developing contemporaneously in Finland, where Julius and Kaarle Krohn were working out a historic-geographic method of folk-narrative research. Their purpose was to create a methodology for locating the time and place of a folktale's origin and then tracing the routes by which it spread. The Finnish School dominated folklore research in Europe and North America for the first half of the twentieth century, though few students using its methodology, which was most applicable to folklore in literate societies, worked with American Indian oral narratives.

A good deal has been written about the life and career of Franz Boas. Perhaps the most comprehensive source is Walter Goldschmidt, ed., The Anthropology of Franz Boas. Essays on the Centennial of His Birth, *published in 1959 as the eighty-ninth* Memoir of the American Anthropological Association. *Included is an essay by Melville Jacobs on Boas' folklore work. Two anthologies of Boas' writings have been published in the twentieth century:* Race, Language, and Culture *(New York: Macmillan, 1940); and George W. Stocking, Jr.,* The Shaping of American Anthropology 1883–1911. A Franz Boas Reader *(New York: Basic Books, 1974). The most fully developed statement of the methods of Boas' Scandinavian contemporaries in diffusionism is Kaarle Krohn,* Die folkloristische Arbeitsmethode, *translated by Roger L. Welsch as* Folklore Methodology *(Austin: University of Texas Press, 1971). The historic-geographic researcher who has worked most assiduously on American Indian materials was Stith Thompson. See his* The Folktale *(New York: Dryden Press, 1946) and especially his model study of a single narrative, "The Star Husband Tale," Studia Septentrionalia, 4 (1953), 93–163. The latter work has been reprinted in Alan Dundes,* The Study of Folklore *(Englewood Cliffs, New Jersey: Prentice-Hall, 1965), pp. 414–474.*

* * * * *

The general character of the Navaho legends recorded by Dr. Washington Matthews[1] differs fundamentally from traditions collected in the northern portion of our continent. Different geographical surroundings and the influence of a different culture convey the strong impression that we have to deal with material that sprang from independent sources. I was much interested in finding on a close examination of the Navaho legends that there was interwoven with a large mass of material foreign to northern tribes many tales undoubtedly derived from the same sources from which the northern tales spring. Most of them are so complex and curious that, taken in connection with the known northern affiliations of the Navaho, they must be considered as a definite proof of either a survival of ancient myths or as proving a later connection.

I will briefly enumerate here the legends or parts of legends which I think must be considered as belonging to the northern area.

Among the Coyote tales is one[2] in which it is told how the Coyote visited the Porcupine, who scratched his nose until blood flowed freely out over it; he then roasted it until it turned into a piece of fine meat. Coyote invited his host to return the visit in two days. He tried to imitate the Porcupine, but failed ignominiously. He next visited the Wolf, who roasted two arrowpoints that were transformed into minced meat. Again the Coyote tried to imitate his host, but failed. Compare with this the tradition of the Chinook, who tell how Bluejay tried to imitate his host;[3] that of the Comox, Nootka, and Kwakiutl of Vancouver island, and of the Bella Coola and Tsimshian of Northern British Columbia,[4] who tell the same story of the Raven; that of the Ponca,[5] who tell the same story of Ictinike, and that of the Micmac,[6] who relate how the Rabbit tried to imitate his host. Although the peculiar method of producing food by magic is not always the same, the whole stories are identical to all intents and purposes.

Later on it is told how the Coyote was playing with his eyes, tearing them out of their sockets and throwing them up; then they fell back into their sockets.[7] We find the identical incident among the Shuswap in the interior of British Columbia[8] and among the Blackfeet.[9]

Once upon a time the Coyote met the Brown Giant. He proposed to him that they should vomit. He placed a large piece of pine bark before each as a dish, and bade the Brown Giant keep his eyes shut till he was told to open them. Coyote vomited bugs and worms, while the Brown Giant vomited fat venison. Coyote exchanged the dishes, and then told the Giant to open his eyes.[10] The Shuswap ascribe the same trick to Coyote when he met the Cannibal Owl.[11]

The people sought to divine their fate. They threw a hide-scraper into the water, saying, "If it sinks, we perish; if it floats, we live." It floated, and all rejoiced. Then Coyote repeated the same test with a stone. It sank, and therefore people die.[12] Among the Blackfeet the first woman asked the "Old Man" if people would be immortal. In order to decide this question he threw a buffalo chip into the water, saying that if it floated people would resurrect on the fourth day after their death. It floated. Then the woman took a stone, saying, "If it floats, we will always live; it it sinks, people must die." It sank, and therefore people die.[13]

One of the most striking resemblances between the myths of the Navaho and those of the Northwest is the visit of the War Gods to their father, the Sun. A brief abstract of this portion of the myth is as follows: The War Gods, the sons of the Sun, leave the earth in quest of their father. On their way they meet the Spider Woman, who advises them in regard to a number of dangers that they will encounter on their way. These were the crushing rocks which close upon those who try to pass them, the reeds with leaves as sharp as knives, a country covered with cane cacti, and the land of the rising sands. They pass these and reach the house of the Sun, the door of which is guarded by pairs of sentinels—bears, serpents, wind, and lightning—two of each kind. When the Sun enters he is angry and tries to kill the intruders on sharp spikes with which the floor of his house is covered. Then he tries to kill them in an overheated sweat-house, and finally by means of poisonous tobacco.[14]

One of the most important legends of northwestern America, which occurs in a great number of versions, tells how one or two boys visited the Sun in quest of a wife. They are warned of the dangers of the road by two women. The last of these dangers is generally the snapping door of the Sun's house. After arriving at the house the young man marries the Sun's daughter. The Sun next tries to kill him by means of the sharp spikes on the floor of his house.[15] The visitor succeeds in crushing these spikes, and is then led to a tree that is being split. The Sun knocks the wedges out of the tree, intending to crush his son-in-law, who escapes in a miraculous way.[16] The other tests vary, but the test of the overheated sweat-house is not absent. It is found among the Chinook[17] and the Ponca.[18] The most striking similarities in these tales are the visit to the Sun with the subsequent attempts on the life of the visitor, the spikes on the floor of the Sun's house, and the test in the overheated sweat-house. In one version of the Navaho legend it is also described how the woman who warned the young men hardened their skins so that the spikes could not hurt them.[19] The same incident occurs in all the corresponding legends from northwest America.

To a similar class of legends belong the attempts of Deer Raiser on the life of his son-in-law, Naci'nescxani,[20] which find their analogy in the tales mentioned above, as well as in the Micmac legend recorded by Rand,[21] in which the wife's mother tries to kill her son-in-law.

The manner in which the people were saved from the deluge also finds its analogy in the Northwest. According to the Navaho legend the people entered a hollow reed, which swayed with the motion of the waters.[22] In the legend of the Tsetsaut, an Athapascan tribe of southern Alaska, they saved themselves in two hollow trees that were swaying to and fro as the water rose.[23]

Another interesting legend which has close analogies in the Northwest is that of the man who was carried to the eyrie of a fabulous eagle. When the eagle drops him into his nest he squirts on the rock some blood that he carried in a bag, and thus makes him believe that he has been killed. The eaglets complain that the food that their father has brought is still alive, but he flies away. Then the man asks the eaglets: "When will your father come back, and where will he sit when he comes?" They answered: "He will return when we have a he-rain (thunderstorm)." Upon being further questioned they said that their mother would return when they had a she-rain (without thunder and lightning). The man then kills the old eagles when they return. He threw the young ones out of the nest, transforming them into an eagle and an owl.[24] The Shuswap tell of a similar incident. A man is carried by an eagle to his nest. He is thrown against a rock and deceives the eagle by squirting red and white paint out of his mouth. Then he threatens the eaglets and by their help induces the old eagle to sit in a position in which he is able to kill her. Then the eaglets carry him down from the eyrie, and upon arriving on level ground he kills them.[25] The Ponca tell of a similar incident, but the eagles are made to reside in the sky.[26] Here it is said that the male eagle returns with the rain, the female with the darkness. Among the Hare Indians we find a tale of a man who climbed an eagle's nest in a fir tree. He awaits the arrival of the old eagles and is told by the eagles that their father arrives with a bright light, while their mother arrives with the night. The man finally killed the eaglets.[27] The Dog Rib Indians tell the same story, but the male brings the snow, the female the rain. The man then kills the old ones and transforms the man-eating eaglet into an eagle living on fish.[28] Petitot records the same story from the Chippewayans.[29]

While I consider that these coincidences have considerable weight as evidence of elements of common origin in the mythologies of the Northwest and of the Southwest, the following are so general that their value is open to doubt. Still in connection with the preceding they are of considerable interest, no matter if we prefer to interpret them as analogous independent phenomena or as due to dissemination.

On page 91 it is told that the vital principle of the Coyote was kept in the tip of his nose and in the end of his tail. The Tillamook of Oregon tell that a certain spirit kept her vital principle in her hat. The Cathlamet of Columbia river tell of a being who kept it in her little finger, while the Kwakiutl relate that a certain spirit was able to lay it aside and kept it in a knot-hole.

The incident of the alien god who flung visitors down a precipice and who is finally flung down himself by the War God, to be eaten by his children at the base of the cliff,[30] reminds us somewhat of the corresponding incident in the Cikla legend of the Chinook and of the Micmac legend quoted before.[31]

In the legend of the visit of the War Gods to their father, the Sun, it is told how the Sun entered his house, hung up the sun on a peg, and gave his visitors irresistible weapons and protective armor.[32] We find the same incident in a Cathlamet myth relating a visit to the Sun, in which the man when carrying the Sun's arms is compelled to kill all whom he encounters.

The legend of Naci'nescxani, who was enclosed in a hollow log and drifted down the river, reminds us somewhat of corresponding tales of the northern Athapascans which were recorded by Petitot.[33]

Other incidents which resemble those of northern legends are so general in character that I do not ascribe any weight to them as proving common origin of these legends. Such are the power of the hunters of reducing the bulk of their game in order to carry it home, which art the Coyote tries to practice among the Navaho[34] as well as among the Kootenay;[35] the magical descent from a great height, which proceeds without danger so long as the person keeps his eyes shut;[36] children formed of the epidermis that a woman rubs from her body,[37] which incident is of very frequent occurrence in northern traditions,[38] and small dishes of food which prove inexhaustible,[39] which compares with [northern] references.[40]

The more elaborate tales which are worked into the fabric of the legends of the Navaho and which are common to their mythology and to that of the northwest coast seem to me to be a certain proof of the complex origin of the Navaho traditions. It is important to note that coincidences with Siouan and Algonquian legends are rare, and that only such are found as occur also on the north Pacific coast. It may be that a more detailed comparison with the mythologies of these tribes would reveal additional material common to them, but so far I have not been able to detect additional striking resemblances of complex tales. If no additional material common to the Navaho and to the tribes of the Mississippi basin and of the Northeast should be found, this would prove that the Navaho mythology has been influenced by those of the northwestern tribes, but not by those of the tribes of the Atlantic coast.

Notes

1. Washington Matthews, *Navaho Legends. Memoirs of the American Folklore Society No. 5* (1897).
2. Matthews, p. 87 [Boas' note].
3. Franz Boas, *Chinook Texts. Bureau of American Ethnology Bulletin No. 20* (1894), p. 178 [Boas' note].
4. Franz Boas, *Indianische Sagen von der Nord-Pacifischen Kuste Amerikas* (Berlin: A. Asher, 1895), pp. 76, 106, 177, 245 [Boas' note].
5. James Owen Dorsey, *The Cegiha Language. Contributions to North American Ethnology No. 6* (1890), p. 557 [Boas' note].
6. Silas Rand, *Legends of the Micmacs* (New York: Longmans, Green, 1894), pp. 300–302 [Boas' note].
7. Matthews, p. 90 [Boas' note].
8. Boas, *Indianische Sagen*, p. 8 [Boas' note].
9. George Bird Grinnell, *Blackfoot Lodge Tales. The Story of a Primitive People* (New York: Scribners, 1892), p. 153 [Boas' note].
10. Matthews, p. 227 [Boas' note].
11. Boas, *Indianische Sagen*, p. 9 [Boas' note].
12. Matthews, p. 77 [Boas' note].
13. Grinnell, pp. 138–139 [Boas' note].
14. Matthews, pp. 109ff. [Boas' note].
15. Boas, *Indianische Sagen*, pp. 39, 66, 111, 118, 136, 171 [Boas' note].
16. Boas, *Indianische Sagen*, pp. 39, 67, 70, 111, 118, 171, 136, 198; Boas, *Chinook Texts*, p. 34 [Boas' note].
17. Boas, *Chinook Texts*, p. 58 [Boas' note].
18. Dorsey, p. 60 [Boas' note].
19. Matthews, p. 232 [Boas' note].
20. Matthews, pp. 186ff. [Boas' note].
21. Rand, p. 90 [Boas' note].
22. Matthews, p. 75 [Boas' note].
23. Franz Boas, "Traditions of the Ts'ets'āut," *Journal of American Folklore*, 9 (1896), 262 [Boas' note].
24. Matthews, pp. 119–120 [Boas' note].
25. Boas, *Indianische Sagen*, p. 4 [Boas' note].
26. Dorsey, p. 30 [Boas' note].

27. Emile Petitot, *Traditions indiennes du Canada Nord-ouest: textes originaux & traduction littérale* (Alençon: E. Renaut de Broise, 1887), p. 144 [Boas' note].

28. Petitot, pp. 323–324 [Boas' note].

29. Petitot, p. 359 [Boas' note].

30. Matthews, p. 122 [Boas' note].

31. Boas, *Chinook Texts*, p. 21; Rand, p. 90 [Boas' note].

32. Matthews, pp. 111–113 [Boas' note].

33. Petitot, p. 56 [Boas' note].

34. Matthews, p. 97 [Boas' note].

35. Franz Boas, "Einige Sagen der Kootenay," *Berliner Gesellschaft für Anthropologie, Ethnologie und Urgeschichte,* Verhandlungen 1891, p. 170 [Boas' note].

36. Matthews, p. 121 [Boas' note].

37. Matthews, p. 148 [Boas' note].

38. Boas, *Indianische Sagen*, p. 358 [Boas' note].

39. Matthews, pp. 165, 199 [Boas' note].

40. Boas, *Indianische Sagen*, p. 360 [Boas' note].

The Scientific Importance of the Folk-Music of Our Aborigines

by John Comfort Fillmore

* * * * *

*As a music theóretician and teacher, John Comfort Fillmore (1843–1898)
enjoyed a good deal of renown during the late nineteenth century. After graduation from Oberlin College in 1865, he studied organ, piano, and music
theory in Leipzig under Moritz Hauptmann, Ernst Richter, and Benjamin
Papperitz. Upon returning to this country, Fillmore taught music at Oberlin,
then at Ripon College in Wisconsin, and then at the Milwaukee College for
Women. He founded the Milwaukee Music School in 1884 and remained its
director until 1895, when he joined the faculty of Pomona College in Clare-
mont, California.*

 *Fillmore's interest in American Indian music was stimulated by Alice
Fletcher. Fillmore provided musicological analysis of Fletcher's collection of
Omaha songs and collaborated with her and Francis La Flesche on the pio-
neering* A Study of Omaha Indian Music, *which appeared in the first*

SOURCE: *Out West Magazine*, 7, No. 1 (June 1897), 22-25. From a paper read
before the Southern California Academy of Sciences [Fillmore's note].

volume of the Archaeological and Ethnological Papers of the Peabody Museum *in 1893. Although his contribution to this study stands as his major effort in "ethnomusicology" (the word was not coined until the twentieth century by Jaap Kunst), Fillmore published, in various periodicals, several articles on Native American music in general and on specific tribal musical traditions.*

In the essay included here, a survey of the scientific importance of American Indian music as a setting for the performance of oral literature, Fillmore evokes the two academic disciplines that must merge in the study of such material: musicology and ethnology. His insistence that music reflects the rest of a group's culture and may infuse all of the group's activities remains central to the thinking of many ethnomusicologists. For instance, cantometrics, the theory that Alan Lomax has been developing over the past several decades, arises primarily from such an assumption. Essentially Lomax asserts that a group's musical style can be shown to reflect most of its cultural values.

Not all of Fillmore's musicological and ethnological conclusions have been as durable as the idea that music can reflect culture. Responding to the evolutionary thought of his day as well as to the concept of the psychic unity of all "primitive" humanity, he sees cross-cultural parallels among musical traditions of societies at an "early" stage of cultural development where such parallels are in fact nonexistent. But Fillmore's view of American Indian music as a subject worthy of study indicates a broadness of mind somewhat unusual for one with a background such as his in elite art music.

Other essays by Fillmore, similar to this one in their general approach to Native American music, include "Harmonic Structure of Indian Music," Music, *16 (1899), 453–472; "Scale and Harmonies of Indian Songs,"* Music, *4 (1893), 478–489; and "What Do Indians Mean to Do When They Sing, and How Far Do They Succeed?"* Journal of American Folklore, *8 (1895), 138–142. Alan Lomax's work on cantometrics can be sampled in* Folk Song Style and Culture *(Washington: American Association for the Advancement of Science, 1968) and* Cantometrics: A Method in Musical Anthropology *(Berkeley: University of California Extension Media Center, 1976). The latter consists of seven casette recordings with an explanatory booklet.*

Scholarly people do not need to be reminded of the importance, to ethnology and anthropology, of study of the mental life, the history, the manners, customs, religious and social ideas of the various races and tribes of our American aborigines. The comparison of the inherited ideas and customs of the different race-stocks with each other and with the races of the Eastern hemisphere, if it could be made thorough and complete, would throw a world of light on many important questions which are still in doubt. The studies already made in this field by American and foreign anthropologists have been decidedly fruitful; but nevertheless serve mainly to show the enormous magnitude of the field and the pressing necessity for its immediate occupation. For it is patent to every observer that the aborigines of this continent are fast vanishing from the face of the earth; and that those who still remain are forced to live under conditions so different from those of their ancestors that their inherited ideas, customs and traditions must very soon perish from the memory of men. Whatever is done to preserve the unwritten records of their past,—records which are priceless in their relations to our scientific understanding of primitive men,—must be done quickly. A short delay and all this incomparably important body of scientific knowledge will have perished without hope of resurrection.

Upon American scientific men and American scientific bodies rests the responsibility of allowing the rich harvest of anthropological and ethnological knowledge which still remains in the domain of American aboriginal life to perish ungathered, or of doing what may be done to collect and record it in permanent form, accessible to students. This responsibility is ours whether we will or no; it is forced upon us by circumstances. It is we who are crowding the Indian to his doom. Our race has destroyed all the conditions of his primitive life. We are pressing upon him our ideas, customs, habits, and are doing all we can to eradicate from his mind, as from his daily life, everything which was characteristic of his ancestors. It will be anything but creditable to our boasted civilization, and professions of interest in the science of man as man, if we shall fail to do what in us lies to preserve whatever can be preserved of the memorials of these fast vanishing tribes.

A vast proportion of the most valuable ethnological and anthropological material to be gathered among our American aborigines is embodied in their folk-music. The Indian is extremely religious. He not only worships, but he does nothing whatever without reference to the superior powers with which he is at all times surrounded. Whether he hunts, plants, harvests, goes to war, makes peace, eats, drinks, sleeps, makes love—no matter what he does—he conceives each special mode of activity as related to the gods. Religious ideas permeate his whole life and affect his every thought, word and action.

Now, it is a curious fact that Indian prayers are *always sung, not said.* At least this is true so far as my knowledge of them extends. Every Omaha mother, for example, teaches her child to sing, not say, "Wakanda, I am poor and needy; have pity upon me." When her son approaches the border-line between childhood and youth, she sends him out to fast and pray, to receive visions and to dream dreams; but the prayer which he is to bring home with him as his own peculiar property must invariably be a song. When he goes out upon the warpath his intention is announced and his departure accompanied by a war-song. The warrior society to which (if he shall distinguish himself in battle) he may have the honor of being admitted, will record his valiant deeds in song and transmit them in this form to posterity. The Haethuska, the warrior society of the Omaha tribe, keeps all the historical chronicles of the tribe in this way.

Children have singing games; young men sing when they gamble, when they make love, when they gossip among themselves. Medicine men sing in their ministrations to the sick and during all their acts of conjuration—and the singing is regarded as essential. The great religious ceremony of the Wa-wan, or Sacred Fellowship Pipes, which I was once permitted to witness, is a full choral service of four or five hours in length, every act of which is sung.

In view of these facts, it is obvious that whoever collects and thoroughly studies the folk-music of any one tribe, thereby acquires a tolerably complete knowledge of the governing ideas of that tribe.

Of course there are serious difficulties in the way of acquiring this knowledge. The Indian is always suspicious of the white man, until his confidence has been completely won. He is always expecting his white visitor to look on his religious ideas and feelings, not with respect and sympathy, but with more or less of contempt. "You will not believe me," said a Sioux priest to a friend of mine who was his guest at the great Sun-dance, "but I pray to God, and I am answered." "Certainly," was the reply, "why not?" The priest looked surprised and said: "But your people think my people are dogs!"

Whoever would study the Indian must absolutely divest himself of all feeling of superiority of any kind and think of his red brethren simply as men like himself, differing, to be sure, in their bringing-up and in their inherited ideas, but as well-intentioned and living up to the light they have quite as well, on the average, as the men of his own race. If he can show himself brotherly and sympathetic he will, sooner or later, overcome the natural suspicion with which the Indian at first regards him, and then the way is open for an intelligent comprehension of the Indian character. Such was the attitude of Mr. Frank Cushing among the Zuñis; and how great and complete was his success you are doubtless aware. One of our own number, Mr. Chas. F. Lummis, was equally successful in Isleta and other Pueblo towns. To him I owe some valuable songs of the Tigua tribe.[1]

To Dr. Franz Boas I owe an introduction to the Kwakiutl tribe of Vancouver Island, whose music I had the opportunity of transcribing at the World's Columbian Exposition; and to Mr. Carl Lumholtz I am indebted for songs of some Mexican tribes and of the cannibal natives of Australia.[2] One of our Pomona College graduates, Mr. David Barrows, learned some valuable songs among the Coahuias two years ago, and I transcribed them from his singing.[3] He has since been studying in Chicago University and Columbia College. He and I purpose visiting the Coahuias this summer to make further collections.

But by far the largest collection of aboriginal folk-songs thus far obtained, (unless it be that of Dr. Washington Matthews), was made by Miss Alice C. Fletcher, a Fellow of Harvard University and an assistant of Professor Putnam, of the Peabody Museum of American Archaeology and Ethnology. She spent several years among the Omahas in Nebraska, won the entire confidence and the devoted love and gratitude of the whole tribe and learned to understand the innermost life of those people. She was admitted to their most sacred religious ceremonies, sang their songs with them, reduced them for the first time to written form and afterward turned them over to me for scientific study, such as could be made only by a professional musician. Both she and I had the invaluable assistance of Mr. Francis La Flesche, a son of the chief whose guest she was during her stay among the Omahas; now her adopted son and a trusted employe of the Indian Bureau at Washington, D.C. He accompanied me to the Omaha reservation in the summer of 1891, enabled me to witness religious ceremonies rarely opened to a white man, helped me to verify Miss Fletcher's records and to attain scientific results never before achieved in the domain of folk-music. The results of all this work were published in 1893, by the Peabody Museum of American Archaeology and Ethnology of Harvard University, in a volume bearing the names of Miss Fletcher, Mr. La Flesche and myself.[4]

Thus the Omaha music has been pretty thoroughly exploited. Of no other tribe has so complete a collection of songs been published. I have a large number of phonographic records of the songs of the Kwakiutls and their neighbors, obtained by Dr. Franz Boas; and Dr. Washington Matthews, U.S.A., formerly stationed at Fort Wingate, N.M., made a larger number of similar records of Navajo songs. A few of them are now in my possession, and a number of them, which I transcribed, have been published. But all these put together form but a small percentage of the enormous amount of material which might, with proper effort, be obtained from our aboriginal tribes.

The value of these Indian folk-songs does not consist alone in their relations to ethnological and anthropological science. They also have important bearings on the science of music. Such questions as the origin of scales, the relations of primitive melody to harmony, the naturalness of our major and minor scales, the progressive development of them and above all, the fundamental question *"What is the line of least resistance for the human voice in primitive man making music spontaneously?"* (which I had the honor of being the first to ask and to answer)—all these have been illuminated, as never before, in the investigations made on the material collected during the last twenty years. I have already mentioned the foremost collections of Indian songs which it has been my privilege to study. The World Columbian Exposition gave me the opportunity of making comparisons, at first-hand, of our Indian folk-music with that of many other races: Chinese, Japanese, Malays, Arabs, Egyptians, Turks, Dahomeyans, South Sea Islanders, Esquimaux, etc.

All this comparative study has already led to important scientific results. It has shown, for one thing, that all folk-melody, the world over, is *harmonic* melody; i.e., implies harmony and is clearly the result of a sub-conscious perception of the harmonic relation of tones. The line of least resistance for the human voice making melody spontaneously is a *harmonic* line; i.e., the voice, when it changes pitch from a monotone, tends to move along the line of the Tonic chord, or chord of the key-note. When it departs from this it fills in the gaps between these chord-tones with tones belonging to the chords most nearly related to the Tonic, viz, the Dominant, Subdominant and Relative Minor chords. These tones are precisely those of our major scale. This scale usually appears at first with the fourth and seventh omitted, making the 5-toned scale so familiar in Scotch and Irish music. A shifting of the center of gravity from the first to the sixth of the major scale gives minor tonality, *without any change in the actual tones of the scale*, the key-note being merely shifted from Do to La, thus:

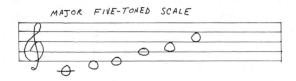

MAJOR FIVE-TONED SCALE

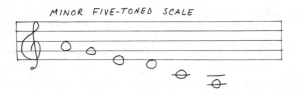

MINOR FIVE-TONED SCALE

These scales are, therefore, natural and not artificial. Primitive man everywhere, no matter to what race he belongs, produces them naturally and spontaneously, as a result of a natural and universal harmonic sense, founded in the immutable laws of acoustics as related to the human ear and vocal organs.

Now the question whether other scales might not be just as natural as those we have was considered doubtful by no less an authority than Professor Helmholtz; so that the discovery, by means of this extended comparative study of primitive folk-music, of the fact that men of all races, the world over, do actually produce songs based on precisely the same major and minor tonalities that we ourselves use, *and on no others*, and the obvious inference that they, *and they alone*, must therefore be natural, is a matter of first importance to the science of music.

It used to be thought (and most if not all the histories of music still say), that the Arabs have a scale of 17 tones within the octave. But Mr. Land, a Dutch student of Arab music,[5] has shown that this is an error. The Arab lute, he says, does indeed provide separate strings for the sharps and flats; but one set is used for the sharp keys and another for the flat keys; the two are never used for the same tonality. By this means each key is in pure tune, instead of being tempered as in our system, so as to make, for example, C sharp and D flat identical. The *tonality* of their music, whether major or minor, corresponds precisely with our own. And this tallies exactly with my own observations of Arab folk-music at the World's Fair.

There are those, I believe, who still imagine that our own aborigines sing quarter-tones or even smaller intervals, producing scales of a different character from those on which our European folk-music is based. But these bizarre scales exist nowhere in the world except in the imaginations of those whom my friend Mr. Lummis aptly calls "armchair students." The Indian does, indeed, often sing more or less out of tune; but singing out of tune is a phenomenon not confined to our American savages nor to any other savages. Nor is it any more intentional in the case of Indians than in the case of our own opera-singers. Numerous and repeated experiments of the most thorough and careful sort have demonstrated that the tonality of all the Indians songs yet studied corresponds precisely to our own. The same is true of the folk-music of all races, so far as yet appears; and I think that enough specimens have been collected and compared to justify such induction.

Nevertheless, the duty of the scientific man is to hold his mind open to the reception of new truth and to be ready at all times to modify or abandon any or all his former opinions, if new light should prove the necessity of so doing. It is conceivable (although I do not think it probable), that further collections of material may modify the views above expressed. For that reason, if there were no other, we ought to preserve as much of it as possible. But when we consider the importance of the ungathered material for the purposes of ethnological study and comparison, and the meagreness of the results thus far accomplished, the necessity of speedy and vigorous action presses upon us with overwhelming weight. When we consider, further, the difficulties of the undertaking, the time which must necessarily be consumed in preliminaries before and after the fields of work are reached and the fewness of the competent investigators whose interest has thus far been enlisted, the necessity of energetic action becomes still more apparent.

Notes

1. Charles F. Lummis (1859-1928) was an important man of letters in the American Southwest. He published several books on Pueblo Indian cultures, including some folktale collections. He served as editor of the periodical *Land of Sunshine*, which became *Out West Magazine*.

2. Karl Sofus Lumholtz (1851-1922) had written *Among Cannibals. An Account of Four Years' Travels in Australia and of Camp Life with the Aborigines of Queensland* (New York: Scribners, 1889) at the time of Fillmore's essay.

His book on Mexico did not appear until some five years after the essay. See *Unknown Mexico. A Record of Five Years' Exploration Among the Tribes of the Western Sierra Madre; in the Tierra Caliente of Tepic and Jalisco; and Among the Torascos of Michoachan* (New York: Scribners, 1902).

3. David S. Barrows published "Some Coahuia [Cahuilla] Songs and Dances" in *Land of Sunshine*, 4, No. 1 (December 1895), 38–41.

4. Alice Cunningham Fletcher, Francis La Flesche, and John Comfort Fillmore, *A Study of Omaha Indian Music. Archaeological and Ethnological Papers of the Peabody Museum*, 1, No. 5 (1893).

5. Jan Pieter Nicolaas Land (1834–1897) wrote *Recherches sur l'histoire de la gamme arabe* (Leiden: E. J. Brill, 1884).

Indian Superstitions
and Legends

by Simon Pokagon

* * * * *

During his lifetime Simon Pokagon (1830–1899) was regarded as the best-educated American Indian of his generation. Son of a Potawatomi chief who had participated in the Fort Dearborn massacre of 1812, Pokagon attended Notre Dame in South Bend, Indiana, for three years, spent another year at Oberlin College, and completed his formal education with two years of schooling at Twinsburg, Ohio. As chief of a branch of the Potawatomi, Pokagan spent much of his life seeking payment of funds owed to his tribe for the sale of the land on which the city of Chicago was built. He also encouraged Native American unity and unsuccessfully tried to organize a congress of American Indians for the 1893 Chicago World's Fair. During the last decade of his life, Pokagon wrote a number of articles on the culture and history of the Potawatomi. But his most important literary achievement was O-Gi-Maw-Kwe Mit-I-Gwa-Ki *(Queen of the Woods), Also Brief Sketch of the*

SOURCE: *The Forum*, 35 (July 1898), 618-629.

Algaic Language (*Hartford, Michigan: C. H. Engle, 1899*), *variously described as a fictionalized autobiography or an autobiographical novel. The work treats Pokagon's romance with his first wife and indicts Euro-American society for introducing alcoholic beverages into Native American life. In fact, the last section of the book is essentially a temperance tract.*

In the essay reproduced here, Pokagon presents an insider's—or emic— view of various aspects of Potawatomi culture, including myths and legends. But his primary purpose is to advise Euro-Americans that they need not feel superior because of the "superstitious" belief and practices of the Indians. His own experience in both cultures has shown him that the civilized Euro-American may employ magic to ensure good fortune or to prevent bad luck and thus is as liable to the charge of being superstitious as is the Native American. Although highly educated, Pokagon does not suggest a preference for the ways of civilization as did his younger Indian contemporary Charles A. Eastman. Nor does he develop any concept of cultural evolution—with Indians at an early stage of cultural progression which will culminate in a lifeway resembling that of European and American civilization—despite his argument for psychic unity, a basic principle for cultural evolutionists.

*A biographical sketch of Simon Pokagon is David H. Dickason, "Chief Simon Pokagon: 'The Indian Longfellow,' "*Indiana Magazine of History, *52 (1961), 127–140. For a thorough discussion of* Queen of the Woods, *see Charles R. Larson,* American Indian Fiction (*Albuquerque: University of New Mexico Press, 1978), pp. 37–46. Pokagon's book was reprinted by Hardscrabble Press in 1972.*

* * * * *

Until twelve years old I could speak only *nin-gaw odaw-naw-naw* (my mother-tongue). Before then I had bitter thoughts of the white men; regarding them as robbers of the worst sort, and destitute of all love or sympathy for our race. When I saw them I fled and hid myself, like the young partridge from the hawk.

About that time I became acquainted with Edward Coles, a travelling Indian missionary, who frequently called at our wigwam in Pokagon, my father's village, in Southwestern Michigan. He had had a fair English education, and was a fine Christian teacher. He saw how bitterly I felt toward the dominant race, and often told me that the better class were as good as our own people, and that I was very prejudiced. No doubt this was the case, and was due to the fact, that the white men who generally came in contact with the Indians were the worst of their kind. He also said that numbers of white men believed in Kigi Manito,—the God we worshipped,—and that many, many years before, He had sent from Waw-kwi (Heaven) to their forefathers His son Jesus, whom they murdered, and that He arose from the dead, and ascended to Heaven; that He now there stood, with open arms, ready to receive all who put their trust in Him; and that when life was ended here, they would dwell with Him in Waw-kwi forever. I could not understand how white men could be so good as red men, and yet be guilty of taking the life of a noble chief who had come to save them. I inquired of him if those white men who had brought ruin upon our people, by selling them fire-water, would be permitted to enter the garden of Waw-kwi. He claimed that if they would quit their accursed business, and humbly repent, and try to repair the great wrong they had done, it was barely possible they might enter the land of promise. This noble Christian missionary greatly impressed me with the wonderful things white men could do, through the mighty inventions and discoveries they had made; and these so excited my love of the marvellous, that my youthful heart thirsted night and day to drink from the fountain of knowledge at the white man's school.

About this time my dear father died; and, soon after, my mother, on the advice of one of the Catholic Fathers, sent me to Notre Dame School, near South Bend, Indiana, where I remained four or five years. But, desiring a more liberal education than I was likely to get there, I sought out my old missionary friend Coles, and laid before him my great anxiety to go to school at Oberlin, Ohio, where race and color were disregarded. The good man finally persuaded my mother to send me to that school. I was about to leave home, when, to my surprise, some of the older members of the Pokagon band objected to my going to the white's man's school; believing it would displease the Great

Spirit for a son of the Great Chief, who had passed into the hunting-ground beyond, to attend the Pale-face school.

I listened to their admonitions and advice; well knowing their objection was too weak for consideration. Yet, I must confess that their words lingered about my heart, and worried me, in spite of all my reasoning; and I said to myself, "Pokagon, such superstition you must inherit from your race." I was troubled; for I thought I should not be able to compete in my studies with white class-mates, who would have better sense than to worry over that which they did not believe.

A short time after this I mentioned to one of the most intelligent of my class-mates, that on the following day I was going into an advanced class. He replied, "You had better wait until Monday." "Why so?" I asked. "Because," said he, "to-morrow is Friday—an unlucky day—and very likely, if you start then, you will always be at the tail-end of your class." This foolish suggestion, coming from such a source, fairly staggered me; and yet it encouraged me to know that my rival had weak points like those which had lessened my faith in myself.

Notwithstanding the superstitions of our Algonquin fathers, they were no idol-worshippers. Their "religion" taught them that each mountain, stream, and lake had its spirit that governed and ruled over it. They also believed that some deity controlled the winds and waves, and rode upon the clouds; commanding the storm, and guiding the whirlwind in its course.

They believed in four sister-deities, who controlled the four seasons of the year. Bi-bon (Winter) brought down from the north *agon* (the snow), and, with her chilly fingers, touched the lakes and streams; leaving them ice-bound, until her sister Sig-wan (Spring) came. She, with her warm breath, melted the snow and ice; letting the imprisoned lakes and streams go free, clothing the naked trees in robes of green, covering the earth with grass and fragrant flowers, filling the air with song-birds and insect life, and the waters with fish, and working with might and main until the arrival of her sister Ne-bin (Summer) on hasty wings, to help on the work Sig-wan had so well begun. Man, beasts, and fowls sought the shade, to avoid the scorching sunshine of her face. Last of all, the oldest sister, Baw-waw-gi (Autumn), came to ripen all the fruit, grain, and nuts; painting in gold and red the forest leaves, which for a few short days flaunted their glories in the breeze, then shed themselves, leaving their parent branches to combat with the winter's storms.

Our forefathers did not grasp the grand idea of an infinite, all-wise being whose presence is everywhere. Hence they believed that these deities, scattered throughout the world, were the agents of a mighty chief, one Mi-chi Ogaw-maw, who ruled all the rest. They saw the beauty of his face in the rainbow; the majesty of his eyes flashed in the clouds; the terror of his voice thundered in the storm, rumbled in the earthquake, and roared in the sea. They taught their children, that Ke-sus (the sun) represented the eyes of this mighty Kigi Manito by day; that Te-bik Kesus and Anong (the moon and stars) were his eyes by night; and that they could not hide their words* or acts from him.

Our tradition show most clearly that the children were obedient to their parents, kind to the old and unfortunate, and respectful to all. They had no cigarettes to smoke, no fire-water to drink, no saloons to lounge in. As a race they were held in great Nature's lap, close to her heart: they listened to her words, and obeyed, as they understood them. All believed in the immortality of the soul.

I never saw nor heard of an Indian atheist. Their Heaven was not paved with gold and precious stones; but it was a grand, romantic paradise of forests and wide, extended plains,—filled with beasts and birds, with lakes and streams swarming with fish close to shore,—where want never came, and where all were contented and happy.

Among the most ancient traditions of our race is one that our first parents found themselves here surrounded by beasts of prey without number, whose physical strength far exceeded theirs, and whose young had greater strength and more knowledge than the Indian children. Stones and clubs were used for weapons, until the bow and arrow were invented; and but for the fact, that a *manito* was impressed upon the human countenance, before which the fiercest brute stood in awe, our first parents and their children would have been destroyed from off the face of the earth.

THE GREAT FLOOD.

One very remarkable character reported in our legends, dimly seen through the mist of untold centuries, is Kwi-wi-sens Nenaw-bo-zhoo, meaning, in Algonquin dialect, "The greatest clown-boy in the world." When he became a man, he was not only a great prophet among his people, but a giant of such marvellous strength, that he could wield his war-club with force enough to shatter in pieces the largest pine-tree. His hunting-dog was a monstrous black wolf, as large as a full-grown buffalo, with long, soft hair, and eyes that shone in the night like the moon. The deity of the sea saw the charming beauty of this wolf-dog, and was so extremely jealous of him, that he was determined to take his life. So he appeared before him in the form of a deer; and as the dog rushed to seize him, he was grasped by the deity and drowned in the depths of the sea. He then made a great barbecue and invited as his guests whales, serpents, and all the monsters of the deep, that they might exult and rejoice with him that he had slain the dog of the prophet.

When the seer-clown learned of the fate of his noble dog, through cunning Waw-goosh (the fox), whose keen eyes saw the deception that cost the wolf-dog his life, he sought to take revenge upon the sea-god. So he went at once to the place where the latter was accustomed to come on land with his monster servants to bathe in the sunshine, and there concealed himself among the tall rushes until the "caravan of the deep" came ashore. When they had fallen fast asleep, he drew his giant bow, twice as long as he was tall, and shot a poisoned arrow that pierced Neben Manito, the water-god, through the heart. Neben Manito rolled into the sea, and cried, "Revenge! Revenge!" Then all the assembled monsters of the deep rushed headlong after the slayer of their king. The prophet fled in consternation before the outraged creatures that hurled after him mountains of water, which swept down the forests like grass before the whirlwind. He continued to flee before the raging flood, but could find no dry land. In sore despair he then called upon the God of Heaven to save him, when there appeared before him a great canoe, in which were pairs of all kinds of land-beasts and birds, being rowed by a most beautiful maiden, who let down a rope and drew him up into the boat.

The flood raged on; but, though mountains of water were continually being hurled after the prophet, he was safe. When he had floated on the water many days, he ordered Aw-mik (the beaver) to dive down and, if he could reach the bottom, to bring up some earth. Down the latter plunged, but in a few minutes came floating to the surface lifeless. The prophet pulled him into the boat, blew into his mouth, and he became alive again. He then said to Waw-jashk (the muskrat), "You are the best diver among all the animal creation. Go down to the bottom and bring me up some earth, out of which I will create a new world; for we cannot much longer live on the face of the deep."

Down plunged the musk-rat; but, like the beaver, he, too, soon came to the surface lifeless, and was drawn into the boat, whereupon the prophet blew into *his* mouth, and he became alive again. In his paw, however, was found a small quantity of earth, which the prophet rolled into a small ball, and tied to the neck of Ka-ke-gi (the raven), saying, "Go thou, and fly to and fro over the surface of the deep, that dry land may appear." The raven did so; the waters rolled away; the world resumed its former shape; and, in course of time, the maiden and prophet were united and repeopled the world.

PICTURES OF GOD BEFORE AND AFTER HE MADE THE WORLD.

About forty years ago two Indians, who were cutting cord-wood near Little Traverse village, one day returned in great haste, pale and excited, to Kaw-kee, their employer, saying, "Oh Kaw-kee, we cut down this morning a large maple-tree; and when we had sawn off the butt cut, behold, we found painted on the end of the log a figure of God before He made the world! It seemed so strange and wonderful that we dared not stay longer on the work; feeling sure that something awful would happen if we did." I will complete the story as it was told me by Kaw-kee about the time it occurred:

"Well," said he, "I laughed at them for such foolish superstition. They then tried to get me to return with them and examine the strange picture. I was sick at the time, and persuaded them to go back and saw off a thin piece of the log, and bring it to me, that I might see the picture for myself.

They started off very reluctantly. Returning in about two hours more excited than before, they exclaimed, 'Oh Kaw-kee, we have cut off the end of the log as you requested; and, as it fell picture-side to the ground—*Na! Mash-Kee!* On the other side was a plain figure of God after He had made the world. And we do not dare to meddle further with it, for we feel that something dreadful will happen if we do.' On the following day I went with them to see what had so alarmed them, and to soothe their fears, if possible.

I must confess that as we approached the fallen tree I felt a curious sort of awe about my heart. I picked up the slice of wood which they had sawn off, and looked it carefully over on both sides. I was indeed astonished; for on each side Nature had traced a wonderful picture!"

At this point I became so intensely interested in his wonderful story, that I said, "Kaw-kee, what has become of that piece of wood?"

"Here it is," he replied; handing it to me as he stepped to one corner of his wigwam.

It was indeed a natural curiosity, well calculated to deceive anyone. On one side appeared the figure of a man with folded arms, and with a blanket wrapped about him, standing in what appeared to be the outlines of the segment of a rainbow. This had been regarded as a picture of God *before* He made the world. On the other side, appeared the same figure, with the right arm extended at full length, holding in his right hand a large ball, apparently in the act of throwing it. This had been considered to be a picture of God *after* He had made the world.

On close inspection, I saw that these pictures were caused in some way by the growth of the timber. The heart, or red part, of the wood forming the figures was surrounded by the white of the wood, which made the outlines clear. As I looked first at one side, and then at the other, I said to myself, "Those pictures might deceive the very elect."

INDIAN SPIRITUALISM.

There is a tradition among the Ottawa branch of the great Algonquin family, believed to this day, that, centuries ago, their first parents migrated westward from the sea-coast, near the mouth of the St. Lawrence River, and settled in the valley of the Ottawa River in Canada, where they lived for untold centuries, and that their main village was at a place they named Ke-tchi-nebis-sing, which name it still bears. There a daughter of the chief of the village went down to the lake to bathe one morning; leaving her infant boy tied to a flat piece of wood, as was the custom. On returning to the spot where she had left her child, he could nowhere be found. Distracted, she ran back to the village; frantically screaming that her child had been stolen. The villagers turned out and searched long and well; but not a trace of the child could be found.

A few days after this two young lovers sat on a mound near the spot where the child had been lost; and while they were kissing and making love, they were startled by hearing, deep in the ground beneath them, an infant crying and sobbing as if its heart would break. They ran in great haste to the village, and reported what they had heard. All the inhabitants believed that it was the lost child which had been heard crying underground. The old chief called together all the magicians,—as is the custom to this day, where the Indians are not under the influence of Christianity,—to hold a *séance*, for communion with the unseen spirits, to

245

divine what had become of the child. I will here briefly describe the manner in which Indians proceed to receive communications from the spiritual world, as I have myself witnessed.

Poles, ten to twelve feet high, are set in the ground, in the form of a circle from six to eight feet in diameter. The top of the lodge is left open. The sides are tightly covered with birch-bark, or the skins of animals. A fire is built close to the lodge for the purpose of enabling the spectators to light their pipes, as they generally smoke during the strange performance. All being ready, a low, tinkling sound is heard, like several small bells at a distance. With a rush, on comes the leading performer, carrying a magician's little, flat rattle-box, somewhat like a tambourine. He sits down by the fire, and begins by telling his audience how he can call up spirits of the dead, as well as of those yet living in the world, and that any present can ask them questions and receive true answers thereto. He next sings a peculiar song, which can scarcely be understood. He then either goes into the lodge by crawling under, or sits outside with the audience; throwing his blanket or some other clothing over the top of it. Immediately the lodge begins to shake, like a creature of life with an ague chill. Then is heard in the lodge a sound like that of a distant, strong wind sweeping through leafless trees, and intermingled with strange voices. When questions are asked by anyone present they are always answered in an unknown tongue; but, luckily, among the spirits there is always a special interpreter to explain what the spirits say.

According to the tradition above referred to, when the performance closed a party was sent to the lake to dig near where the lost child was left by its mother. They did so; and, as deep down in the ground as they were tall, they found the remains of the child in a cavern, from which fled, through an underground channel into the lake, a spirit monster. The magicians then declared that the country was ruled by Mau-tchi Manito, the evil one, who was an enemy seeking to do them all the harm possible; that all the misfortunes which had befallen them came from that source alone; and that their only means of safety was to seek a new land toward the setting sun. Thus is was, that those tribes of the great valley of the Ottawa moved westward along the northern limits of Lake Huron and Lake Michigan and all about Ot-chip-we-ki-tchi-gami (Lake Superior), where many of them remain to this day.

ORIGIN OF OUR TRIBAL FLOWER— THE TRAILING ARBUTUS.

Many, many moons ago, there lived an old man alone in his lodge beside a stream in the thick woods. He was heavily clad in furs; for it was winter, and all the world was covered with snow and ice. The winds swept through the woods; searching every bush and tree for birds to chill, and chasing evil spirits over high hills, through tangled swamps, and valleys deep. The old man went about, and peered vainly in the deep snow for pieces of wood to sustain the fire in his lodge. Sitting down by the last dying embers, he cried to Kigi Manito Waw-kwi (the God of Heaven) that he might not perish. The winds howled, and blew aside the door of his lodge, when in came a most beautiful maiden. Her cheeks were like red roses; her eyes were large, and glowed like the fawn's in the moonlight; her hair was long and black as the raven's plumes, and touched the ground as she walked; her hands were covered with willow-buds; on her head were wreaths of wild flowers; her clothing was sweet grass and ferns; her moccasons were fair white lilies; and, when she breathed, the air of the lodge became warm and fragrant. The old man said, "My daughter, I am indeed glad to see you. My lodge is cold and cheerless; yet it will shield you from the tempest. But tell me who you are, that you should come to my lodge in such strange clothing. Come, sit down here, and tell me of thy country and thy victories, and I will tell thee of my exploits. For I am Manito." He then filled two pipes with tobacco, that they might smoke together as they talked. When the smoke had warmed the old man's tongue, again he said, "I am Manito. I blow my breath, and the lakes and streams become flint." The maiden answered, "I breathe, and flowers spring up on all the plains." The old man replied, "I breathe, and the snow covers all the earth." "I shake my tresses," returned the maiden, "and warm rains fall from the clouds." "When I walk about," answered the old man, "leaves wither and fall from the trees. At my command the animals hide themselves in the ground, and the fowls forsake the waters and fly away. Again I say, 'I am Manito.' " The maiden made answer: "When I walk about, the plants lift up their heads, and the naked trees robe themselves in living green; the birds come back; and all who see me sing for joy. Music is everywhere." As they talked the air became warmer and more fragrant in the lodge; and the old man's head drooped upon his breast, and he slept. Then the sun came back, and the bluebirds came to the top of the lodge and sang, "We are thirsty. We are thirsty." And Sebin (the river) replied, "I am free. Come, come and drink." And while the old man was sleeping, the maiden passed her hand over his head; and he began to grow small. Streams of water poured out of his mouth; very soon he became a small mass upon the ground; and his clothing turned to withered leaves.

Then the maiden kneeled upon the ground, took from her bosom the most precious pink and white flowers, and, hiding them under the faded leaves, and breathing upon them, said: "I give you all my virtues, and all the sweetness of my breath; and all who would pick thee shall do so on bended knees."

Then the maiden moved away through the woods and over the plains; all the birds sang to her; and wherever she stepped, and nowhere else, grows our tribal flower—the trailing arbutus.

GOD'S KETTLE.

About two hundred and fifty years ago Weme-gen-debay, a noted chief and a great hunter, discovered, while hunting in the wilderness east of Traverse Bay, Michigan, a great kettle made of pure copper. It was nearly covered with earth; and the roots of large trees had grown over and around it. When taken out of the ground it had the appearance of never having been used. The kettle was so large that a full-grown bear could be cooked whole in it. It was regarded as *Manito aukick* (God's kettle).

Hence it was considered a sacred relic, was treated with a sort of reverential awe, and was kept securely hidden in a wild retreat unfrequented by man; never being used except when Tchibekan-kewin (the feast for the dead) was celebrated.

When the Indians in the Grand Traverse region became civilized this magic kettle lost its sacred influence, and was used to boil maple sap to sugar, instead of for cooking bear at feasts. Blackbird, a noted Indian now living at Harbor Springs, Michigan, as late as 1840, made a bail for this kettle while he was at work in the Government blacksmith-shop at the old Mission on Grand Traverse Bay. When I asked him, a short time since, what had become of that magic kettle, he replied, "I do not know, but must believe Manito has taken it home; for it disappeared as mysteriously as it came."

THANKSGIVING FEASTS, AND FEASTS FOR THE DEAD.

In the spring-time of each year our forefathers held Ma-gosh-e-win—a religious feast of prayer and thanksgiving,—rejoicing that winter had passed, and that all nature was alive again. At such times they erected in the centre of their camping-ground a high pole, on which they hung all their old, cast-off garments. Around this pole men, women, and children would sing and dance. The prayer of their song was, that Kigi Manito, who had brought back Ke-sus, the sun,—melting the snow and unlocking the ice-bound lakes and streams,—would look down upon his dependent children with love and compassion, and give them peace and plenty through another year. After the close of this feast they celebrated the feast for the dead.

All would march among the camp-fires; shaking hands whenever they met, singing in plaintive tones, "Ne-baw-baw-tchi-baw-yew ash-an-dis-win at-chak ne-bod" ("We are wandering about as spirits feeding the souls of the dead"), and at the same time eating, and throwing part of their food into the fire. This practice of feasting the dead, and of burying their weapons and utensils with them, was done in the same spirit as that in which the dominant race provides clothing, flowers, and marble for its dead. I believe there is no race on earth that has more reverence for its dead than ours. Our greatest sorrow, in being driven from our homes, has been our separation from the graves of our fathers, which we loved so much.

No greater insult can be given to Indians than to speak evil of their dead; for, say they, "The dead cannot speak for themselves; and the living that will not defend them are worse than Mau-tchi Manito (the Devil)."

LOVE AND MARRIAGE.

My feelings have often been mortified in reading in American histories that it was a custom among our people to marry for so many moons. There never was a greater misstatement. All our traditions most clearly show that, in our primitive state, we were a very virtuous people. Love and marriage were regarded as of divine origin. The false reports quoted in histories were made by white fur-traders, who, in early days, came among us, and, in order to get in closer touch with our people, intermarried. They afterward deserted their Indian wives and children; returning to their own people, and branding us with the lie in order to hide their own shame.

When our boys and girls become warmly attached to each other, they confidently talk the matter over with their parents, who always sympathize with them in their love affairs; for, believe me, our children are never laughed at and tormented, as is the case with white people, as though it were a crime to fall in love.

When lovers are married they repeat, generally in presence of both families, the following: "We now marry each other for life, before all our friends, now here assembled, by the command of the Great Spirit, who has united our hearts in one."

Then the lovers simply join hands; their lips in mutual concert meet, and the marriage-knot is tied for life.

THE SACRED WHITE DEER.

There is a very old superstition, still extant among our people, that white, or albino deer—which are very rare—are sacred. They have for time out of mind been called *Manito sucsee wabe* ("the sacred white deer").

It is believed that if anyone should shoot at and miss a white deer, he would be sick in consequence; and, that should he kill one, death would soon be the result. I once encamped while hunting with a white man for partner. Returning to our lodge one night, I told him how, during the day, I had had a chance to kill a most beautiful white buck, having the most perfect antlers I had ever seen, but that I had not had the heart to take his life, for I had always heard our old hunters say that the white deer was sacred, and that they never knew a hunter who killed one to live long. He called me many hard names, and among other things, said: "Pokagon, you are as superstitious as an uneducated redskin. Don't you know anything? Why, we could have sold that deer for more than fifty dollars!"

Yet this same man, a few days later, when we had started on our morning hunt, went back to the lodge, a distance of at least half a mile, to get an old horse-chestnut which he claimed had brought him good luck for years.

He would not hunt on Friday; fearing he might get shot. I suggested to him one Friday morning that, if he should fill his pockets with chestnuts, he would be perfectly safe. He talked very eloquently to me for some time; but he did not thank me for my advice.

In conclusion, permit Pokagon to say that he once thought that man's proneness to trust in superstitions was such a reflection on his natural ability, as to declare him unworthy of being considered spiritual and immortal. But, after having associated with the dominant race, as well as his own, for more than fifty years, and after having learned that trust in superstitions creeps into the hearts of all races, whether savage, or civilized and enlightened, he has been forced to a contrary opinion; and he now believes with all his heart, that such trust in superstitions most emphatically declares that man is spiritual and immortal, and has a higher life beyond the grave. In fact, it appears to him just as natural for man to trust in some intelligence higher than himself, who he believes brought him into being, as it is for children to trust in their parents.

As reasonable beings, without prejudice, we cannot for a moment believe that heathens who bow down to idols, or savages who trust in totums, or the civilized who have faith in mascots, believe there is any power in the object itself, but simply that there is somehow or other, a spiritual intelligence connected with it, which they cannot understand or explain, independent of the thing itself. They only know that it satisfies their nature to confide in it. As beings of common sense, we cannot believe otherwise than that their feelings are akin to those of the little girl who pets and caresses her doll, sleeps with it; and embraces it with all the tenderness of a devoted mother, and yet not for a moment believes it real. She is actuated to love and caress it in order to satisfy that parent love born in her own soul, which the God of nature has so wisely implanted in the breast of all human-kind.

Those mother-like caresses of the little girl, as she plays with her doll, declare no more emphatically to our reason that she inherits maternal love, than do those acts of rational beings who idolize totums and mascots declare that they are spiritual beings connected in some way with a higher Intelligence, who created them and governs all, and to whom all are accountable in this life and in the life to come. Pokagon does not wish to be understood, because he has reasoned by way of analogy in proof of spirituality, that he wishes to encourage idol-worship, after the relation between God and man has been revealed to men. Nor can he understand how it is possible for true Christians to trust or confide in anything this side of eternity beyond the revealed God of Heaven, to satisfy their spiritual wants.

Notes

*Indians never swear in their own language; and, as they generally believe all white men to be Christians, they do not understand why so many should indulge in profanity [Pokagon's note].

Traditions of Descent

by William W. Warren

* * * * *

William Whipple Warren (1825–1853), son of an Ojibwa woman and a New England fur trader, received his formal education at mission schools and at the Oneida Institute in New York. He served as interpreter for the Indian agency at La Pointe, Wisconsin, before being elected to the legislature of Minnesota a few years before his early death. During his last few years, he wrote several sketches on Ojibwa customs for The Minnesota Democrat. *In 1852 Warren completed a history of the Ojibwa, but it was not published until 1885, when it appeared as "History of the Ojibways, Based upon*

SOURCE: *De Lestry's Western Magazine*, 3, No. 2 (December 1898), 40–47. The article is subtitled as follows: "Ojibway lore relating to their origin. A possibility of an early connection with the lost tribes of Israel. Religious beliefs in harmony with the Old Testament. With additional views of Leech Lake. From the Manuscript of WILLIAM W. WARREN." Five photographs are interspersed throughout the article, but they have little pertinence to what Warren is writing about.

Traditions and Oral Statements,'' in the fifth volume of the Collections of the Minnesota Historical Society.

The origin of the American Indians, the issue raised in Warren's post-humously published essay included here, posed a problem that began to intrigue European and American commentators almost as soon as contact was established with the Indians early in the sixteenth century. Beginning probably with Lumnius' De Extremo Dei Judico et Indorum Vocatione in 1569, the most widely held theory, accepted well into the nineteenth century, was that Native Americans represented remnants of the ten lost tribes of Israel. Although other theses were advanced—for example, that the Indians derived from the Chaldeans, Welsh, Canaanites, or nonsemitic children of Noah—the Hebrew ancestry theory prevailed and was endorsed by such luminaries as Cotton Mather, John Eliot, and William Penn. Perhaps the most thorough presentation and development of the theory appeared in James Adair's The History of the American Indians . . . (London: E. and C. Dilly, 1775), wherein are catalogued a plentitude of Hebrew–Native American parallels. However, literally dozens of eighteenth- and nineteenth-century writers espoused the notion in their works. And, of course, it became a religious article of faith when it was incorporated into the Book of Mormon in 1830.

A major part of the rationale behind this theory must have come, as it does in Warren's essay, from the need to integrate the existence of the American Indians into the Old Testament version of world history. Other peoples who had been encountered by the Christian cultures of Europe had been accounted for in scriptural terms; for instance, blacks of sub-Saharan Africa could be traced to Noah through his son Ham. Viewing Native Americans as descendants of the lost tribes of Israel served the same purpose. At the same time it explained a vexing problem for Old Testament historians: the disappearance of ten of the twelve tribes of Israel from the chronicles of Hebrew history after the Promised Land had been attained.

For William Warren the theory served still a third purpose: it elevated his tribal group, the Ojibwa, above other Native Americans through the Ojibwa's kinship with God's chosen people. Aside from his a priori assumption that the Bible must be utilized to explain American Indian origins, Warren's position manifests some sensibleness. For example, he clearly recognizes that Native Americans do not constitute a single homogeneous entity but exist as separate groups of differing origins. He thus rejects the monistic hypotheses about Native Americans that still characterize the ideas of some commenta-

tors. Furthermore, Warren's suggestions about what occurred to their culture as the lost tribes of Israel migrated through Asia to North America reveals some insight into the processes of culture change through culture contact. Admittedly, his parallels between Ojibwa and Hebrew myths and rituals appear strained, but no more so than those offered by most other nineteenth-century comparativists attempting to explain the origin of American Indian cultures.

Although several works of intellectual history have explored the theory of Hebrew origin of Native Americans, among the most useful sources are Don Cameron Allen, The Legend of Noah. Renaissance Rationalism in Art, Science and Letters *(Urbana: University of Illinois Press, 1963), pp. 113–167; and Allen Howard Godbey,* The Lost Tribes a Myth. Suggestions Towards Rewriting Hebrew History *(Durham, North Carolina: Duke University Press, 1930).*

* * * * *

EDITOR'S INTRODUCTION.

The lines which follow here, taken from Mr. Warren's history of the Ojibway nation, may perchance be read, and have no doubt already been read with some peculiar ideas, by the scientists who are engaged in unraveling the mysteries surrounding the origin of the Red races of America. Yet after all, the subject is still unsolved and no one can say for certain that his own pet theory is correct. The story here related comes from the pen of a man who has all his life resided with the Ojibway, being of their blood and closely allied to their chief men. It is the oral history of the tribe, taken from the lore of ages. If it should aid the reader to form any opinion as to the descent of this red race, well and good.—Editor.*

ORIGIN OF THE OJIBWAY.

Ever having lived in the wilderness, even beyond what is known as the western frontiers of white immigration, where books are scarce and difficult to procure, I have never had the coveted opportunity and advantage of reading the opinions of the various eminent authors who have written on this subject, to compare with them my crude impressions which have gradually, and I may say naturally, obtained possession in my own mind during my whole life, which I have passed in a close connection of residence and blood with different sections of the Ojibway tribe.

Respecting their origin the Ojibway are even more totally ignorant than their white brethren, for they have no Bible to tell them that God originally made Adam, from whom the whole human race is sprung. They have their beliefs and oral traditions, but so obscure and unnatural, that nothing approximating to certainty can be drawn from them. They fully believe, and it is a part of their religion, that the world had once been covered by a deluge, and that we are now living on what they term the "new earth." This idea is fully accounted for by their vague traditions; and in their Me-da-we-win, or religion, hieroglyphics are used to denote this second earth.

They fully believe that the Red men mortally angered the Great Spirit which caused the deluge, and at the commencement of the new earth it was only through the medium and intercession of a powerful being, whom they denominate Man-ab-o-she, that they were allowed to exist, and means were given them whereby to support life; and a code of religion was more lately bestowed upon them, whereby they could commune with the offended Great Spirit, and ward off the approach and ravages of death. This they term their Me-da-we-win.

Respecting their belief of their first existence, I can give nothing more appropriate than a minute analysis of the name which they have given to their race—An-isch-in-aub-ag. This expressive word is derived from An-ish-aw, meaning without cause or "spontaneous" and in-aub-a-we-se, meaning the "human body." The word therefore translated literally means "spontaneous man."

The belief of the Algics is, as their name denotes, that they are a spontaneous people. They do not pretend, as a people, to give any reliable account of their first creation. It is a subject which to them is buried in darkness and mystery, and of which they entertain but vague and uncertain notions; notions which are fully embodied in the word An-isch-in-aub-ag.

It requires a most intimate acquaintance with them as a people, and individually with their story tellers, also with their language, beliefs and customs, to procure their real beliefs and to analyze the stories they seldom refuse to tell, and separate the Indian or original from those portions which they have borrowed or imbibed from the whites. Their innate courtesy and politeness often carry them so far that they seldom if ever refuse to tell a story when asked by a white man, respecting their ideas of the creation and origin of man.

These tales, though made up for the occasion by the Indian sage, are taken by his white hearers as their bona fide belief, and as such many have been made public, and accepted by the civilized world. Some of their sages have been heard to say, that the Great Spirit from the earth originally made three different races of men—the white, the black and the red race. To the first he gave a book, denoting wisdom; to the second a hoe, denoting servitude and labor; to the third or red race he gave the bow and arrow, denoting the hunter state. To his red children the Great Spirit gave the great island on which the whites have found them; but because of having committed some great wickedness and angered their Maker they are doomed to disappear before the rapid tread and advance of the wiser and more favored place face [?].

It is however plainly to be seen that these stories are not their original ideas, for they knew not, till they came amongst them, of the existence of a white and black race, nor of the characteristic symbols of the book and the hoe.

Were we to entertain the new belief which is being advocated by able and learned men, who have closely studied the biblical with the physical history of man, that the theory taught us in the Sacred Book, making mankind the descendants of one man—Adam—is false, and that the human family are derived originally from a multiplicity of progenitors definitely marked by physical differences, it would be no difficult matter to arrive at a certain conclusion respecting the manner in which America became populated. But a believing mind is loth to accept the assertions, arguments and opinions of a set of men, who would cast down at one fell swoop the widely received beliefs inculcated in the minds of enlightened mankind by the sacred book of God. Men will not fall blindly into such a belief, not even with the most convincing arguments.

Throw down the testimony of the Bible, annul in your mind its sacred truths, and we are at once thrown into a perfect chaos of confusion and ignorance. Destroy the belief which has been entertained for ages by the enlightened portion of mankind, and we are thrown at once on a level with the ignorant son of the forest, respecting our own origin. In his natural state the Indian would even have the advantage of his more enlightened brother, for he deduces his beliefs from what he sees in nature and her work, and possessing no certain proof or knowledge of the manner of his creation, he simply but forcibly styles himself "spontaneous man."

We pause therefore, before we take advantage of any apparent discrepancy or contradiction in the Bible which may be artfully shown to us by unbelieving writers, and to make use of it to more easily prove any favorite theory which we may imbibe, respecting the manner in which America first became peopled.

Taking the ground that the theory respecting the origin of the human race taught us in the Bible, is true, I will proceed to express my humble opinion respecting the branch of the human race from which originates that particular type of the aboriginal race of America, comprised by the term Algic or Algonquin, of which grand family the Ojibway tribe forms a numerous and important section.

During my long residence among the Ojibway, after numberless inquiries of their old men, I have never been able to learn by tradition or otherwise, that they entertain the belief that all the tribes of the red race inhabiting America have ever been at any time since the occupancy of this continent one and the same people, speaking the same language and practicing the same beliefs and customs. The traditions of this tribe extend no further into the past than the once concentration or coalition under one head, of the different and now scattered tribes belonging to the Algic stock.

We have every reason to believe that America was not peopled from one nation or tribe of the human family, for there are differences amongst its inhabitants and contrarieties, as marked and fully developed, as are to be found between European and Asiatic nations—wide differences in language, beliefs and customs.

Assuming the ground that America has been peopled from the eastern and northeastern shores of Asia (a ground which has been proved both probable and practicable by different eminent authors) it is easy to believe that not only one, but portions of different Asiatic tribes found their way thither, which will account for the radical differences to be found in the languages of the several stocks of the American aborigines. Taking these grounds, the writer is disposed to entertain the belief that, while the original ancestors of the Dakota race might have formed a tribe or a portion of a tribe of the roving sons of Tartary, whom they resemble in many essential respects, the Algics, on the other hand, may be descended from a portion of the lost tribes of Israel, whom they also resemble in many important particulars.

Of this latter stock only can I speak with any certainty. I am fully aware that the surmise here advanced, is not new, but is one which has already elicited much discussion, and although later writers have presented it as an exploded idea, yet I cannot refrain from presenting the ideas on the subject which have gradually inducted themselves into my mind. Unlike other writers who have had the advantage of books, the belief which I have here expressed has grown on me imperceptibly from my youth, ever since I could first read the Bible, and compare it with the lodge stories and legends of my Indian grandfathers, around whose lodge fires I have passed many a winter evening, listening with parted lips and open ears to their interesting and most forcibly told tales.

After reaching maturity I pursued my inquiries with more system, and the more information I have obtained from them— the more I have become acquainted with their anomalous and difficult to be understood characters, the more insight I have gained into their religious and secret rites and faith, the more strongly has it been impressed on my mind that they bear a close affinity or analogy to the chosen people of God, and they are either descendants of the lost tribe of Israel, or they have had, in some former era, a close contact and intercourse with the Hebrews, imbibing from their beliefs and customs and the traditions of the patriarchs.

To enter into all the details of the numerous trivial causes which have induced me to entertain this idea would take up too much space. So I will confine myself to stating a few general facts, some of which have missed the attention of my predecessors on this road of inquiry and which none but those intimately acquainted with the Indians and possessing their fullest confidence, are able to obtain.

It is a general fact that most people who have been discovered living in a savage and unlightened state, and even whole nations living in partial civilization, have been found to be idolaters—having no just conception of a great first Cause or Creator, invisible to human eyes, and pervading all space. With the Ojibway it is not so. The fact of their firm belief and great veneration in an overruling Creator and Master of Life has been noticed by all who have had close intercourse with them, since their earliest discovery. It is true they believe in a multiplicity of spirits which pervade all nature, yet all these are subordinate to the one Great Spirit of good. This belief is as natural (if not more so) as the belief of the Catholics in their interceding saints, which in some respects it resembles, for in the same light, as intercessors between him and the Great Spirit, does the more simple Red man regard the spirits which in his imagination pervade all creation.

Ke-che-mun-e-do (Great Spirit) is the name used by the Ojibway for the being equivalent to our God. They have another term which can hardly be surpassed by any one word in the English language, for force, condensity and expression, namely Ke-zha-mune-do, which means pitying, charitable, overruling and merciful spirit; in fact it expresses all the great attributes of the God of Israel. There is nothing to equal the veneration with which the Indian regards this unseen being. They seldom mention his name unless in their Me-da-we and other religious rites and in their sacrificial feasts; and then an address to him is always accompanied with a sacrifice of tobacco or some other article deemed precious by the Indian. They never use his name in vain and there is no word in their language expressive of a profane oath.

All other minor spirits whom they court in their dreams of fasting appear to them in the shape of animals or some inanimate object in nature, as the moon, the stars, etc. The dream itself, which has appeared to the faster on entering manhood, guides in a great measure his future course in life, and he never relates it without offering a sacrifice to the spirit of his dream. Their beliefs and rites, connected with their fasts and dreams are of great importance to themselves, more so than has been generally understood by writers who have treated of the Algics. These facts are mentioned to show an analogy with the ancient and primitive customs of the Hebrews—their faith in dreams, their knowledge and veneration of the unseen God and the customs of fasting and sacrifice.

The Me-da-we rite contains most that is ancient amongst them, but it is still a mystery to the white man. Songs and traditions have descended in it for a long line of generations not orally but in hieroglyphics. In this rite is also perpetuated the purest and most ancient idioms of their language, which differs somewhat from the language of every day usage. The writer has learned enough of the Me-da-we to strengthen his belief of an analogy with the Hebrews. They assert that the rite was granted them by the Great Spirit in a time of great trouble and death, through the intercession of Man-ab-o-she, the universal uncle of An-isch-in-aub-ag. Certain rules to guide their course in life were given them at the same time, and are represented in hieroglyphics. These great rules of life which the writer has often heard inculcated by the Me-da-we initiators in their secret teachings to the novices, bear a strong resemblance to the ten commandments revealed by the Almighty to the children of Israel, amidst the awful lightning and thunder of Mount Sinai.

They have a tradition of a great pestilence, which suddenly cut off many while encamped in a great village. They were saved by one of their number, to whom a spirit in the shape of a serpent, revealed a certain root, which to this day they name Ke-

261

na-big-wushk or snake root. The songs and rites of the medicine are incorporated in the Me-da-we. The above circumstance is told to have happened when the "earth was new," and taking into consideration the lapse of ages, and their being greatly addicted to figurative modes of expression, this tradition bears some resemblance to the plague of the children of Israel in the wilderness, which was stopped by the brazen serpent of Moses.

Another peculiar trait among the Algics is that of the Totemic division. There is nothing to which I can compare the purity and rigid conformity with which this division into families has been kept for centuries and probably ages, amongst the Ojibway, as the division of the Hebrews into tribes originating from the twelve sons of Jacob. Another peculiarity which has most forcibly struck my mind and which in fact first drew my attention to this subject, is the similitude which exists between the oral traditions and the lodge stories of the Ojibway and the tales of the Hebrew patriarchs in the Old Testament.

They tell of one set of traditions which treat of the adventures of eight, ten and sometimes twelve brothers. The youngest of these brothers is represented in the many traditions which mention them, as the wisest and most beloved of their father and lying under special guardianship of the Great Spirit. In one tradition under the name of Wa-jeeg-e-wa-kon-ay (Fisher skin coat) he delivers his brethren from divers difficulties, entailed on them from their own folly and disobedience. In another tradition he is made to supply his brethren with corn. The name of the father is sometimes given as Ge-tub-e. The similarity between these and the Bible stories of Jacob and his twelve sons cannot fail to attract the attention of any person who is acquainted with both versions. The tradition of the deluge and of wars between the different Totemic clans all bear an analogy with tales of the Bible.

To satisfy my own curiosity I have sometimes interpreted to their old men portions of Bible history and their expression invariably has been: "The book must be true, for our ancestors have told us similar stories generation after generation, since the earth was new." It is a bold assertion, but nevertheless a true one, that were the traditions of the Ojibway written in order and published in a book, it would as a whole, bear a striking resemblance to the Old Testament, and would contain no greater improbabilities than may be accounted for by the loose manner in which these traditions have been perpetuated, naturally losing force and truth in descending orally through each succeeding generation.

Discard then, altogether, the idea of any connection existing between the Ojibway and the Hebrews, and it will be found difficult to account for all the similarities existing between many of their rites, customs and beliefs.

It is not supposable however, that the ten lost tribes of Israel emigrated from the land of their captivity in one body, and proceeding direct to the eastern shores of Asia, crossed over to America (by some means which through changes and convulsions in nature, have become extinct and unknown to the present age) there to resume the rites of their religion, practice the Mosaic laws and isolated from the rest of mankind perpetuated, in their primitive purity, their language and beliefs.

On the contrary, if the Algics are really descendants of the lost tribes, it must be only from a portion of them, as remnants of the lost tribes have been discovered in the Nestorians of Asia. To arrive in America these portions must have passed through strange and hostile tribes of people, and in the course of their long wanderings and sojourns amongst them, they might have adopted portions of their languages and usages, losing thereby the purity of their own. It is natural to surmise that they were driven and followed into America by hostile tribes of Asia and that they have been thus driven and followed until checked by the waves of the broad Atlantic. This would account for the antagonistical position in which they and the Dakotas were first discovered.

Notes

*Edmond Louis De Lestry (1860-1933), editor of his *Western Magazine* (which later became *Northwest Magazine*), also worked on newspapers in Minnesota.

The Red Indian Imagination

by Andrew Lang

* * * * *

The consummate Victorian man of letters, Andrew Lang (1844–1912) earned his living and reputation through witty journalism and eclectic scholarship. The range of his literary efforts included a variety of genres: poetry, the essay, history, biography, autobiography, literary criticism, and the novel. His far-flung scholarly interests encompassed the history of his native Scotland, the Homeric epics, psychic research, anthropology, and folklore. The breadth of his concerns is indicated by the articles which he contributed to the ninth edition of the Encyclopedia Britannica *(1875–1899): "Apparitions," "Ballads," "The Casket Letters," "Crystal-gazing," "Fairy," "Family," "Edmund Gurney," "Hauntings," "La Cloche," "Molière," "Mythology," "Name," "Poltergeist," "Prometheus," "Psychical Research," "Scotland," "Second Sight," "Tale," and "Totemism."*

As a folklorist, Lang was Britain's leading spokesman for the theory of the unilinear evolution of cultures and championed that theory in a series of pub-

---

SOURCE: *The Independent*, 52 (18 January 1900), 163–165.

lished interchanges with comparative mythologist Max Müller. Most of Lang's thinking evinced the influence of Edward Burnett Tylor, but he did himself contribute some innovative ideas to cultural evolutionism, especially the notion that primitive peoples were capable of conceiving of a high god. Lang's ideas about the evolution of cultures and of how folklore and mythology fit into that evolution are clearly presented in Custom and Myth (London: Longmans, Green, 1884), the first chapter of which is a primer of cultural evolutionist methodology.

Lang showed no particular interest in Native American folklore during his career. American Indian cultures were regarded as examples of the sort of primitive cultures from which he could draw data for his theories, though Lang preferred the cultures of Australian aborigines because they had been less tainted by contact with European civilization. Actually, the brief essay included here illustrates the profundity of misunderstanding that can result from a superficial overview of American Indian oral literature. After a passing suggestion that the study of Native American oral poetry can contribute to an appreciation of the Homeric epics, a conventional idea of the cultural evolutionists about the relationship between the cultures of contemporary "primitives" and of the ancestors of modern civilized societies, Lang begins to disparage the oral narratives of American Indians. His criticisms, that the myths and folktales collected in the New World lack form, development, and consistency, have been common among those commentators who have made comparisons between these narratives and European materials. It was not until Alan Dundes's The Morphology of North American Indian Folktales appeared in 1964 as Folklore Fellows' Communication No. 195 that a different view was fully articulated. Dundes suggested that critics such as Lang were looking only at the surface content of narratives, which at times might seem chaotic. That content, though, was grounded in clearly developed and consistently structured patterns. The key to the artistry of American Indian folktales, Dundes argued, lay in their structure, or morphology. Even when a story was borrowed from another culture, it would soon lose much of its original focus in order to conform to the structural aesthetic of the Native American storytellers.

Andrew Lang has been the subject of several books and articles, but the best account of his folklore work appears in Richard M. Dorson, The British Folklorists. A History (Chicago: University of Chicago Press, 1968), pp. 206–220. Incidentally, Lang's idea for an anthology of American Indian oral poetry, with which he begins his essay, was soon accomplished in *such works as Alice C. Fletcher,* Indian Story and Song from North America *(Boston: Small Maynard, 1900) and Natalie Curtis,* The Indians' Book. An Offering by the American Indians of Indian Lore, Musical and Narrative, to Form a Record of the Songs and Legends of Their Race *(New York: Harper and Brothers, 1907).*

* * * * *

It would not be a profitable, but it would be a pleasant task for some American man or woman of letters to give us an anthology of Red Indian poetry and prose. The materials are easily accessible in the volumes of the Bureau of Ethnology (the Smithsonian Institute's publications), in the philological works of the regretted Dr. Brinton, in the chaotic miscellany of Schoolcraft, in the reports of the Jesuit and other old missionaries, and in many volumes of travel. No doubt there are plenty of other sources, which would need critical handling. I am now writing mainly from memory, and without book, and merely wish to offer a suggestion to a collector better qualified than myself.

The idea first occurred to me when reading a book of Dr. Brinton's, whereof even the name has escaped me. He printed, with the original texts, a number of short songs by red men and women, in prose translations. One of these, a love song by a woman, contained the same ideal theory of love as Lovelace's famous lyric:[1]

> "If to be absent were to be
> Away from thee,"

and, even in English prose, the expression was beautiful. Again, the Ethnological Bureau has published a long report of that strange religious phenomenon, the Ghost Dance of the Arapahoes and Sioux.[2] This new creed, much influenced by Christianity, promised the restoration to us of the beloved dead, and its rites were an esthetic kind of dances, accompanied by hypnotic phenomena. But the real interest lay in the published songs of yearning affection, composed for themselves by the dancers.

Many were truly poetical. Even in Schoolcraft there is a strange and beautiful pantheistic hymn, by a Meda maiden, or prophetess, taken down from her lips after her conversion to the Christian religion. These things, and many more, lie embedded in vast scientific collections, only opened, now and then, by some special student, whose researches are not literary. But it is the literary merit of the poetry of a wild people that is of rather more general interest. Such absolutely popular work is the wild stock of our cultivated or garden poetry, for all our poetic literature is only elaborated out of, and refined upon, conception much older than any civilization. Yet while the other arts and the social institutions of savages are closely scanned in Europe and America, their poetry seems to be neglected by students of literary origin. Till we go back to the poetry of the natives of America, Africa and Australia we are not in a position to deal with the Homeric questions and the problems of popular ballads. These problems, of course, are *practically* unimportant, but the mere literary merits of savage songs will sometimes delight and surprise the reader. For example, the "Hymns of the Maoris," and the religious traditions of the Zuñis, are often couched in language worthy of the old Greek poet philosophers, like Empedocles.

Of prose tales and myths, current among many American races, there is great plenty. I fear that neither in Schoolcraft's Algonquin legends, nor in Mr. Leland's,[3] can we be sure that we have the unadulterated native fancy. In both books one is driven to suspect recent borrowing by the Indians from European popular tales, heard beside the camp fire. The plots are often, too, like those in the stories of Grimm. Now, except for the recurrence of scattered incidents, talking hearts, and metamorphoses, and so forth, Australian stories are not like ours. The regular round of plots, as Cupid and Psyche, Cinderella, the Sleeping Beauty, Puss in Boots, the Boy and the Giant's Daughter, and so on, do not occur. The society of the black fellows is not developed, in rank and property, to the point from which stories like these would possibly be evolved. How this may be among red Indians (who had chiefs, and some property), I do not clearly know.

There lies before me "The Cegra Language," by Mr. James Owen Dorsey, the sixth volume of "Contributions to North American Ethnology."[4] It is full of tales from the Ponka and Omaha tribes. I looked into it, to see if the stories could be made amusing to white children. They could *not*! Leaving out tales of a mythological sort, accounting for the beginnings of things and the characteristics of animals, the yarns were long, dull and confused. One is about a boy, a written scroll, and a gun—modern innovations. Then we come to the Seven Headed water monster, who wants to swallow the chief's daughter. This is Perseus and Andromeda in Omaha or Ponka, but is it of native origin? The sword of the boy is not a red Indian weapon. He keeps the tongue of the monster as a proof of his prowess, a feature in scores of European tales. Is that, can it be, an unborrowed idea? A black man finds the heads of the monster, and claims the chief's daughter; the boy produces the tongues, better evidence. The negro is burned for his imposture. How orthodox, how familiar all this is, despite native touches! Surely we must decide that a European tale has somehow filtered through to the Ponkas. Mrs. La Flèche (half-breed wife of the Ponka narrator), remarks the European nature of the gun, sword, table and white man's food, but "agrees with the others in considering the rest of the myth as of Indian origin." This can hardly be. The tale has far more of plot than most of the others, and must have come from a hunter who had heard it among Europeans. In several other inordinately tedious stories an isolated familiar incident occurs here and there, such as the choice of a lady or of half dozen, all alike; or the mangy dog, who is really a great hero in that disguise. These things are common in the tales of the Old World, but in the Indian tales they have no relations to the familiar plots and sequences of our stories. Religious traits occur; men pray to Wakanda. "You being the Cause, you have made life for me, Wakanda." Now Wakan, like the Maori *mana*, means the unknown magical or magnetic force in things and people, dimly surmised. But if Wakanda be the mysterious All Powerful, author of life, is the idea native to the Indians? A weary controversy has been waged over this topic. I see no reason why, given the conception of *Wakan,* disembodied power (which is native), the Indians should not have developed for themselves the idea of a Powerful One. But into this tale comes the Nebelkappe, or cap of darkness, of our stories, and a sword, and a magic wishing ring. In other respects native, the story seems to have borrowed these European properties, and wedged them at haphazard into a tale vaguer than a dream, or than the narratives which very young children improvise in the nursery.

None of the Ponka and Omaha tales are like the improvisations of children of four years old. The idea of the Medea's cauldron, wherein a mutilated body is resuscitated, the ideas of magical metamorphosis, and of getting information by knowledge of the talk of animals occur, but in all a mist of the dreariest hunting adventures. These Indians have imaginative materials, like other people, but cannot make good use of them. Even when they have conspicuously borrowed from Europeans they lose the threads and forget the finish of the story, resembling those very stupid people who tell you a Joe Miller[5] and have to be reminded by you of the point of the anecdote. Here is a case, Joseph La Flèche being the narrator. There was a beautiful woman, many wooed her vainly, but one young man, on his way to her home, met a fellow who bounded so far that he had to handicap himself by tying stones to his feet; another fellow who would drink up whole lakes; another who drew so good a bow that the arrow, fired upward, did not return to earth for days; and a fourth, who could hear the grass growing. Now these gifted companions are commonly in European popular tales. In Kingsley's "Heroes"[6] you find their ancient Greek counterparts, the swift, keen-eyed, strong comrades of Jason in the legend of the Golden Fleece. In European tales their gifts are used with marvelous effect when occasion arises. And they are used in this Indian story, but in a bald, conventional way, without any pleasing turns and surprises. Joseph La Flèche is clearly telling a European story which he does not remember distinctly. He "speaks Canadian French," as Dorsey says, and so the mystery is explained. His wife is white on the paternal side; perhaps some of the stories which resemble ours were introduced by her.

Another of Mr. Dorsey's informants is called "He who is always thinking about the Great Spirit," "Great Spirit" being elsewhere used to translate *Wakanda*. But Wakanda appears really to mean "the Powerful One;" in one place it is translated "the Mysterious Power." So we come to the question, Is Wakanda a borrowed Christian idea, like the borrowed popular tales; or is it like the notion of Wakan (mystic power) native to the Ponkas and Omahas? In an Omaha letter we read about "God (Wakanda) and his Son," and the combination of the two seems to be due to missionary influence. "A missionary is here at Ponka River," says the letter writer. Do these missionaries translate "God" by "Wakanda," and did they adopt or introduce the term? These are questions which have some importance, but cannot be decided except by experts who know the tribes.

On the whole, the Ponkas and Omahas seem to have little original imaginations and never stumble on a coherent plot, except when there is every reason to suppose that the plot is borrowed. But other Indians have a very charming and pathetic version of the myth of Orpheus and Eurydice, which seems to be native; and native in character is the myth of the Beaver Bride, who is lost when she crosses running water; a story with variants in Eskimo, Maori, Sanskrit, Greek and so forth. The notions might occur to the human fancy anywhere. But the Ponkas and Omahas have clearly become so contaminated with European beliefs and legends that they are of little use for purposes of study, except as examples of the way in which European influences work in the savage mind. We must go further afield, and examine much older records, if we would find out which is native and authentic in Indian real literature. This is the task which I have suggested to some student with leisure, and with access to some rich library of Americana.

Notes

1. These two lines introduce "To Lucasta, Going Beyond the Seas" by the seventeenth-century poet Richard Lovelace.

2. James Mooney, "The Ghost-Dance Religion and the Sioux Outbreak of 1890," in *Fourteenth Annual Report of the Bureau of American Ethnology, 1892–93* (Washington: Government Printing Office, 1896).

3. Henry R. Schoolcraft (1793–1864) published a number of books which included oral narrative collected during his researches with Algonquin-speaking groups in the midwest, so it is unclear if Lang has a specific publication in mind. Charles Godfrey Leland (1824–1903) published less on American Indian folklore, and Lang is most likely referring to his *Algonquin Legends of New England* (Boston: Houghton Mifflin, 1884).

4. Lang's title is incorrect. He means James Owen Dorsey, *The Cegiha Language. Contributions to North American Ethnology No. 6* (1890).

5. *Joe Miller's Jests* was a jokebook published in 1730 by John Mottley, who took the name from an eighteenth-century London actor and humorist. A "Joe Miller" has come to mean a worn-out joke.

6. Charles Kingsley, *The Heroes; or, Greek Fairy Tales for My Children* (Boston: Ginn, Heath, 1885).